Orchids
of
BRAZIL

D1571713

Orchids of BRAZIL

JIM & BARBARA McQUEEN

TIMBER PRESS
Portland, Oregon

Published in North America, 1993
Timber Press, Inc.
9999 S.W. Wilshire, Suite 124
Portland, Oregon 97225 USA.
ISBN 0 88192 248 X.

First published 1993

The Text Publishing Company Pty Ltd
220 Clarendon Street
East Melbourne Victoria 3002
Australia

Printed and bound in Australia by Brown Prior Anderson Pty Ltd
Typeset by Guntar Graphics Pty Ltd, North Melbourne, Victoria, 3051 Australia

ACKNOWLEDGEMENTS

This book is dedicated, with much affection, to our friend and fellow orchidophile, Gerald McCraith.

The authors gratefully acknowledge the assistance of the following people who have most kindly lent photographs for inclusion in this book. In Australia: Stafford Betteridge, Dick Cahill, Lea Crawford, Graham and Marion Gamble, Gary Yong Gee, Athol Gilson, Sandy Holmes, Gary Knight, Gerald McCraith, Bill Pamment, Bev and John Woodward, Hal Young. In Brazil: Sandra Altenburg Odebrecht, Dr Sérgio A. A. Oliveira. In the USA: Dr J. A. Fowlie.

CONTENTS

INTRODUCTION

The prospect of writing a book about the orchids of Brazil was at first rather a daunting one. After all, Brazil is a country about the size of Australia or the continental USA, with a great range of climates and habitats and perhaps two and a half thousand orchid species. Also, Brazilian orchids have been popular in cultivation for over a hundred and fifty years, and a great deal has already been written about them.

But when we took a closer look we found that in fact there is quite a gap in the literature available. There are a number of orchid flora available: Pabst and Dungs, Cogniaux, Hoehne, and so on. But these are quite expensive, and often difficult to obtain. They are also perhaps too technical for the average hobbyist, and lack detailed cultural information. There are books on specific genera, such as oncidiums, laelias and cattleyas, but none that we know of which present — at a moderate price — an introduction to the wide range of Brazilian species.

Even so, had we not travelled in Brazil and seen many of the orchids growing in their natural habitat, we would probably not have begun this book. But Brazil is so vast, so varied, a country of such botanical richness, that once we had experienced a little of it we wanted to share our pleasure

in it. For an orchid lover, there is probably no greater joy than to travel in a new country rich in orchids. What have been cherished and coddled plants in a greenhouse are suddenly unregarded inhabitants of the roadside scrub, the river bank and the swamp. Orchids, like prophets, are often given scant honour in their own countries, and the orchids of Brazil are no exception. It is true that in southern Brazil there are orchid nurseries and orchid societies, and throughout Brazil some dedicated amateur growers. But, in general, the farther we ranged from the cities, the less interest we found in orchids. On the Amazon and the Rio Negro, it took us some time to educate our guides in the difference between orchids and the variety of other epiphytic plant life — bromeliads, ferns, philodrendrons and so on — that crowded the tree tops. In the great Ver O Peso market in Belém we found among the numerous stalls of the plant sellers only one man who even knew about orchids, and who had a few unidentified encyclias and cattleyas tucked away behind the rest of his stock in trade.

It is true that when we went aboard the little river boat which we had hired for our trip up the Rio Negro almost the first thing we saw was a plant of *Cattleya violacea* in an old glass jar, collected by the boatman's wife. But this was an exception; on the great rivers orchids are of little interest or concern to the local inhabitants.

This is not altogether surprising, of course. While the wealthy middle class of Rio or São Paulo can afford the luxury of an orchid collection, the poor *caboclo* of the Rio Negro has neither the time nor the money for something as unproductive as orchids.

It is hardly a surprise, then, to find that until halfway through the present century the sum of the outside world's knowledge of Brazilian orchids was largely the result of the efforts of non-Brazilians. Fortunately, that situation has changed dramatically in the last generation, and today there is a growing number of enthusiastic and knowledgeable Brazilians who are actively engaged in discovering, growing, describing and classifying the orchids of their native land, and publishing their results in more or less accessible journals and books. This change is taking place not only in Brazil, but in many other Latin American countries. Thanks to such efforts we are learning more and more each year about the thousands of orchid species of the New World.

It is a sad fact that in the ever increasing quest for economic development, orchid species are being rapidly depleted by habitat destruction as civilisation impinges more and more on the wild places of the Earth. Nowhere is this more obvious, more dramatic, and more tragic than in Brazil. On the credit side, there is a growing consciousness in Brazil that the richness of the country's botanical heritage is at risk, and that something must be done before it is too late.

Readers of this book may note that,

The beautiful and easily grown *Laelia purpurata* is Brazil's national floral emblem.

in quite a number of cases, our descriptions of flowers and plants differ in some details of size, shape and colour from those in a number of the popular reference works. This raises an interesting point. In most, although not all, cases, our descriptions are based upon firsthand examination of plants and flowers. After describing the material to the best of our ability, our next step was to check the results against descriptions in a number of standard references from our library. And at this stage a curious fact often emerged. We found that in many cases the description of a particular species was repeated almost word for word in a number of references dating back a century. And the original description, in most of these cases, seems to have appeared first in Veitch's *Manual of Orchidaceous Plants* published in 1887–94. It seems obvious to us that many more recent authors have copied their entries either directly from Veitch, or from other works which have copied from Veitch.

The similarities in text and mensuration are too frequent to admit of any other conclusion. This is not a matter about which we care to make any judgment; but readers should be aware that many modern books contain references which are virtual copies of 100-year-old descriptions, most probably based on limited plant material.

It has been said that one does not write a book because one is an expert, but that one may become an expert in the course of writing a book. We would disclaim any pretension to expertise in the field of Brazilian orchids, but in the course of researching and writing this book we have learned a little more about the subject than we knew before, and hope to learn even more as time goes by. In the course of our labours we have leaned heavily on the real experts in the field; the botanists, the writers, the nurserymen and amateur growers, all those who have contributed to the sum of knowledge about Brazilian orchids. We are deeply indebted to them all, and conscious of the limitations of our own work. Our objective, however, was a fairly modest one — to provide an interesting and useful introduction to the fascinating world of Brazilian orchids — and we hope that we have gone some way towards achieving this goal. We hope that our readers will be encouraged to a wider and deeper interest in the species inhabiting one of the world's great 'orchid' countries.

1 · GEOGRAPHY AND CLIMATE

GEOGRAPHY

Within its 8,511,965 square kilometres, Brazil encompasses a wide diversity of geological forms and climatic variations. It is hardly surprising that against the background of this physical diversity there is to be found an enormously varied plant life, of which orchids constitute a small but fascinating part.

Brazil has virtually no coastal plain and very little plains country, except for the upper part of the Amazon Basin and a limited area adjacent to the Paraguayan border. The rest of the country is largely comprised of low mountain ranges, plateaux and rolling hill country. The highest mountain in the country, Pico da Neblina, is only 3,014 m. Although there is no true coastal plain, there are many beaches, swampy areas, dune systems, sandbars and lagoons. In some places the escarpment plunges steeply to the sea, in others it descends in a series of steps. The coast is provided with many good harbours.

Three main river systems drain the Brazilian highlands. The river which everyone associates most readily with Brazil, the Amazon, rises in the north, where it is fed by the Andean snowfields and mountain streams. The Amazon is in many ways less a single river than a river system, comprising a number of large and small tributaries. Close to its source in the Andes, the Amazon Basin achieves its greatest breadth. It begins to narrow as the river's course moves eastward. Between Manaus and the Atlantic Ocean, it occupies a relatively narrow band of flood plain which separates the Brazilian highlands to the south from the Guianan highlands to the north. The flood plain widens again as it nears the sea, and the mouth of the river becomes a complex delta system.

The Rio São Francisco is the second of the great rivers of Brazil, and the only one wholly within Brazil. It is a river which for the Brazilian people has a special meaning, a special feeling closely associated with their national identity. The São Francisco rises in the high plains of western Minas Gerais and southern Goiás, about 1,200 m above sea level, near the site of the modern capital, Brasília. The Tocantins

States of Brazil

and the Paraná rivers also rise in this area. The course of the São Francisco is northward, and it flows more than 1,500 km through the states of Bahia and Pernambuco before emptying into the Atlantic Ocean. Unlike the mighty Amazon, which is navigable for ocean-going ships as far up as Manaus, only the last 200 km or so of the São Francisco are deep enough for such traffic.

The other major river system of Brazil is the Paraguaya-Paraná-Plata complex. Like the São Francisco, it rises in western Minas Gerais. It flows southward, passing through the Iguaçu Falls where the borders of Brazil, Paraguay and Argentina meet, and then through Argentina, emptying into the sea near Buenos Aires.

In addition to the three main river systems, there are many other important rivers in Brazil, most of which drain into the ocean via the heavily populated coastal belt.

CLIMATE

In view of the size of the country it is hardly surprising that Brazil has a wide range of climates within its borders, from equatorial in the north to temperate in the south. For the sake of convenience the climate range can be divided into five types. There are intergrades, of course, and many localised microclimates and anomalies, depending upon topography, altitude, wind direction, etc.

Rainforest

There are two major areas of rainforest

in Brazil. The first is the northern tropical rainforest, or selva, of the Amazon Basin. This vast area covers the two large states of Amazonas and Pará, together with Amapá and Acre, parts of Maranhão, Mato Grosso, Rondônia and Roraima.

The forest consists mainly of tall trees and contains an enormous variety of species; as many as 1,000 in a square kilometre. These trees form a thick canopy which excludes most of the sunlight from the forest floor. As a result of this, and the periodic flooding of the low-lying areas, there is little undergrowth. Most bird and other animal life, and most plant life is confined to the canopy of the forest. The soil is very poor owing to heavy leaching by the rains. Few orchids are evi-

dent unless you are a good climber, or enter the edges of the forest by boat during the season when the forest is flooded and the lower canopy accessible.

Lowland tropical areas generally contain fewer orchid species than do tropical and subtropical montane areas; yet, perhaps because of its vastness, the basins, plains and hills of the Amazon river system contain quite a diverse population of orchids. *Cattleya eldorado*, *C. violacea* and *C. lawrenceana* are found here, together with many *Catasetum* species (*C. discolor* is perhaps the most common), *Cycnoches pentadactylon*, *Rodriguezia lanceolata*, *Acacallis cyanea*, many *Oncidium* species including *O. nanum*, *O. lanceanum*, *O. cebolleta*, as well as *Mormodes*, *Brassia*, *Galeandra* species, the beautiful *Encyclia randii* and *Epidendrum nocturnum*, and

Vegetation

6

many more *Encyclia* and *Epidendrum* species.

Although this enormous expanse of rainforest spans the equator at low elevations, temperatures are not extreme. Contrary to general perceptions, maximum temperatures in this area never reach 38°C. Average temperatures in November, the warmest month, are about 27–28°C and are only about 2–3°C lower in March, the coldest month. Surprisingly, night temperatures can fall to as low as 10°C. The temperatures in Manaus itself seem just as high at night as during the day, probably due to the thermal mass of the city. But a hundred kilometres up the Rio Negro, we found that we needed sweaters from midnight to dawn.

The Amazon Basin is generally subject to heavy annual rainfall, especially on the upper Amazon and near its mouth. Belém, a pleasant town in the delta, has the reputation of being one of the wettest cities on the continent. Most of the annual rainfall in the Amazon area occurs between January

Amazonian igarapés, or small tributaries, like this one are the habitat of orchid species such as *Schomburgkia crispa* and *Cattleya eldorado*.

and June, but the other months are only slightly less rainy.

The second great area of rainforest occupies much of the Atlantic coastal strip. It extends in a broad band from Rio Grande do Sul in the south, through the states of Santa Catarina, Paraná, São Paulo, Rio de Janeiro, the south-eastern portion of Minas Gerais, to Espírito Santo. Just south of the city of Salvador, at about 15°S it is constricted into a narrow coastal strip, which extends all the way north to the state of Maranhão, where it meets the Amazonian selva. In the south the rainforest covers the main mountain ranges, including the Serra Geral, Serra do Mar, Serra Mantiquiera and the Serra dos Orgãos. As in the Amazon Basin, a great deal of the forest has been cleared for agriculture and mining.

The climate in the south is generally

Coastal swamps such as this abound in the state of Rio de Janeiro, and are the habitat of orchid species such as *Cattleya harrisoniana* and *Oncidium flexuosum*.

mild and equable. In Rio de Janeiro, the average temperature in January, the warmest month, is 26°C, dropping 6°C in June, the coldest month. Temperatures in northern coastal areas are warmer, but in the mountains, particularly in the south, temperatures are lower. Curitiba, in Paraná, has an average of about 12°C for the coldest month. The climate of the southern mountain areas, where annual rainfall is in the region of 150 cm per annum, is typical of subtropical montane areas throughout the world, with warm summers and cool dry winters. Light frosts may be experienced at times, but these seldom last long. Mists and fogs are frequent, and there is sufficient moisture to guarantee a rich diversity of plant life.

This part of Brazil is home to a large number of the country's most sought-

after orchid species. In fact, about 80 per cent of all Brazilian orchid species are found within this southern moun-

In south-eastern Brazil the moist mountain forests, such as this one near Teresópolis, are the habitat of a multitude of orchid species.

tain region. It is the home of all the lovely *Sophronitis* species, most of the Brazilian *Cattleya* and *Laelia* species, many *Oncidium* species, the beautiful *Promenaea* genus, *Miltonia*, *Maxillaria* and an enormous number of tiny 'botanicals' in such genera as *Pleurothallis*, *Stelis*, *Ornithocephalus*, and so on.

This is not only one of the richest orchid areas of the world, with 2,000 or more species, it is also very accessible, even to the casual visitor. From Rio de Janeiro, an hour or so in a comfortable bus takes you to Petrópolis (where a section of the Florália nursery is located, with most of its cooler-growing species) or to Teresópolis high in the Serra dos Orgãos (Organ Mountains). Teresópolis is especially rewarding. Only two or three kilometres from the centre of the town there is an extensive national park. Admission is free, and you can wander for as long as you like among trees literally encrusted with orchids, bromeliads and other epiphytic plant life.

The Organ Mountains near Rio de Janeiro, home of many outstanding orchid species

Cerrado

This area is named for the campo cerrado, or woodland savannah, which covers much of the tablelands or chapadas of the central western plateau. This area covers most of the state of Goiás, parts of Maranhão and Piauí, western Minas Gerais and the southern portion of Mato Grosso. It is a vast raised plateau, standing 1,000 m above sea level, which has been subject to ancient erosion by numerous stream beds, a process which has produced flat-topped tablelands and deep valleys. The level land on the tops of the individual chapadas is covered with savannah and light woodland, while the slopes and valleys bear semi-deciduous forest, sometimes quite dense. Annual rainfall is about 100 cm, concentrated in the months between October and April. Due to its unusual topography, this area is largely unsettled.

The chapada country of southern Mato Grosso, with its dramatic landscape of table-lands and deep forested gorges, is home to a wide variety of orchid species.

This is unusual and spectacular country, with a wide range of micro-climates. There are high dry plains, steep rocky slopes, lush river gorges and open savannah. In the eastern part, particularly in the state of Minas Gerais, many of the rupicolous or rock-dwelling *Laelia* species are found — *L. flava*, *L. reginae*, *L. crispilabia*, *L. endsfeldzii* and so on. Also found in this area, which experiences a dry cold winter, are such species as the unusual terete-leaved *Pleurothallis teres*, *Oncidium jonesianum*, semi-terrestrial *Oncidium* species such as *O. spilopterum* and *O. blanchetii*, and *Bifrenaria tyrianthina*.

Caatinga

Except for a narrow coastal belt which experiences regular rainfall, this zone covers most of the north-east portion of Brazil between the eastern extremities of the Amazonian rainforest and the Atlantic coast. It occupies the northern part of the state of Bahia, much of Piauí, and most of Ceará, Rio Grande do Norte, Paraíba, Pernambuco, Alagoas and Sergipe. The severity of the climate in this densely populated area, which is beset by recurrent floods and droughts, accounts for its reputation as the poorest part of Brazil. There is some irony in the fact that this part of the country was the first to achieve great wealth from large-scale sugar plantations worked by African slave labour.

Except for the coastal belt the summer rainfall is light and irregular and the interior is covered with scrubby woodland, much of it deciduous in the dry season. With wide diurnal variation in temperatures, mists and fogs provide some moisture for vegetation. This is the hottest region of Brazil, with summer temperatures exceeding 38°C. There is little really high country, with

the most elevated parts of the mountain ranges reaching only about 1,000 m.

Despite the aridity of the land and the severity of the climate, there is a variety of orchid species found here which is second only to the rainforest and the Cerrado.

Cattleya labiata and its many varieties are found in the interior of Pernambuco, often growing in exposed conditions in full sunlight. The beautiful *Laelia sincorana* occurs in northern Bahia, often sharing its habitat with *Cattleya elongata*. Other beautiful, and increasingly rare, species from the inhospitable north-east include *Cattleya porphyroglossa* and *C. granulosa* and *Brassavola tuberculata*.

Campo Limpo

There are two small areas of Campo Limpo, or open grassland or tall-grass prairie, in Brazil. One, the more southerly, stretches across the width of the country at its southern extremity, extending across the borders with Uruguay and Argentina, and occupies

The vast wetlands of the Pantanal are the home of a wide variety of wildlife, including the capybara, a giant rodent; but orchids are rare.

much of the state of Rio Grande do Sul. The other lies in a small pocket in the south of Mato Grosso do Sul. In addition to the open prairie, some forest is found in the south, mainly of pine and deciduous broadleaf trees. Frosts may occur down to sea level in the more southerly parts.

Most of the orchid species found in this southernmost part of the country occur on the eastern coastal strip, where the mountains reach their southern extremity. Much of the Campo Limpo itself is devoted to agriculture, producing beef, rice, wine and timber.

Pantanal

The Pantanal is an enormous flood plain covering almost a quarter of a million square kilometres, two-thirds of which lies in the Brazilian central west, the remainder extending across the borders into Bolivia and Paraguay. It covers the north-western part of Mato Grosso do Sul and extends into the southern part of Mato Grosso, almost as far north as the city of Cuiabá, which lies in an area of transition from flood plain to the northern chapada country.

The Pantanal comprises a vast flat plain intersected with river systems which flood each year, covering much of the area. The only relatively high ground is found in the lightly forested hummocks or knolls which stud the area, and to which most of the animal life retreats during the wet season. The margins of the rivers are mostly thickly covered with low scrub and trees, the tops of which are above flood level. The Pantanal contains the greatest concentration of wildlife — particularly bird life — in the New World; it is the home of the alligator, the anaconda,

the jaguar and the capybara. Because of the annual flooding, there is no agriculture. Cattle are grazed on the plains during the dry season, being trucked out or driven on to the hummocks in flood time.

Despite the presence of trees on the hummocks and along the river banks, this area is almost devoid of epiphytic plant life. It is the only part of Brazil we have seen without at least some bromeliads in the tree-tops. The only orchid we found (in November) was a flowering terrestrial species by a roadside near the Pixaim River. We were not able to identify it, and our pressed specimen, left outside at night to dry, was destroyed by a marauding animal. We were puzzled — and remain so — by the apparent absence of epiphytic orchids, as the chapada country only a short distance to the north is rich in such species.

2 · HISTORY

Although Brazil was first colonised almost five hundred years ago, its orchids — and for that matter its plant life generally — have remained poorly chronicled until fairly recent times, and have been less generally reported than the orchid flora of other countries which experienced colonial rule. It is a little odd to reflect that this situation was due to the geo-political situation in Renaissance times, and to the power of a fifteenth-century Pope.

In the century before Britain emerged as a great sea power, the oceans of the world were largely the province of Spain and Portugal, countries which, consequently, produced the greatest of the navigators and maritime explorers of the era. It was just as natural that the two greatest sea powers should also have been the most important colonisers, and that on occasion conflicts would arise over areas of influence.

Columbus's first voyage presented the two countries with immediate problems. Popes of the day were as much political as religious figures, with enormous influence over the Catholic countries of Europe, and, to resolve the problems which had risen between Spain and Portugal on colonial matters, Pope Alexander VI in 1493 virtually divided the colonial world between the two powers by drawing an imaginary line from pole to pole 100 leagues west of the islands of Cape Verde in the Atlantic. To the west of this line, Spain was given exclusive rights; to the east, Portugal.

This was quite a satisfactory arrangement to both parties, protecting Spain's American colonies and those of Portugal in Africa and India. A year later, envoys of both countries met at Tordesillas in Spain, modified the arrangement a little, and signed a treaty. The dividing line was moved further westward so that it now ran through the bulge of (as yet undiscovered) north-eastern Brazil. In April of the year 1500 the Portuguese navigator Pedro Alvares Cabral, on a voyage to India, sailed westward to avoid the calms of the African coast, sighted Brazil, and landed at Porto Seguro, in Bahia. As the land lay to the east of the line of demarcation, Cabral immediately claimed it for Portugal. Despite the fact that the settlements were later extended westward beyond the demarca-

Salvador de Bahia, on the east coast of Brazil, was the capital of the country between 1549 and 1763.

tion line, the whole country remained Portuguese, the only Portuguese colony among all the Spanish settlements of the New World.

For the next three hundred years Brazil remained totally closed to foreigners (including, of course, botanists). The Portuguese were interested in profits rather than knowledge. They had no interest in botany, and the floral riches of the vast country remained unreported. In the colonies of the British, and even the Spanish, the situation was different, and the new wave of scientific exploration gradually began to fill the blank pages with the natural histories of India, Burma, Australia, South Africa, as well as the Spanish colonies of the Americas.

The isolationism of the Portuguese was not the only factor which led to such a paucity of botanical knowledge about their South American colony.

The Portuguese originally divided the country into fifteen separate fiefdoms or captaincies which were formed by creating boundaries every fifty leagues up the coast, each one extending inland for an indefinite distance. Each captaincy was ruled by a donatario who, while owing allegiance to the Crown, pursued profit in his own way, independent of the other captaincies. Most of the donatarios were tyrannical and incompetent, and the country lacked any sort of social, legal or commercial unity. It was a bad start, and led to three centuries of intellectual stultification.

If one had to choose an example of the attitude of Brazilian authorities to outsiders perhaps the best would be that of botanists Humboldt and Bonpland, who in 1800, after exploring in Venezuela, reached the Brazilian border via the Rio Negro. They were both immediately arrested by Brazilian border guards.

The Brazilian authorities were aware of Humboldt's impending arrival and the Governor of Pará had issued the order to arrest him on charges including the suspicion that Humboldt 'may be planning to spread new ideas and religious principles amongst the faithful subjects of the region . . .'.

In fact, in the years between 1637 and 1805 only three scientific collections, those of Marggraf, Hoffmannsegg and von Langsdorff were made. It took the Napoleonic wars to end Brazil's isolation.

When Napoleon invaded Portugal, Britain's ally, in 1807, the Portuguese prince regent fled to Brazil. Thus for a time, a colony became the seat of government of its own mother country. Dom John, the regent, brought a new era to Brazil, an era of relative enlightenment; one of his most significant acts was to open the country to foreign trade.

But by then it was already too late for Brazil to benefit from the work of the botanists who had begun to shed light on the flora of other parts of the world. Within a few decades the great orchid boom of the nineteenth century had begun, and it was the collectors who flooded the unknown places of the world. And their job was collecting. Their sole purpose — in Brazil as in other places — was to provide quantities of new species for their masters, the plantsmen and nurserymen of Europe. By and large they did not write, they did not draw, they did not describe. And mostly they concealed — for commercial reasons — the locations of their finds. Their employers would most probably send material to a botanist so that a particular species might be described, largely to assist in its sale, but they were miserly with both their material and their information. Lindley was just beginning his

work on orchids, and Reichenbach and Schlechter were yet to come.

Apart from the expeditions of Martius, Pohl, Saint-Hilaire and Sellow, most of the nineteenth century's discoveries and descriptions of orchid species resulted from material which found its way from commercial collections to European botanists and taxonomists. The names which appear time after time in the roster of new species — the Harrison brothers, the Earl of Stanhope, Linden, Gardner, Morel, Lobb, Roezl, Wallis, Sander — are European, and often English, for England was the centre of the world orchid trade at the time.

The history of orchid botany in Brazil is largely one of delay and frustration, and nowhere is this better exemplified than in the case of von Martius and the *Flora Brasiliensis*. In June of 1820 von Martius completed an expedition which had lasted almost three years, and had taken him from Rio de Janeiro to São Paulo, Minas Gerais, Bahia, Maranhão, Pernambuco, Ceará, Pará and Amazonas. Back in his native Germany, he enlisted the help of a number of other botanists in order to compile a monumental *Flora* of Brazil. The first volume was produced in 1840 but, owing to lack of funds, the last did not appear until thirty-eight years after his death, in 1906. Cogniaux, curator of the Brussels Herbarium, wrote five of the forty volumes, including the three covering the orchid family. Much of his work was based on the unpublished work of Barbosa Rodrígues.

The experience of J. Barbosa Rodrígues is perhaps the saddest of all. He was born in Minas Gerais in 1842, was director of the Botanical Gardens in Manaus from 1883 until 1889, when

Rio de Janeiro, the country's capital from 1763 to 1960, when Brasília assumed that role. This view shows clearly the lack of any true coastal plain.

he was appointed director of the Botanical Gardens in Rio de Janeiro. He collected widely and wrote extensively about Brazilian orchids, creating a truly great masterpiece, the six-volume *Iconographie des Orchidées*, which sadly was never published, although his illustrations were used to illustrate the orchid volumes of the *Flora Brasiliensis*. Barbosa Rodrígues' problem was a financial one; he was unable to raise sufficient funds to publish his work, and the Brazilian government, already committed to subsidising Martius's work, would not assist him. He described a great number of species, but most were never validly published, and the relatively small number which are valid today do not reflect the true merit or achievement of this great Brazilian botanist.

In the early twentieth century relatively little new work was done in the field of Brazilian orchids, due in some measure to the interruption of World War I. The work that was done was often on a small scale, carried out by dedicated amateurs. The next great step forward in terms of published work was the revision of the *Flora Brasiliensis* by Hoehne, Director of the Botanical Institute of São Paulo, who began his career as a gardener in the Botanical Gardens of Rio de Janeiro, and was a self-taught botanist. In the 1940s he also published the incomplete *Flora Brasílica*, with four volumes devoted to orchids and covering about half the country's species, and also *Iconografia de Orquídeas do Brasil*, a less technical work. Unfortunately, this work was published only in Portuguese, limiting its accessibility.

The last of the truly monumental works on Brazilian orchids is the *Orchidaceae Brasilienses* (1977) by Guido Pabst and Fritz Dungs. Pabst was a native Brazilian, while Dungs lived in Brazil from the age of eight.

Theirs is an important, well-illustrated and accessible work, being trilingual in Portuguese, German and English, but is marred by its lack of adequate keys.

In addition to non-Brazilians, such as Dr J. A. Fowlie and Margaret Mee, who have contributed to our knowledge of Brazilian orchids over the last forty years or so, there have also been Brazilians such as Ghillany, Kautsky and Richter. And today there is an entirely new generation of active professional orchid botanists and taxonomists at work in Brazil, as well as an energetic body of amateurs, all of whom are continuing and enhancing the native tradition which began with the persistence and vision of Barbosa Rodrígues.

3 · ORCHID CONSERVATION IN BRAZIL

Brazil is such an enormous country with such a large range of habitats that it is very difficult to arrive at any kind of general overview of the status of orchid species in the wild. Two *Laelia* species — *L. jongheana* and *L. lobata* — are listed in Appendix I of CITES (the Convention on Trade in Endangered Species), together with all species of *Phragmipedium*, which signifies that they are considered by that body to be endangered, and many other species, such as *Cattleya porphyroglossa*, are rare nowadays in their native habitat. The beautiful red *Laelia milleri* has a very limited natural distribution, and is said to be threatened by mining operations. Yet, with the exception of the phragmipediums, all these species are so popular horticulturally and so well represented in collections around the world that, although they may disappear from their habitats, there is no real risk of their becoming extinct. And while healthy and genetically diverse populations exist in cultivation, there is always the possibility of their re-introduction into the wild.

It is interesting in this context to consider the case of Tijuca Forest, a 120-square-kilometre national park within the boundaries of the city of Rio de Janeiro, and perhaps the only large national park in the world within a major city. Guide books generally represent this park as being a remnant of the forests which once surrounded Rio. In fact, Brazilian friends tell us, Tijuca was cleared over a hundred years ago for a coffee plantation. The climate proved unsuitable for coffee, and the owner — a most enlightened gentleman for those, or any, times — replanted the area with the original tree species, all of which he knew well. Today the area is almost indistinguish-

Once a coffee plantation, Tijuca Forest in Rio de Janeiro was replanted with the original tree species. Now orchids, such as this *Encyclia patens*, are re-establishing themselves naturally.

able from any other area of local forest, except that epiphytic plant life is not quite so abundant. But it is returning, slowly but naturally, as seeds are borne by wind and birds and insects, and orchid and bromeliad species are becoming more abundant as time passes.

There is no doubt that over-collecting, especially in the nineteenth century, has led to a vast reduction of species in the wild, especially those restricted to small areas where access is relatively easy. However, the great threat to the majority of orchid species today, in Brazil as in other countries, lies in the continuing destruction of tropical and temperate forests. There is probably no need to labour this point; no informed person can be unaware today of the rate at which the world's forests are being depleted. And nowhere is this more evident than in Brazil. In 1989 alone, in the state of Rondônia, 30,000 square kilometres of forest, an area equal in size to Belgium, was cleared and burned. When every square kilometre can contain as many as 750 separate tree species, 125 different mammals, 400 bird species, 100 reptiles, dozens of orchid species, there is a great deal to be lost.

Although habitat destruction clearly remains by far the major threat to wildlife everywhere, there has been a distinct lack of inclination by governments in most countries to address this problem. Instead, most governments have become signatories to the twenty-year-old Convention on Trade in Endangered Species, better known as CITES. This international convention had wild animals as its major initial preoccupation. Plants (including orchids) were added to the convention in haste and almost as an afterthought.

The Convention has, by and large, been a signal failure. As an example, it has sought since its inception to protect the African elephant by proscribing the trade in ivory. Yet at the time of writing the only African country remaining with a large — even superabundant — population of elephants is Zimbabwe, which manages its herds on sound economic grounds and sells its ivory. The Convention has had little more success with plants than with animals, and is largely irrelevant in relation to orchid conservation.

The broad-scale failure of CITES is hardly surprising as it attempts to solve a problem which in any substantial sense has ceased to exist — over-collection and trade — while failing to address the real problem of this century, which is clearly widespread habitat destruction. CITES, in our opinion, must be viewed as a fairly cynical exercise by politicians of all countries by which they appear to be doing something about plant and animal extinction when in fact they are not. To attack the real problem of habitat destruction would involve measures totally at variance with the commitment of most politicians and governments to expanding economies and the consequent demands for greater resource consumption and ever-increasing markets. The best chance for the world's endangered species probably lies in the increasing public pressure for the establishment of more national parks, wildlife reserves and land rights for indigenous people.

A factor which may play a significant part in retaining fairly extensive areas of relatively undisturbed forest in Brazil is the increasing agitation by indigenous people for retention of their traditional tribal lands. In 1991

Charcoal burners are responsible for significant damage to the rainforest along the Amazonian rivers.

the Brazilian government set aside 97,000 square kilometres of land — an area the size of Portugal — for the Yanomami, an Amazonian tribe numbering less than 10,000. In fact, since 1990, 131 reserves totalling 306,000 square kilometres, in nineteen states have been created for tribal people. These reserves, it is to be hoped, will suffer a minimum of intrusion from outsiders and may serve as valuable core habitats for the preservation of unique plant species, including orchids.

The species which are truly at risk are those which are of limited interest to horticulture, such as the hundreds of pleurothallids. Even animal primate species new to science are still being discovered in the Amazonian forests, and there is no doubt in our minds that there are many plant species in Brazil as yet undiscovered and undescribed, which may well disappear forever as their habitats are destroyed.

In 1989 we visited the Amazon and the Rio Negro. We were particularly interested in the status of two *Cattleya* species on the Rio Negro, *C. violacea* and *C. eldorado*. Neither species is common in cultivation, and is seldom listed in Brazilian nursery catalogues. We feared that over-collecting had decimated the natural populations. We need not have worried. On the banks of the river, in the region of the Anavilhanas archipelago — the largest inland archipelago in the world — we saw numerous examples of both species as we cruised by. The only apparent threat to these species must be from forest clearing or charcoal burning as the cost of commercial collecting is obviously too great to make it profitable — travel in Brazil, as in most other places, is expensive. But the forest clearing goes on, more it seems each year, and as the trees disappear so do the orchids, so there is no room for complacency.

The equatorial forests of the Amazon Basin grow in a very thin layer of poor soil — soon eroded or exhausted once the trees are removed.

Nevertheless, commercial collecting of orchids in Brazil no doubt still causes the depletion of some orchid species as it does elsewhere (the case of a number of *Sarcochilus* species in Australia comes to mind), and may reduce certain species, especially populations of the more accessible lithophytes and terrestrial species, to the danger level. L. C. Menezes, writing in the *Orchid Digest* in 1992, mentions the case of *Encyclia chapadensis*, a new species with its habitat in the state of Goiás. 'Contrary to the usual run of things with Brazilian orchids', Menezes writes, 'being decimated by the cutting and burning of the forests; by the constructions of dams; and by demographic growth it can be said that in the case of *Encyclia chapadensis* the imminent extinction is due to this indiscriminate and illegal collecting done by orchidophiles and commercial nurserymen'.

Although some amateur and professional growers in Brazil continue to collect plants from the wild for resale as well as for personal interest, it is very doubtful if any significant quantities are exported. Since 1990, Brazilian authorities have clamped down on exporters who lack the facilities to produce artificially propagated plants. But some pressure exists from local growers, particularly on the larger more colourful species such as *C. porphyroglossa*, which are now very rare in their habitat, having been over-collected in the past, particularly in the nineteenth century. Most miniature and 'botanical' species are not popular with the general run of Brazilian growers and nurseries and so suffer little from over-collection, leaving habitat destruction, again, as the major risk to their continued existence.

The clearing of the Amazonian rainforest for farming or timber has been extensive and well-publicised, and charcoal burners have also added to

Caboclo families on the Rio Negro clear land for their manioc plantations using the traditional 'cut and burn' technique. This is very limited in scale, and contributes little to forest destruction.

the problem. Due to the permanently impoverished nature of rainforest soil due to heavy leaching, and the thinness of the topsoil layer, once the land is cleared it deteriorates very rapidly; in general it is useless for anything after a few seasons cropping, a pattern which has become well established through Central and South America. The cut and burn practices of the *caboclos*, who live along the river and who generally grow manioc, a tuber root plant, are small in scale and have relatively little appreciable effect. But profiteering, through continuous subdivision of leases, has led to serious depletion of the forest.

Much publicity has been given to the destruction of the forests of the Amazon basin by timber-getters; yet ninety per cent of clearing is done to provide additional land for the production of beef for export. And this is an uneconomic industry, heavily subsidised by the Brazilian government. It is obvious that until this situation changes the major threat to the Amazonian forests will remain. Much of the forest still stands, however, and we should give our support to all efforts to preserve it, together with its diverse and unique flora and fauna.

4 · GROWING BRAZILIAN ORCHID SPECIES

There are few, if any, countries in the world which have more to offer to the grower of orchid species than Brazil. Not only does it have a large number of species in a wide range of genera, but many of the most horticulturally desirable species are fairly readily available commercially, and many more may be found with a little perseverance.

But perhaps the greatest advantage for the grower who specialises in Brazilian species is that about eighty per cent of all Brazilian species originate from the area in the south-east of the country roughly situated between 15° and 30° south of the Equator. Because of the lack of any true coastal plain, most of this area consists of the montane or sub-montane forest which extends on both sides of the Tropic of Capricorn. And the narrow strip of coastal lowland, where this occurs, is cooled by sea breezes from the Atlantic. Thus most of the desirable species, including such taxa as *Cattleya loddigesii*, *C. harrisoniana*, *C. intermedia*, *C. forbesii*, *C. schilleriana*, *C. bicolor*, *C. velutina*, *Laelia purpurata*, *L. lobata*, *L. perrinii*, *L. tenebrosa*, *L. pumila*, *L. jongheana* and all the *Sophronitis* species, are found in this area.

From a horticultural point of view, the advantage of plants originating from this part of the country is that their habitat is not subjected to great climatic extremes. There is neither the chill, high-altitude cloud-forest of the Andes nor the year-round heat and humidity of the coastal lowlands of the Guianas. Most orchid growers round the world live in areas where it is difficult, expensive, and often impossible to replicate such extreme conditions. Most species from south-eastern Brazil will respond well for growers who can provide intermediate to cool conditions, with winter minima to the order of about 8–10°C and summer maxima in the low thirties.

However, even plants originating

Laelia pumila, mounted on a slab of tree-fern, soon grows into a large plant.

from the Amazonian lowlands need not necessarily be excluded from the average mixed collection. Much depends on the tolerance of individual species to divergences from the conditions of their habitat. And in this, few rules can be laid down; it is often a matter of experimentation to determine just how much tolerance a particular species possesses. This factor was brought home to us many years ago when we first ventured into the Australian coastal mangrove swamps near Cairns in north Queensland. Growing side by side on the low trees were two very common orchid species, *Dendrobium discolor* and *D. teretifolium* var. *fasciculatum*. The first of these is fairly intolerant of low temperatures, and does not do well in higher latitudes unless given fairly high temperatures. On the other hand, *D. teretifolium* var. *fasciculatum* will grow without heat even as far south as Tasmania, Australia, at latitude 44°S. This plant obviously has much greater tolerance of extremes that does *D. discolor*, and similar differences in tolerance will usually be found, regardless of the country, wherever two or more species share a habitat.

Most orchid growers we know will admit to difficulty in growing or flowering some easily cultivated species; there are some species, too, which are generally regarded as difficult to flower. A good example of the latter among Brazilian species is probably the beautiful *Laelia lobata*, which often refuses to bloom until it is trailing well beyond the pot or basket. Another species which, in Australia, has a longstanding reputation as a shy flowerer is *Bifrenaria harrisoniae*. For at least thirty years, and possibly longer,

The beautiful *Laelia lobata* is a shy bloomer, flowering best when allowed to grow beyond its mount or container.

this species has been the cause of much frustration. Yet, because of its hardiness and ease of cultivation, it has often been recommended as a good beginner's orchid.

We have owned a clone of this species for over thirty years and, like many other growers, have tried it in every conceivable condition of light, shade, heat, cold, humidity and so on. It has rewarded us sparsely over the year, and apparently in complete disregard to the conditions it has been given. It has flowered just as rarely in bright light as in shade, in warmth as in coldness. After many years of this we imported new plants from Brazil with some trepidation. Yet the new imports have flowered unfailingly for us each November, year in, year out, without any special attention and in a variety of conditions. This leads us to suspect that the reputation of this species as a shy flowerer may be due in fact to its very ease of cultivation and rapidity of propagation. It seems likely that the original plants imported many years ago to this country came from a limited population with some genetic inadequacy. Because it grew so easily and propagated so readily, there were very few further importations. Few people a generation ago ever actually bought a plant of *B. harrisoniae*; they were so plentiful that most new orchid growers were given a plant. We would recommend, then, that anyone having problems flowering this species should discard their recalcitrant plant and secure either a seedling or a freshly imported clone. We should point out that plants which enjoy this bad reputation have flowers which are identical to those most often seen in illustration, having creamy-white petals and sepals. The free-flowering plants which we have imported are those with rose-flushed sepals, called sometimes in Brazil 'variety *grandiflora*' although its flowers are no larger than the white variety. The two varieties most probably come from separate locations.

Aside from the difficulties sometimes experienced in flowering particular species, there are few Brazilian orchids which will not respond, in the long term, to persistence and experimentation by the dedicated grower. One we have failed with, however, is *Constantia cipoensis*, a pretty miniature from Minas Gerais, where it seems to grow mainly on *Vellozia* bushes. We have imported a number of these over the years, well-established plants on their natural hosts, and all have eventually given up the ghost, despite our best efforts. We would certainly not go so far as to say that this species cannot be grown away from its native habitat, but we know of no one outside Brazil who has successfully

grown the species over an extended period. Even in Brazil, nursery people we know have told us that they find it extremely difficult to keep the species in cultivation. It may be that plants raised from seed may be more tolerant than their wild ancestors of variations in growing conditions. We have noted that this is true of some bromeliad species, and hope to try to raise seedlings of *C. cipoensis* when we can obtain seed.

Luckily, this is the exception when it comes to cultivating Brazilian species, as most of them will respond well to conditions in a mixed collection, as long as some thought is given to providing them with something approaching conditions in their native habitat.

With few exceptions, the Brazilian

A *Cyrtopodium* species growing in bright light in the Botanical Gardens of Rio de Janeiro.

cattleyas all do well for us if given intermediate conditions — some, such as *C. harrisoniana*, *C. forbesii* and *C. intermedia*, will grow cool — and plenty of bright light. *C. araguaiensis* seems to prefer a little more shade, and we find that although *C. loddigesii* grows well in bright light, it flowers best for us if given moderate shade once buds begin to form. Extremely bright light seems only to intensify flower colour in the case of *C. harrisoniana*, but in the case of *C. loddigesii* may cause the flower buds to burn. All the *Cattleya* species may be potted or grown on mounts, and in almost all cases we use treefern.

Obviously, in the matter of substrates — mounts or potting mixes — it is sensible to use materials which are inexpensive and readily available locally. We have plentiful supplies of treefern in Tasmania. We use quite large slabs as suspended mounts, and coarse chunks as potting material. We find that *C. araguaiensis*, which seems a rather fragile plant, does well when mounted on an aged treefern slab with a covering of natural moss. The only Brazilian cattleyas which we do not grow on or in treefern are *C. aclandiae*, *C. walkeriana* and *C. nobilior*, which seem to prefer a mount of natural cork bark. All plants, whether potted or mounted, are suspended well above the benches in our greenhouses, where they experience adequate light and good air movement.

The genus *Laelia* is very well represented in Brazil, and indeed is one of the country's true floral glories. It is entirely appropriate that *L. purpurata* should have been chosen as the nation's floral emblem. For many reasons this species might be called the perfect orchid; it is a plant of moderate size and easy cultivation; it is relatively easy to obtain; it flowers, unlike its close relative *L. lobata*, with ease and regularity; its flowers are large and handsome, and appear in a wide range of dramatic colours. A visit to a southern Brazilian nursery or collection in late spring, when this species is in flower, is an experience not to be forgotten.

Plants of this species are, from our observation, mostly grown in terra cotta pots by Brazilian growers. The most popular substrate seems to be *xaxim*, the local soft treefern fibre. We grow most of our plants in pots, too, but as we like to suspend them high in the greenhouse for maximum light we use plastic pots for lightness. We too use treefern, our hard dark brown variety, chopped into small chunks. The plastic pots are well crocked — for lightness, once again, we use broken polystyrene pieces — for drainage.

Laelia purpurata is one of those species about which it is possible to enthuse almost endlessly; yet there are other Brazilian laelias hardly less beautiful and just as easy to grow. And many are so spectacular and so modest in their spatial requirements that they have remained favourites with growers for generations. In our own collection there are few plants which flower so regularly year after year — with so little attention — than the laelias of section *Hadrolaelia* which include *L. dayana*, *L. spectabilis*, *L. sincorana*, and *L. pumila*. We grow these small plants on quite large slabs of treefern fibre in moderate to bright light. They get lots of water during the growing season, followed by a fairly dry cool winter. They grow quickly into large plants, covering their slabs and extending beyond the edges. At this time, when they have reached the limits of their host, they may be divided or pruned back. But usually we simply tie the old slab to a newer larger one and allow to plants to extend naturally on to their new host.

The so-called 'rupicolous', or rock-dwelling, laelias have been known and grown for over a hundred and fifty years. Yet, with the discovery of many species over the last thirty or so years, this group has experienced a greatly increased popularity. Mostly quite small plants, they do not differ greatly in flower shape. But they have such a range of colour and are so modest in their requirements, that it is well worth growing at least a few in any collection. There are (as will be seen from the illustrations in this book) brilliant reds, vibrant yellows and sparkling pinks and whites. As a group, they are not difficult to cultivate, bearing in mind that the greatest concentration of species is in Minas Gerais, where plants grow at fairly high elevations in an area which experiences hot wet summers and cold dry winters. Plants are accustomed to very bright light, to long periods of drought tempered only by nightly dews and cooling breezes. They are, rather naturally, fairly tolerant plants in cultivation, and will grow happily in a wide range of conditions. The one thing they do resent above all is poor drainage and the resultant 'wet feet'. We have at times found them to be a little difficult to establish after importation, owing to a disinclination to put out new roots. The only answer is patience and, once re-established, plants are trouble-free and easy to grow. We grow ours in suspended

The rupicolous or rock-dwelling laelias, such as this *L. tereticaulis*, make ideal subjects for suspended pots in bright light.

pots of treefern fibre mixed with broken sandstone and leaf mould or moss.

Closely related to both *Cattleya* and *Laelia* is the genus *Sophronitis*, one of Brazil's endemic treasures. Species of this genus have enjoyed continuous popularity since their introduction, mostly in the first half of the eighteenth century. As well as being grown for their own sake, they have been much used in hybridisation, imparting their brilliant reds and oranges — as well as their dwarf habit — to their progeny. In general, *Sophronitis* species are of montane origin and are suited to cultivation only in cool or, at the most, intermediate conditions. They will tolerate neither high summer temperatures nor the lack of a cool dry resting period. They are amenable to pot culture, but most of ours are grown on small treefern slabs in semi-shade to moderately bright light. The exception is *S. cernua*, which tolerates fairly warm dry conditions, and is more suited to cultivation by growers in tropical areas. We have seen this species growing happily in full sunlight on the bare trunk of a palm tree in Rio de Janeiro. We grow our plants on slabs of natural cork bark in intermediate to warm conditions.

Sophronitella violacea, closely related to *Sophronitis*, is another species which will tolerate higher temperatures. This very attractive little species, however, detests 'wet feet', and in our experience we have found it most unhappy when either potted or grown on a treefern mount. We have found that the best mount, by far, is a piece of paperbark (*Melaleuca* sp.) branch or trunk. Natural cork is a good second best. Apart from that, our plants grow happily in the same conditions as our *Sophronitis* species.

Of all indigenous Brazilian orchids, few genera have been as popular over the years with collectors as the oncidiums. Most people seeking to build a mixed collection of orchid species will number among their early acquisitions one of the better-known species from this genera — *O. gardneri*, *O. forbesii*, *O. crispum*, *O. marshallianum*, *O. concolor* perhaps, or that wonderful beginner's orchid, *O. flexuosum*. The popularity of such species — and their hybrids — seems never to diminish. One of their greatest charms, perhaps, is that so many of them flower in autumn, enlivening the shortening days with their brilliant golden displays. But there are many more wonderful species, hardly known at all beyond their native country, which deserve a place in any collection.

O. trulliferum is one of our favourites, with its large clustered mass of small flowers, as is the wonderfully

An easily grown species, *Oncidium flexuosum* is happiest when allowed to ramble with its roots hanging freely in the air.

floriferous *O. macronix* with its delicate 'rhinoceros-horn' flowers. And it has always surprised us that the so-called 'terrestrial' oncidiums (which in fact are only semi-terrestrial) such as *O. hydrophyllum* and *O. gracile* are not more widely grown than they are. Their habitat, among tall grasses, has encouraged them to produce very tall stems which display their flowers to perfection, and of all oncidiums they are perhaps the most amenable to pot culture. While many oncidiums may be grown in pots, their rather scrambling habit lends itself better to culture on slabs of treefern or cork or on branches of trees with persistent bark. Of these, none likes to scramble more, perhaps, than *O. flexuosum*. Our favourite method with this species is to tie several plants to a long rather narrow slab of treefern and hang it high in the greenhouse. Its roots trail in the air and as the rhizome extends it may be severed well behind the leading bulb to encourage new leads. In a surprisingly short time a specimen plant results. Oddly, this species, which is often encountered in the hot humid coastal swamps of Rio de Janeiro and is generally regarded in Brazil as a warm grower, will tolerate cool, even quite cold, winter conditions.

Most Brazilian oncidiums are of relatively easy culture and, provided they receive plenty of water in summer and a cool dry winter rest, will thrive. They need good air movement and perhaps more shade than is generally thought, though certainly less, we believe, than many of them receive in their native habitat.

Many growers, being aware of the difficulties of growing the high altitude *Miltoniopsis* (previously *Miltonia*) species of northern South America, have fought shy in the past of attempting to grow Brazilian *Miltonia* species. Happily this situation is changing as more and more people come to realise that these plants present little difficulty in cultivation. If anything, we find them easier to grow than oncidiums. With the exception perhaps of *Miltonia spectabilis* and its varieties, they are quite rampant growers, scrambling happily over quite large treefern slabs and preferring if anything a little brighter light than the general run of oncidiums.

Stanhopea species tend to go in and out of fashion a little as times change, but they are so unusual and spectacular in flower — even if they do not last long — that every collection should have at least one or two species. It has

been the custom for many years, in consequence of their habit of projecting their flower spikes vertically downward, to grow these plants mostly in wire baskets. And this is certainly a satisfactory method. But even better results can be obtained by mounting them on large treefern slabs. The roots, which relish a free run, will penetrate the mount extremely quickly. The flower spike will be free to grow downward, and the plant will relish the heaviest of waterings in the growing season and still dry out quite rapidly between applications.

Another genus which has been present in collections for a long time and is lately achieving renewed popularity is *Catasetum*. This intriguing genus, which produces both male and

A *Catasetum* species (possibly *C. discolor*) growing in full sunlight in the Amazonian forest.

female flowers from the same plant (but not usually at the same time — bright light tends to produce female flowers, subdued light male flowers), was one with which we had had little success until we actually saw plants growing in their native habitat. In early summer we saw plants of *C. discolor* growing on the banks of the Rio Negro, close to the equator. It was the dry season (as much as there is a dry season on Amazonian rivers) and the plants were growing on bare tree-trunks exposed to the full sun. They were all plump and healthy. Since then we have changed our methods, wintering our *Catasetum* species (and plants of the related genera *Clowesia* and *Mormodes*) in warm humid conditions with bright light, and almost no direct water at all.

Schomburgkia crispa, the only species of this genus found in Brazil, grows in the same general area and under much the same conditions as catasetums. *Cattleya eldorado* and *Cattleya violacea* are also found along the river banks in this area, although growing generally a little closer to the forest canopy and thus enjoying a little more shade.

There seems to be an increasing number of growers in recent years who, whether from conviction or due to constraints of space, are concentrating their efforts on cultivating the miniatures of the orchid world. The smallest plants of the orchid world are just as rewarding as their larger brethren, and Brazil provides an enormous range of species in this field. Unfortunately, the miniatures of the country are not generally popular among Brazilian growers, so the country's nurseries don't carry many examples. But it is well worth while

Cattleya violacea flowering in November on the banks of the Rio Negro

taking the trouble to track them down. Not only do they have their own special charm, but they may be fitted without difficulty into the mixed collection, often occupying those small corners and niches left among the bigger plants. A dozen *Pleurothallis* or *Stelis* plants, or half a dozen of the smaller *Maxillaria* species, will take up little more space than a single *Cattleya* plant. Most will grow happily in the shade of larger plants and will flower regularly and prolifically.

As mentioned before, the substrates we use are those we have available locally. These are treefern, fresh *Sphagnum* moss and the bark and branches of paperbark, and we rely heavily on these materials. In other areas, growers will use different materials such as bark (pine, fir or *Casuarina*) cork, leaf mould, peat moss, etc. Improvisation is one of the keys to successful orchid growing, and intelligent growers will adapt methods of potting, watering, and so on, to the materials available in their own locality. Perhaps the most important point to bear in mind is that the type of substrate will affect significantly the amount and quantity of water given to plants. The type of material — treefern, moss, etc. — which we mostly use is fairly water retentive. If we used cork mounts and open bark mixes then we would need to water more frequently and more copiously than we do.

In this brief survey we have covered only a few of the many Brazilian genera which are commonly cultivated. Many more will be found under the Alphabetical Listing of Species, together with recommendations as to their treatment in cultivation. Few Brazilian species present serious problems for the orchid grower with some knowledge of natural habitat, who is willing to experiment a little.

5 · THE ORCHID FAMILY IN BRAZIL

When we think of Brazilian orchids, the genera which probably first come to mind are those which have been so popular in cultivation for the last hundred years or so — the brilliant multi-flowered *Oncidium*, the vibrant orange and red *Sophronitis*, the wonderful bifoliate *Cattleya*. Yet, even when added together, the members of these three genera account for no more than about five per cent of the orchid species found in Brazil. There are over one hundred and fifty *Encyclia* and *Epidendrum*, one hundred *Octomeria*, more than three hundred *Pleurothallis*, sixty-odd *Catasetum*, one hundred *Maxillaria*; not to mention dozens of smaller genera containing exciting and often spectacular flowers such as *Acacallis, Cycnoches, Bifrenaria, Huntleya, Miltonia, Promenaea* and so on.

The botanical order in which all orchids are arranged by botanists is largely determined by variations in floral structure which have been developed by the plants to attract specific pollinators. While botanists are using new diagnostic aids, such as chromosome numbers and variations in pollen structure (through electron microscopy), floral variation remains the most significant factor. And, from a horticultural point of view, this means that often comparisons of these floral variations enable us to see quite clearly the relationships between particular genera and species.

For ease of reference, the species listed in this book are set out in alphabetical, rather than botanical, order. While this method makes it easier to find the illustration and reference for a particular species, it has the disadvantage of obscuring the botanical relationships between closely related genera and species. Both the genera *Leptotes* and *Cattleya*, for instance, belong to the same subtribe (*Laeliinae*) and the same alliance (*Epidendrum*), but this relationship is not apparent in an alphabetical listing. For this reason we have included the following table, which sets out the botanical organisation of Brazilian orchids (following the system of Pabst and Dungs). We hope this will assist readers in placing the various genera in their appropriate botanical context.

Subfamily	Tribe	Subtribe	Alliance	Genus
Cypripedioideae	Cypripedieae	Cypripedilinae		Phragmipedium Selenipedium
Orchidioideae	Orchideae	Orchidinae		Habenaria
Neottioideae	Neottiae	Caladeniinae		Codonorchis
		Chloraeinae		Chloraea Geoblasta Bipinnula
		Vanillinae		Vanilla Epistephium
		Pogoniinae		Cleistes Pogoniopsis Triphora Psilochilus Duckeella
		Sobraliinae		Elleanthus Sobralia Palmorchis Xerorchis
	Cranichideae	Gastrodinae		Uleiorchis
		Cranichidinae		Cranichis Prescottia Baskervilla Ponthieva Wullschlaegelia Stenoptera
		Spiranthinae		Hapalorchis Beloglottis Disciphus Mesadenus Brachystele Sauroglossum Cyclopogon Sarcoglottis Eurystyles Pelexia Cogniauxiocharis Lankesterella Mesadenella Stenorrhynchus Lyroglossa Pteroglossa Eltroplectris Buchtienia
		Goodyerinae		Erythrodes
		Tropidiinae		Corymborchis
Epidendroideae	Epidendreae	Liparidinae		Liparis Malaxis

Subfamily	Tribe	Subtribe	Alliance	Genus
		Dendrobiinae		Polystachya
				Galeandra
				Bulbophyllum
		Laeliinae	Epidendrum	Amblostoma
				Hexisia
				Pinelia
				Jacquiniella
				Caularthron
				Dimerandra
				Encyclia
				Epidendrum
				Lanium
				Cattleya
				Laelia
				Schomburgkia
				Renata
				Pseudolaelia
				Brassavola
				Isabelia
				Sophronitis
				Sophronitella
				Constantia
				Pygmaeorchis
				Leptotes
				Loefgrenianthus
			Ponera	Reichenbachanthus
				Scaphyglottis
				Tetragamestus
				Ponera
				Orleanesia
				Isochilus
				Hexadesmia
		Pleurothallidinae		Lepanthes
				Cryptophoranthus
				Stelis
				Phloeophila
				Physosiphon
				Masdevallia
				Lepanthopsis
				Platystele
				Pleurothallis
				Pleurobotryum
				Barbosella
				Brachionidium
				Octomeria
				Pleurothallopsis
	Vandeae	Phajinae		Bletia
		Catasetinae		Mormodes
				Catasetum
				Cycnoches

Subfamily	Tribe	Subtribe	Alliance	Genus
		Eulophidiinae		Eulophidium
		Cyrtopodiinae		Eulophia
				Pteroglossaspis
				Cyrtopodium
				Cyanaeorchis
				Govenia
				Grobya
		Gongorinae		Promenaea
				Eriopsis
				Peristeria
				Houlletia
				Paphinia
				Polycycnis
				Stanhopea
				Gongora
				Coryanthes
				Cirrhaea
		Zygopetalinae	Lycaste	Xylobium
				Bifrenaria
				Rudolfiella
				Lycaste
			Zygopetalum	Pabstia
				Zygopetalum
				Neogardneria
				Zygosepalum
				Batemannia
				Mendoncella
				Aganisia
				Acacallis
				Otostylis
				Koellensteinia
				Paradisanthus
				Warrea
			Huntleya	Cheiradenia
				Hoehneella
				Chaubardia
				Bollea
				Huntleya
				Cochleanthes
			Maxillaria	Maxillaria
				Ornithidium
				Scuticaria
				Mormolyca
				Trigonidium
			Dichaea	Dichaea
		Oncidiinae	Oncidium	Gomesa
				Binoti
				Rodrigueziella
				Solenidium

Subfamily	Tribe	Subtribe	Alliance	Genus
				Oncidium
				Baptistonia
				Otoglossum
				Miltonia
				Brassia
				Aspasia
				Macradenia
				Warmingia
				Sigmatostalix
				Leochilus
			Trichocentrum	Trichocentrum
				Centroglossa
			Comparettia	Comparettia
				Plectrophora
				Rodriguezia
				Ionopsis
			Capanemia	Trizeuxis
				Sanderella
				Ornithophora
				Diadenium
				Rodrigueziopsis
				Quekettia
				Capanemia
			Trichopilia	Trichopilia
				Leucohyle
			Ornithocephalus	Dipteranthus
				Zygostates
				Ornithocephalus
				Chytroglossa
				Phymatidium
				Platyrhiza
				Thysanoglossa
			Lockhartia	Psygmorchis
				Lockhartia
			Saundersia	Saundersia
			Notylia	Notylia
		Pterostemminae		Pterostemma
		Cryptarrheninae		Cryptarrhena
		Sarcanthinae		Campylocentrum

36

ALPHABETICAL LISTING OF SPECIES

As we are not professional taxonomists or botanists, and as this book is intended for a horticultural rather than a scientific audience, we have adopted a fairly conservative stance on matters of taxonomy. It is clear from the continuing publication by botanists and taxonomists, both in Brazil and in other countries, that we can expect to see a continuing revision of many Brazilian genera for some time to come; but this is not the place to anticipate such revisions.

We have, in general, followed the classification set out in Pabst and Dungs' *Orchidaceae Brasilienses* (which in turn generally follows Garay). We have preferred Fowlie's more recent revision of the genus *Sophronitis*, although even in this revision minor puzzles remain, and

Formerly known as *Stenocoryne racemosa*, this species is now regarded as a *Bifrenaria*.

we have given consideration to Withner's recent treatment of the genera *Cattleya* and *Laelia*.

Although we treated Lindley's genus *Stenocoryne* as a distinct genus in *Miniature Orchids*, the first book in this series, we have reverted to the classification used by Pabst and Dungs whereby *Stenocoryne* appears as a section of the genus *Bifrenaria*. It is not clear to us exactly what criteria those authors have used to justify the inclusion. They state that the presence in the genus *Bifrenaria* of a bifurcated caudicle differentiates the genus from *Maxillaria*; yet in one, *Bifrenaria (Stenocoryne) stefanae*, the caudicle does not appear to be split. Given that we are writing from a horticultural rather than a botanical viewpoint, we have been tempted to revert to Lindley's original concept of *Stenocoryne* as a separate genus; after all, they are much smaller plants than the true *Bifrenaria*, have smaller flowers and more of them, and bear them on much longer more slender spikes. However, contemporary Brazilian botanists have followed Pabst and Dungs and are naming new species accordingly so, despite our reservations, we have gone along too. We also acknowledge the recent monograph by Castro on the *Stenocoryne* as a section of the genus *Bifrenaria*.

There are some other arguments in which we do not feel disposed to engage.

The beautiful *Cattleya harrisoniana*, often found in the hot coastal swamps of eastern Brazil, is tolerant of a wide range of temperatures in cultivation.

One such is the vexing question of *Cattleya harrisoniana* and *C. loddigesii* — do they constitute two separate species, two races within one species, one species and one subspecies, or indeed a single species? Frankly we do not know, and the more we read about the subject the more confused we become. A century ago, Veitch said that the stems of *C. loddigesii* were longer that those of *C. harrisoniana*; Sander said the reverse. Veitch said *C. loddigesii* flowered in spring, *C. harrisoniana* in autumn; Sander said the former flowered in late summer, the latter in summer. Cogniaux was thwarted in his first attempt to clarify matters when the captions of his illustrations were transposed by the printer. To complicate matters, until recent times, *C. harrisoniana* was sometimes known (incorrectly) as *C. harrisoniae*.

The habitats of the two species are adjacent: *C. loddigesii* at higher elevations in the state of São Paulo, *C. harrisoni-*

ana at lower elevations in Rio de Janeiro; where the two meet in the region of the Rio Paraíba, intergrades between the two species occur. This further complicates correct identification. It is Fowlie's opinion, after extensive study, that the two are separate species, and we are happy to accept this view, and his evidence on this vexed question. It is certainly a satisfactory answer from a horticultural viewpoint, although some Brazilian writers (though not Pabst and Dungs) still regard *C. harrisoniana* as a subspecies of *C. loddigesii*.

There has also been much discussion concerning the flowering habit of *Cattleya walkeriana*. Some plants flower, as is the general case with *Cattleya* species, on a spike which rises from the apex of the matured pseudobulb. Others flower on what Braem calls 'a special flower stalk

This clone of *Cattleya walkeriana* flowers in autumn from a basal rather than an apical spike.

generated from the base of the pseudo-bulb' (although our own observation suggests that this flower stalk rises not from the base of the pseudobulb, but from the extending rhizome). Braem regards the plants with basal spikes as the true *C. walkeriana*, and those which flower from the apex as natural hybrids with *C. loddigesii*, occurring where the habitats of the two species overlap. Fowlie gives some consequence to this view, although he suggests that the influence of *C. loddigesii* may be small except for a residual genetic predisposition to apical flowering due to occasional hybridising. He points out that plants of *C. walkeriana* which flower from the apex are more commonly found near the western limit of the species' range, where *C. loddigesii* is found.

Fowlie also makes the observation that basal-flowering plants 'flower from the base of the most recently matured pseudobulb atop a vestigial and highly modified stalk, formed from the abortification of a regular pseudobulb growth but superficially given the appearance of a stalk'. This is an interesting observation, especially when considered in the context of flowering times. *C. walkeriana* has two well-established flowering seasons. Some plants flower in Brazil (also in Australia, and presumably in other southern hemisphere countries) from March to May (autumn), while others flower from October to December (spring to early summer). It has been our experience that apically flowering plants bloom in spring, while basally flowering plants do so in autumn. Synanthous flowering (where flower spikes appear concurrently with new growth) is common in many genera such as *Zygopetalum* and *Dendrochilum*, but not in *Cattleya*. Yet the autumn-blooming basal-flowering plants

After its initial discovery, *Cattleya labiata* was lost to cultivation for many years until rediscovered by accident.

of *C. walkeriana* present what appears to be a case of synanthous flowering although, as Fowlie points out, the new growth fails to develop into a full-sized pseudobulb. Perhaps the onset of winter dormancy serves to abort the new pseudobulb. We have not seen enough material to do more than suggest this as a possibility, and it may be due to genetic or merely climatic factors.

The monofoliate *Cattleya* species of South America — probably the largest and showiest orchids of the continent — have been the subject of much argument over the years: are there in fact many species, or just one, *C. labiata*? Over the years we have compared flowers, and pictures of flowers, and drawings of flowers from many of these species and we are still not much the wiser. There are so many differences between clones and varieties of *C. labiata*, and so many similarities between *C. labiata* and other monofoliate *Cattleya* species, that it is exceptionally hard to reach an opinion. In the end, we can do no better than agree with Guido Braem, who says in the introduction to his book on the unifoliate *Cattleya*:

Some authors consider most of the unifoliate cattleyas to be varieties or synonyms of *Cattleya labiata* Lindley and it is certainly not difficult to find enough arguments to support that view ... [the] differences can mostly be explained by the different geophysical data of the areas where the plants grow ... In spite of all this, I have decided to treat most taxa as separate species as far as they have been initially described as such, but I certainly do not feel entirely happy in doing so.

We feel we can do no more than follow Braem, although we share his attitude and his feeling of unease.

Cattleya labiata, the species on which Lindley founded the genus, has an interesting history. It has been recounted often but, as it bears strongly on the geographical location of the species, it probably bears repeating here.

The first plants were sent from Rio de Janeiro to William Cattley, a wealthy amateur orchid grower in England, in 1818. Lindley named the genus after Cattley, who first flowered it. Swainson, the original supplier of the plant, was not a resident of Brazil, and not an orchid specialist, and apparently had no detailed knowledge of the location of the species in its native habitat. It was assumed — rather boldly — that the species came from the Rio de Janeiro area, and it was largely in that area that it was sought for the next seventy years.

However, in 1836 the naturalist George Gardner thought he had found it. He wrote in his book, *Travels to the Interior of Brazil*:

Near the sea and about 15 miles from the city (of Rio de Janeiro) rise the Gavea, or Topsail Mountain, so called from its square shape ... On the face of the mountain we observed some large patches of one of these beautiful large-flowered orchidaceous plants which are so common in Brazil. Its large rose-coloured

flowers were very conspicuous but we could not reach them. A few days afterwards we found it on a neighbouring mountain, and ascertained it to be *Cattleya labiata*.

Unfortunately, within the next few years these sites were stripped of trees, and the true identity of the plants which Gardner saw is uncertain. Louis Forget, who collected for the great orchid firm of Sander later in the century, thought that Gardner might have seen *Laelia lobata*, which comes from the area in question. However, in view of our present knowledge of the distribution of *Cattleya* species in Brazil, it is more than likely that Gardner actually saw *Cattleya warneri*, one of those species so close to *C. labiata* in appearance that it is sometimes regarded as no more than a variety of that species.

C. warneri, appears to be restricted to a relatively small area near the coast, centred on the state of Espírito Santo, but extending northward as far as the southern part of Bahia and southward into the state of Rio de Janeiro. *C. labiata*, in fact, occurs in another restricted area in the far north-east, centred on the states of Pernambuco and Paraíba, and extending into northern Bahia and southern Ceará.

Because of its beauty, *C. labiata* (or *C. labiata vera* as it became known, to distinguish it from the other unifoliates) was sought by collectors over the ensuing half-century with great persistence but no success. Many other beautiful orchids were found in the process, but *C. labiata* remained known only from propagations of the original importation. All the great orchid importers of Europe — Sander, Low, Veitch, Bull, Rollison, Charlesworth — sent out collectors to Brazil, but to no avail. Yet odd specimens kept turning up in out of the way collections. Two plants were found in, of all places, the Zoological Gardens in Regent's Park, London. In 1885 a few plants turned up in the Imperial Gardens at St Petersburg. No one seemed to know where they had come from.

No one was more anxious than Sander to find the lost species. Not only would it be a great commercial coup, but such a rediscovery would enhance his reputation. He sent out collector after collector to South America — Clarke, Arnold, Chesterton, Bartholomeus, Kerbach, the Klaboch brothers, Oversluys, Smith, Bestwood, Osmers, Digance. But in the end it was a simple piece of good luck which put Sander on the right track. In late 1892 or early 1893 Sander visited a French entomologist named Moreau who was also a keen amateur of orchids. And there, in Moreau's Parisian glasshouse, he found several magnificent specimens of *C. labiata* in full flower. Moreau did not even know the name of the species but, to Sander's enormous joy, was able to identify the Brazilian habitat of the plants. His collectors, searching for something quite different, but knowing of Moreau's passion for orchids, had collected fifty plants and sent them back to France.

Sander made his own — and very secret — arrangements for collecting the rediscovered species. No mention of the venture appears in his correspondence files for the period. But by the beginning of 1894 Sander was marketing vast quantities of the species. It seems likely that the collector Louis Forget might have been involved in Sander's operation, because in 1897 he wrote an article for *Le Jardin* in which he described the habitat of *C. labiata*.

The *Cattleya labiata* grows in the mountains of the interior, in the state of Pernambuco and in the neighbouring, to the north of Parahyba, and to the south of Allagoas . . . During the rainy season which is of three months' duration, the vegetation grows with incredible rapidity, after which, owing to the torrid heat, the leaves fall from the trees, giving the region the aspect of winter in Europe. No stranger could ever dream that *Cattleya labiata* or its allies could exist here. But towards the summits of the mountains, one discovers here and there ravines and gorges where virgin forest still persists. It is here that the plant is found, growing on the large trees whose trunks are garnished with Aroids, Begonias, ferns etc. The *Cattleya* grows chiefly on the lateral branches of the trees . . . in the shade of the evergreen foliage . . .

It certainly seems at first glance an unlikely place to find a species which, in cultivation, thrives in much more moderate conditions. What Forget did not mention is that it is found generally at elevations of 600 to 1,000 m above sea level where it is subject to cooling breezes. Its habitat, in fact, has much in common with some of the South-east Asian dendrobiums which have their home in the hot deciduous forests in montane and sub-montane areas. It is hardly surprising, in view of its isolated and unlikely habitat, that it took collectors so long to rediscover *C. labiata*.

The genus *Sophronitis* has also presented some difficulties for taxonomists. This is another instance where, due to the lack of early botanical work on Brazilian flora, it has been left to later taxonomists to do most of the pioneering work on what has proved to be quite a complex, if numerically small, genus. The situation was not improved by the perpetuation of errors, made by early taxonomists, which prevailed up to the time of Hoehne's *Iconografia de Orquídeas do Brasil* in 1949. Pabst and Dungs' *Orchidaceae Brasilienses*, lacking as it does adequate keys, is of little help, and it was not until Fowlie's monograph of

1987 that it was possible to identify many *Sophronitis* species with any certainty at all.

Over the years we have imported many *Sophronitis* species from Brazil, often wrongly named, and we are still uncertain of the correct identification of many of the plants in our collection. The genus is scattered over a wide range of isolated montane habitats in southern Brazil, and presents a wide variation in flower form and colour and in vegetative appearance, even within a single species. Flowering times, on occasion a valuable aid, fortunately seem fairly constant. Fowlie's keys are, at the time of writing, the best available, but they rely to some extent on vegetative form and growth habit. There is obviously more work needed on this genus, and it may be that the problems will not be completely solved without the use of electron-microscopy of pollen, or DNA profiles. No doubt some readers will find fault with our identification of some of the *Sophronitis* species pictured in this book. We would be very pleased to hear from anyone able to offer us valid corrections or suggestions.

The rupicolous laelias are another group which often present problems of correct identification. Many of them are relatively recent discoveries, and it is not unlikely that still other species remain to be discovered in the future. In many species vegetative form, as well as flower structure, is very similar, and differentiating characteristics are not always consistent. We have been guided in our identifications by the 1984 monograph by Pabst, which although incomplete in the light of more recent discoveries has useful keys, and by Withner's later work, *The Cattleyas and Their Relatives: Vol. II* (1990).

In the following pages we have included for each species suggestions concerning growing conditions — temperature, water, light, substrates and so on. These suggestions are based largely on our own experience, on results achieved by other growers, and on climatic habitat conditions. They are suggestions only, and their value will be mainly as a guide for adaptation and experimentation. While we are very conscious of the deficiencies of the conventional classification of growing conditions into **cool, intermediate** and **warm**, we have retained them for the simple reason that we have been unable to propose a better method. It is, however, necessary for us to define precisely what we mean by each term.

Cool: minimum winter night temperatures of 5°C, rising to about 15°C in the daytime. Summer maximum temperatures seldom exceeding 25°C.

Intermediate: minimum winter night temperatures in the region of 8–10°C, rising to about 20°C in the daytime. Summer maximum temperatures usually no higher than 30°C.

Warm: minimum winter night temperatures seldom falling below 12–15°C, and rising to 25°C in the daytime. Summer temperatures rising as high as 35°C.

In all cases summer night temperatures may fall to 10°C or lower.

It should be pointed out that in our collection we do not have separate areas dedicated solely to these three climates. Instead, we rely a great deal on the utilisation of temperature differentials within greenhouses. Thus in a greenhouse where general temperatures might be classified as intermediate, we might have heat- and light-loving species, such as some cattleyas, hung high up near the roof, with dendrobiums or oncidiums hung at middle levels, and cool-growing masdevallias on low benches where temperatures are lower and shade heavier. At floor level we might find terrestrial species from cool-temperate bushland. The sensible orchid grower will find a huge variation between one greenhouse microclimate and another, and will use such variations to accommodate a wide range of species within the restrictions imposed by space, finance and geography.

A final note: an asterisk after a species' name in the text indicates that a separate entry for it may be found in the alphabetical listing.

Amblostoma armeniaca (Ldl.) Pabst?

Also found in Peru and Bolivia, *A. armeniaca* was described by Lindley in 1836 as *Epidendrum armeniacum*, using material from Brazil. In the 1970s it was transferred to *Amblostoma* by, we believe, Pabst. *Encyclia macrostachya* and *Epidendrum alopecuros* are conspecific. In Brazil it is found in the cooler humid mountain areas of Pernambuco, Minas Gerais, São Paulo, Rio de Janeiro, Espírito Santo and all southern states.

The clustered pseudobulbs are usually 8.5–15 cm tall, but may reach 24 cm. Only 0.3–0.5 cm in diameter, they are flattened near the apex. Each pseudobulb comprises several nodes, from which new stems may be produced, and is covered with brown sheaths. Near the apex there are two to five fleshy alternating leaves 6–14 cm long and 1.0–1.6 cm wide. They are lanceolate with an acute tapering point and a prominent mid-rib below. A spike 15–18 cm long rises from the apex of the pseudobulb in summer. It carries a conical raceme of seventy to one hundred tiny yellow-green to burnt orange flowers which open over a period of ten to fifteen days until all are open together. They are quite fleshy and last well. The spreading lateral sepals are 0.3–0.4 cm long, and are wing-like with an acute tapering apex. The shorter lanceolate dorsal sepal and the linear 0.2 cm-long petals are held forward. The three-lobed lip is usually up to 0.28 cm long (rarely to 0.4 cm). The rounded lateral lobes are erect, with a large callus between them, while the mid-lobe is triangular.

A. armeniaca, as is suggested by its habitat, prefers a humid, cool to intermediate environment with year-round moisture and moderate light. It grows well when mounted on treefern slabs.

Actual flower size: 0.6–0.8 cm across.

Amblostoma cernua Scheidweiler

Scheidweiler used this species as the type for the genus *Amblostoma* in 1838. Its several synonyms include *A. tridactylum* (1863) and *A. dusenii*. It is reported from Mexico, Bolivia and Peru, as well as Brazil. In Brazil, *A. cernua* is widely distributed, growing epiphytically in Pernambuco, Minas Gerais, Espírito Santo and south to Rio Grande do Sul, occurring at up to 1,000 m.

The narrowly spindle-shaped pseudobulbs are closely set on a creeping rhizome, 10–30 cm tall and 0.5–1.5 cm in diameter and covered with papery sheaths. Up to six alternating linear to oblong-lanceolate leaves are carried on the upper part of the pseudobulbs. They are 8–22 cm long and up to 1.4 cm wide. An erect to arching, branched spike 9–30 cm long rises from the apex of the pseudobulb in late autumn or winter with many rather fleshy flowers. The tepals, which curve inward at the apex, are typically pale yellow, yellow-green or brownish yellow. The elliptic to oblong sepals are 0.3–0.5 cm long and up to 0.3 cm wide, while the sub-spathulate petals are about 0.4 cm long with a very narrow base. The column is joined to the strongly three-lobed lip for its entire length. The rather triangular mid-lobe of the lip is shorter than the slightly more rounded spreading lateral lobes, which have in-rolled margins. The disc has vague lateral calli which are joined to the column.

A. cernua does best in an intermediate environment with moderately bright indirect light.

Actual flower size: approximately 0.4 cm wide.

Aspasia lunata Lindley

Introduced into cultivation in 1843, this species was described by Lindley soon afterwards. *Odontoglossum lunatum* and *Trophianthus zonatus* are synonyms. *A. lunata* grows epiphytically in cool mountain areas of Minas Gerais, São Paulo, Rio de Janeiro, Paraná and other southern states.

The yellow-green to pale green pseudobulbs are set 1–2 cm apart on a creeping rhizome. From 5–7 cm tall and 1.5 cm wide, they are strongly compressed, elliptic and very narrow at the base. There are one or two leaf-bearing bracts at the base and two narrow leaves, up to 20 cm long, at the apex. One or two flowers are produced from spring to early autumn on short spikes from the base of the pseudobulb. The 2.6–3.5 cm sepals and the slightly shorter petals are about 1.5 cm wide. They are apple green with dark purple-brown to maroon blotches on the basal half. They are keeled on the reverse, and have acutely tapering apices. The three-lobed lip, which is 2.5–3.0 cm long, is joined to the column for half the length of the latter. The lip is white with a purple blotch near the base of the rounded undulating mid-lobe. The slightly reflexed lateral lobes are more or less rounded, and there are several ridges in the throat.

A. lunata may be mounted or potted in fairly fibrous material such as treefern chunks. An intermediate environment with fairly high humidity and moderate shade is recommended. It requires plenty of water when in growth followed by a drier resting period after new growths have matured. However, enough water should be given to avoid shrivelling of the pseudobulbs.

Actual flower size: 5–6.5 cm long.

Baptistonia echinata Barbosa Rodrígues

Barbosa Rodrígues described this epiphyte in 1882, naming the monotypic genus for a Brazilian ethnologist, Dr Baptista Caetano d'A Nogueira. However, Reichenbach's *Oncidium brunleesianum* of 1883 is the name by which it was better known until Garay re-established Barbosa Rodrígues' classification in 1970. It differs from *Oncidium* in column shape, callus and mode of flower opening. Brunlees first introduced the species into cultivation in 1879. *O. vellozoanum* and *Epidendrum tetrapetalum* (Velloso, not Jacquin) are conspecific. *B. echinata* grows in the coastal mountains of Rio de Janeiro and São Paulo in subtropical rainforest at 50–800 m.

The clustered, slightly compressed pseudobulbs are 6–12 cm long and about 1 cm across, with several bracts at the base and two acute leaves up to about 18 cm long at the apex. Many flowers are borne on a pendulous spike 25–45 cm long, which rises from the base of the pseudobulb. The 1.2 cm-long tepals are pale yellow-green with pinkish streaks, especially on the strongly recurved petals. The concave dorsal sepal is held forward over the column, while the lateral sepals are joined for almost their entire length. The lip has large, bright yellow lateral lobes 1.3 cm long, which are more or less erect, and a small strongly recurved maroon-purple to almost black mid-lobe. The crest is a glossy plate with purple markings and two erect white 'teeth' near the middle.

B. echinata does well on treefern mounts in an intermediate environment with moderate humidity and light. Good ventilation is important.

Actual flower size: 2–2.5 cm across.

Barbosella miersii (Ldl.) Schlechter

A member of a small genus named by Schlechter in honour of J. Barbosa Rodrígues, one-time director of the Botanical Gardens in Rio de Janeiro, this tiny epiphyte was originally described as *Pleurothallis miersii* by Lindley in 1842. Schlechter transferred it to his new genus in 1918. In 1981 Luer transferred it to his new monotypic genus *Barbrodria*, but it is still most generally regarded as a barbosella, and we have chosen to retain this usage. The reason for Luer's transfer was the presence of a ball-and-socket arrangement between the lip and column foot, unique among *Barbosella* species. *Barbosella miersii* grows in the cool moist mountains of the southern Brazilian states of Rio de Janeiro, São Paulo, Paraná and Santa Catarina.

This tiny creeping plant can form dense mats and is attached to its host by very short roots. The 0.3 cm fleshy paddle-shaped leaves rise almost directly from the branching rhizome. This species may flower more than once a year with single straw-yellow to pale greenish-yellow flowers borne on 1.0 cm spikes. The flowers are only about 0.3 cm long with pointed segments. The narrow petals are minutely serrated along their outer half. The tiny lip sits on the lateral sepals which are joined for about one third of their length.

A cool to intermediate shady environment is recommended for this species. It does well when grown on a fibrous mount such as treefern, and should be kept moist all year round.

Actual flower size: approximately 0.3 cm long.

Bifrenaria atropurpurea (Lodd.) Lindley

Warre discovered this species near Rio de Janeiro in 1828 and sent plants to Loddiges, who described it as *Maxillaria atropurpurea*. In 1832 Lindley used it as the type species for the genus *Bifrenaria*. Brade's *B. caparaoensis* is conspecific. It inhabits the high rocky mountains of Espírito Santo, Rio de Janeiro, São Paulo and Minas Gerais.

The four-angled pseudobulbs are 4–7 cm tall, 2–4 cm across near the base. There is typically a single elliptic to lanceolate leaf at the apex. From 12–27 cm long and 6–9 cm wide, the leaves have three to five prominent veins. Flower spikes are produced from the base of the pseudobulb in early summer. From 6–8 cm long, they carry three to five very fleshy flowers which are pleasantly fragrant but do not open widely. The tepals are purple-maroon with yellow-green central markings. The oblong sepals are 2.6–4.0 cm long and 1.2–2.0 cm wide, with the concave dorsal sepal having a sharply pointed apex. The lateral sepals are keeled and joined at the base to enclose a spur formed by the purple column and the hinged lip. The narrower petals are 1.7–2.5 cm long, somewhat diamond-shaped, point forward and curve inward. The fiddle-shaped lip is 1.6–2.0 cm long. The triangular lateral lobes are whitish with purple-maroon veins, as is the base of the recurved mid-lobe. The remainder of the 1 cm-wide mid-lobe is purplish pink with darker edges. Near the base there is a thickened callus ending in three raised lobes.

B. atropurpurea is an easy plant to grow, potted or mounted, and does well in moderately bright intermediate conditions.

Actual flower size: approximately 3 cm across.

Bifrenaria aureo-fulva (Hook.) Lindley

This species, which comes from the mountain regions of southern Brazil, was first described by Hooker as *Maxillaria aureo-fulva,* but was later transferred by Lindley to the genus *Bifrenaria*. Kraenzlin later transferred it to the genus *Stenocoryne,* but most botanists today treat it as a member of the *Stenocoryne* section of *Bifrenaria.* Other synonyms include *Maxillaria stenopetala* and *Stenocoryne secunda.*

The clustered, strongly four-angled pseudobulbs are dark yellow-green or brown-green. From 2.5–3.5 cm tall, they bear a single 12–20 cm leaf with a prominent midvein and an acute apex. The erect to pendulous spike appears from the base of the pseudobulb in late spring. From 12–30 cm long, it bears three to fifteen nodding orange flowers which are tinged with green on the outside. The 1.6 cm sepals and petals are elongated and taper to acute apices. The recurved dorsal sepal and petals are held forward. The lateral sepals join at the base to form a spur. The 1.6 cm lip is an elongated diamond. The callus at the base is three-lobed at its apex, the mid-lobe short and triangular, the outer ones larger and rounded.

This species grows well in bright intermediate conditions with plenty of water in the growing season and a drier rest in winter. It may be potted in any well-drained fibrous material or grown on slabs of treefern or cork with a little moss about the base of the plant.

Actual flower size: approximately 2 cm across.

Bifrenaria calcarata Barbosa Rodrígues

Barbosa Rodrígues described this species at about the end of the nineteenth century. It is confined to the cooler mountains of Rio de Janeiro and Espírito Santo.

The clustered pyramidal pseudobulbs are strongly four-angled, 4–6 cm tall and up to 3 cm wide. Each bears a single tough leaf 25–40 cm long and 4.0–4.5 cm wide which has several prominent veins below. In spring a spike about 5 cm long from the base of the pseudobulb bears one to three fleshy flowers which do not open fully. The 3 cm-long sepals, which have recurved apices, are green, strongly suffused with maroon-purple. The lanceolate dorsal sepal is 1.7 cm wide, concave at the base, and projects forward over the column. The lateral sepals are joined to the column to form a spur 1.2–1.5 cm long, which curves back towards the ovary. The petals are pale yellow-green with wide violet margins which are irregular and slightly wavy. The rhomboidal petals are 2.5 cm long, 1.5 cm wide, and recurved at the apex. The hinged lip is 2.8 cm long, including a 0.4 cm-long narrow claw. The basal half is yellow, spotted with maroon-purple. Above this is a narrow cream band, followed by violet on the rounded apical lobe. The apical one-third of the erect 1.7 cm-long lateral lobes is also violet. The apical lobe and the front edges of the lateral lobes are furnished with silky hairs. There is a white callus in the centre of the lip.

B. calcarata is, like most of the bifrenarias, an easy subject in cultivation, requiring cool to intermediate conditions with bright indirect light. It may be potted or mounted, and needs a dry winter rest.

Actual flower size: 4–5 cm across.

Bifrenaria charlesworthii Rolfe

Described by Rolfe about the end of the nineteenth century, this species was later transferred to *Stenocoryne* by Hoehne, but today is generally treated as a member of the *Stenocoryne* section of *Bifrenaria*. It comes from cooler mountain areas of Minas Gerais.

The matt green to brownish-green pseudobulbs are 2.5–3.5 cm long and 1.5–2.5 cm wide, compressed and four-angled. Each bears a single tough dull green leaf 9–15 cm long and 2.0–3.5 cm wide. The leaf is more or less elliptic with a sharply pointed apex. Flower spikes approximately 17 cm long rise from the base of the pseudobulb in summer, and bear about six flowers. The acute tepals are greenish yellow. The 2 cm-long sepals are 1.2 cm wide with slightly recurved edges except at the apex, where they curve inward. The lateral sepals are joined at the base to form a small spur which is held perpendicular to the flower stalk. The dorsal sepal is curved over the column, which is covered with tiny white hairs, and over the 1.5 cm-long petals. The petals are held forward above the column. The almost round to triangular lip is 1.0–1.2 cm across and joined to the base of the column by a 0.4 cm claw. The pale yellow lip, which is sparsely covered with coarse white hairs, is veined with red-purple on the basal half, which curves up on either side of the column. The outer half has frilly edges, while the centre of the lip bears a large erect orange callus which is three-lobed at the front.

This species may be potted, but grows best for us when mounted on treefern. Cool to intermediate conditions with fairly bright light.

Actual flower size: approximately 4 cm across.

Bifrenaria harrisoniae (Hook.) Reichenbach (f.)

In about 1821 William Harrison sent plants of this species from Rio de Janeiro to his brother in Liverpool. Hooker described it as *Dendrobium harrisoniae* in 1825, naming it in honour of William's relative and avid orchid collector Mrs Arnold Harrison. Reichenbach transferred it to *Bifrenaria* in 1854. Synonyms include *Maxillaria harrisoniae* and *Colax harrisoniae*. Mostly epiphytic, this species is also found growing on rocks, often in full sun. It occurs from Minas Gerais and Espírito Santo south to Santa Catarina and Rio Grande do Sul.

The four-angled ovoid to pyramidal pseudobulbs are yellow, green or brown-green, 3.0–7.5 cm tall and up to 3 cm wide. Each bears a single leathery leaf 10–32 cm long and 5–10 cm wide. In spring one or two fleshy very fragrant flowers are produced on a short spike. The tepals are usually ivory-white, yellowing with age. The 4.0–4.5 cm-long dorsal sepal is about 2.4 cm wide, concave and more or less oblong with a rounded apex. The slightly longer and wider lateral sepals form a 2 cm-long spur at the base. The vaguely rhomboidal petals are shorter and narrower. The hinged lip is white or cream, heavily veined and streaked with very dark maroon to pale pink, and is covered with fine silky hairs. The oblong lateral lobes are erect, while the notched mid-lobe is reflexed. In the centre of the lip is a large orange-yellow callus covered with hairs.

This species is a very easy grower, tolerating a wide range of conditions, but grows best given intermediate to cool conditions, moderate light, and a dry winter rest. It does well for us when grown in suspended pots.

Actual flower size: approximately 7.5 cm across.

Bifrenaria harrisoniae var. *alba* Kraenzlin

One of the most sought-after varieties of *B. harrisoniae*, the variety *alba* was described by the German botanist Fritz Kraenzlin. The habit of *B. harrisoniae* var. *alba* is the same as that of the type species and, like the type, one or two flowers are born on short sub-erect to almost horizontal spikes which rise from the base of the pseudobulbs. Flowering time, as with the type species, is mid- to late spring.

In this variety of *B. harrisoniae,* the waxy sepals and petals are white, with a clearly visible network of veins, especially on the irregularly edged petals. The undulating apical lobe of the lip is white, while the throat and trilobed callus are yellow or orange-yellow. The erect lateral lobes show the same colour range as the throat, with white slightly reflexed apical margins.

As well as the variety *alba,* there exists the very rare variety *alba-plena*, the flowers of which have a pure white lip and callus, showing no trace of yellow, as well as white sepals and petals. It was first collected by Roberto Kautsky, who discovered it in Espírito Santo in 1974. Guido Pabst described it soon afterwards.

B. harrisoniae var. *alba*, like the type and the other varieties, is a very hardy plant, and does well in baskets or suspended pots of treefern chunks and sandstone pieces, or some other freely draining material. A light airy position in intermediate to cool conditions suits it well. Good ventilation or air movement is essential, especially in winter when plants are dormant. Pseudobulbs often become a little shrivelled and 'ribby' at this time of the year, but soon fill out when new growth begins.

Actual flower size: approximately 7.5 cm across.

Bifrenaria harrisoniae varieties

The flowers of *B. harrisoniae* are fairly uniform in regard to size and shape, but quite variable in colour. This has resulted in the naming of a number of varieties based on flower colour. As with the type, the flowers of the varieties are very fleshy and quite long-lasting, with an intense but pleasant rose-like fragrance. We call the variety pictured here *rosea*, a purely informal and horticultural name. The pale sepals are pale pink to dark purplish pink, while the petals are white. The recurved mid-lobe of the lip is pale pink to blood-red with darker maroon veins. The erect lateral lobes, which have irregular apical margins, are heavily veined with dark maroon on a paler background colour than that of the mid-lobe — pale pink to pale orange.

This variety most closely resembles Hoehne's variety *typica*, which has similarly coloured sepals and petals. However, the lip of var. *typica* is described as pale yellow with purple to blood-red veins. The variety *pubigera*, originally described by Klotzsch as *Maxillaria pubigera*, has a more compact habit. The flowers open more widely, presenting a more rounded appearance. The tepals are white, tinged with rose. The lip has a darker rose-coloured mid-lobe and yellow lateral lobes, which are veined with dark rose-purple. The rare variety *citrina*, also known as *Lycaste citrina*, was so named by Stein because of its lemon-yellow tepals. The lip is white with lilac markings. The variety *grandiflora*, which is a horticultural not a botanical variety, has flowers which are distinctly larger than those of the type.

Actual flower size: approximately 7.5 cm across.

Bifrenaria magnicalcarata (Hoehne) Pabst

Hoehne described this species as *B. tyrianthina* var. *magnicalcarata*, and it was later elevated to specific status by Pabst. It grows mostly as a lithophyte in the savannah country of Minas Gerais and São Paulo.

The strongly four-angled pseudobulbs are 5.0–6.5 cm tall, 2.5–3.0 cm in diameter, and elongated to pear-shaped. They are dull olive-green in colour, often marked with brown at the base. Each bears a single leathery leaf 15–30 cm long and 4–5 cm wide with an acutely tapering apex. From one to four very fleshy flowers are borne in spring on a spike up to about 12 cm long. The sepals are maroon-brown with green at the base and, like the petals, which are green and heavily suffused and edged with maroon-brown, have recurved apices. The concave lanceolate to oval dorsal sepal is 3.6–4.0 cm long, about 2 cm wide, and is held forward. The longer lateral sepals, which are oblong with an obtuse apex, are extended and joined at the base to form a 1.5–2.0 cm-long spur. The shorter narrower petals are rhomboidal, while the 4.0–4.5 cm-long lip has a short claw at the base and a deflexed rounded apical lobe. It is creamy-white with pinkish-mauve on the apical lobe and the front sections of the large, erect lateral lobes. The mauve section is furnished with long silky hairs. An oblong white callus runs from the base to the middle of the lip.

B. magnicalcarata may be mounted or grown in baskets or pots of coarse treefern fibre and broken sandstone. It likes a fairly bright position in an intermediate to cool environment and should be given a dry winter rest.

Actual flower size: 6–7 cm across.

Bifrenaria melanopoda Klotzsch

Klotzsch originally described this species, which was later transferred by Hoehne to the genus *Stenocoryne*. Today, however, *Stenocoryne* is generally treated as a section of *Bifrenaria*. The specific epithet probably refers to the dark foot-like projection at the base of the column. Epiphytic and endemic to Brazil, this species comes from cool damp mountain areas in the states of Rio de Janeiro, São Paulo and Minas Gerais.

The compressed 2–4 cm-tall pseudobulbs are vaguely four-angled, somewhat wrinkled and clustered on a stout rhizome, often lying flat against the host. The single, sharply pointed leaf which rises from the apex of each pseudobulb is dark green, broad, and 10–18 cm long, including the short stalk. In spring the arching to pendulous spikes which rise from the base of the pseudobulbs carry four to ten well-spaced flowers about 2.0–2.5 cm across. The flowers typically do not open widely, but may do so in some clones. They are greenish-yellow suffused with pinkish brown, and have two bright red spots at the base of the lip. The 1.6 cm dorsal sepal is hooded over the column. The 1.3 cm oval petals are pointed and usually held forward, but sometimes curve outward. The elliptic lateral sepals are widest at the base, where they join to form a small chin. The single-lobed lip is much crisped, with turned-up edges and a yellow callus in the middle.

This species needs intermediate conditions and moderately bright light. It may be potted, but does very well when mounted on treefern slabs. Keep on the dry side in winter.

Actual flower size: 2–2.5 cm across.

Bifrenaria racemosa (Hook.) Hooker

This species was first described as *Maxillaria racemosa* by Hooker, who later transferred it to the genus *Bifrenaria*. Kraenzlin later transferred it to the genus *Stenocoryne* which is now generally accepted as a section of *Bifrenaria*. This epiphytic species comes from the southern states of Rio de Janeiro, Espírito Santo, Paraná and São Paulo, where it grows in cool montane habitats.

The clustered pseudobulbs, 2–5 cm tall, are vaguely four-angled, compressed, and rather wrinkled. Sometimes slightly curved, they are light to mid-green, often marked with dull brownish-yellow. The single leaf, which is folded at the base to form a short stalk, is 11–15 cm long and up to 2.5 cm wide, tapering to an acute point. It is quite leathery, dark green, and has a prominent mid-vein underneath. In spring sub-erect to pendulous spikes 8–15 cm long (occasionally to 30 cm) carry three to ten nodding flowers about 2.5 cm across. The 1.2 cm tepals may be white suffused with pink, greenish-white, or green, and have slightly recurved margins and a sharply pointed apex. The dorsal sepal is held forward and the spreading lateral sepals are joined at the base to enclose the 0.3 cm spur formed by the claw of the lip and the base of the column. The petals project forward. The 1.2 cm roundish lip is very wavy, with its sides curved upward at the base, and a white or yellow three-lobed callus.

This species does well for us mounted on treefern slabs and hung in moderately bright light. Intermediate conditions suit it well. Give a dry winter rest.

Actual flower size: approximately 2.5 cm across.

Bifrenaria stefanae Castro

Considered until recently a form of *B. vitellina*, which has more widely opening flowers, this taxon was given specific rank by Castro in late 1991. It was named in honour of Stefana Solacolu, a Brazilian supporter of orchidology. It occurs in São Paulo at 500–600 m, and also in Minas Gerais.

The pseudobulbs are four-angled, 3.5–5.0 cm tall and up to 2.5 cm in diameter, each with a single arching apical leaf 19–40 cm long. About six nodding flowers are borne on arching spikes 18–20 cm long in late summer or autumn. The yellow tepals are faintly suffused with pink and are held parallel to the column and lip. The asymmetrical lateral sepals are keeled on the reverse and form a short spur at the base to enclose the base of the lip and the column. At 1.5–1.8 cm long and 0.8–0.9 cm wide at the base, they are longer and wider than the slightly concave lanceolate dorsal sepal. The somewhat elliptical petals are 1.1–1.6 cm long, up to 0.8 cm wide, and turn outward at the acute apex. The yellow lip has a few reddish streaks near the base and a large maroon blotch on the mid-lobe, which is wider than it is long, very frilly at the bilobed recurved apex, and has sparse fine hairs. The large triangular lateral lobes are 1.3 cm long, meet above the column, and are rounded at the crisped front edges. Near the base of the mid-lobe is a yellow three-lobed callus about 0.2 cm wide.

B. stefanae prefers an intermediate to cool environment with semi-shade to moderate light and a drier winter rest. Plants do best for us when mounted on treefern slabs.

Actual flower size: approximately 1.7 cm across.

Bifrenaria tetragona (Ldl.) Schlechter

Originally described by Lindley as *Maxillaria tetragona*, this species was reclassified as a bifrenaria by Schlechter It comes from the mountain areas of Rio de Janeiro, São Paulo, Paraná, Santa Catarina and Rio Grande do Sul.

The four-angled tapering pseudobulbs, 5.5–10.5 cm tall and 3.0–5.0 cm wide at the base, carry a single leathery leaf. This leaf is 25–45 cm long and up to 8 cm wide, elliptic with an acute apex and several prominent veins. One to three flowers are produced in summer on 1–4 cm spikes from the base of the pseudobulbs. The flowers are very fleshy with a strong, rather unpleasant musty odour. The tepals are yellow-green to green with purple to dark maroon streaks. The concave lanceolate dorsal sepal is approximately 3.5 cm long and 2–2.3 cm wide. The 4 cm-long lateral sepals have a large dark maroon blotch at the base and are almost triangular. They are joined at the base to form a short spur. The forward-pointing petals are 2.5–3.0 cm long and 1.2–1.8 cm wide. They are irregularly edged and pointed at the apex. The hinged lip is 2.4–2.7 cm long and 1.0–1.3 cm wide, mostly white on the outside and heavily blotched and marked with purple-maroon on the inside. The erect lateral lobes are 1 cm long. The mid-lobe is almost entirely dark maroon, with the very glossy basal half forming a 'shelf' over a small saccate cavity. The velvety apical half has some minute hairs and a pointed apex.

B. tetragona grows well either mounted or in baskets of freely draining coarse material. It prefers an intermediate environment with moderately bright light and a dry winter rest.

Actual flower size: 4–5 cm across.

Bifrenaria tyrianthina (Lodd.) Reichenbach (f.)

Loddiges originally described this species as *Lycaste tyrianthina* and Reichenbach later transferred it to *Bifrenaria*. *Lycaste d'allemagnei* is another synonym. It inhabits both the cool mountains of Espírito Santo, Rio de Janeiro and São Paulo, and also the rocky outcrops of Minas Gerais, where it experiences a continental climate.

The clustered yellowish-green pseudobulbs are strongly four-angled, 6–13 cm tall and 3–5 cm wide at the base. They bear a single very tough leaf which is tapered at both ends. It is acutely pointed, has usually five prominent veins beneath, and is 18–28 cm long and 6–10 cm wide. The flower spike, from 6–9 cm long, rises from the base of the pseudobulb in summer and usually carries two or three very fleshy violet-purple to mauve-pink flowers. They are long-lasting, with broadly elliptic sepals 4.0–4.5 cm long and 2.3–2.5 cm wide with slightly recurved acute apices. The dorsal sepal is concave, while the lateral sepals form a 3 cm spur which is pale with darker purple spots. The more or less rhomboidal petals have slightly irregular edges. The three-lobed 4 cm-long lip is joined to the column by a 1 cm claw. The triangular lateral lobes curve up towards the column. They are whitish with dark purple stripes and mauve suffusions. The more or less rounded mid-lobe is red-purple, paler on the basal half, with darker stripes. The recurved, crisped apical section has several white hairs. A ridge-like callus forms a shelf above the outer half.

We grow this species as we do *B. tetragona*. It is a fairly temperature-tolerant plant.

Actual flower size: 5–7 cm across.

Brassavola tuberculata Hooker

Still commonly known and sold as *B. perrinii*, this species was discovered near Rio de Janeiro by Harrison, who sent plants to England where they flowered in 1828. Hooker described it in 1829. *B. fragrans* is another synonym. It grows as an epiphyte or lithophyte in a variety of habitats — cool mountains, hot lowlands and savannahs. It occurs in Sergipe, Minas Gerais, Rio de Janeiro, Paraná, Santa Catarina and Rio Grande do Sul. It is also reported from Bolivia.

The more or less terete and shallowly grooved pseudobulbs are 2–15 cm long. They have one to four internodes and bear single pendent to sub-erect leaves, which are semi-terete with a deep central groove on the upper surface. The leaves are 12–24 cm long and 0.4–0.8 cm wide at the base, slightly to strongly curved, and taper to a very sharp point. In late spring or summer 5–8 cm spikes carry two to six starry flowers on very long peduncles. They have a faint perfume of vanilla. The pale lemon-green tepals, often with a few purple spots on the reverse, are 3.5–4.5 cm long and 0.5–0.7 cm wide. The lanceolate recurved dorsal sepal is longer than the more or less falcate lateral sepals and petals. The ovoid, 3.0–3.7 cm-long lip is glistening white with a lemon-green blotch in the throat and several raised veins. The irregular edges are more or less wavy.

B. tuberculata prefers an intermediate to warm environment with moderately bright light and high humidity. It should be given plenty of water when in growth, with a slightly drier winter rest. We grow our plants on cork or treefern mounts.

Actual flower size: 6–8 cm across.

Campylocentrum micranthum (Ldl.) Rolfe

One of thirty-four *Campylocentrum* species found in Brazil, this monopodial was originally described by Lindley in 1835 as *Angraecum micranthum*. Rolfe transferred it to the genus *Campylocentrum* in 1903. Other synonyms include *C. stenanthum* and *Angraecum panamense*. Widespread from Mexico south to Brazil and Peru, this species grows epiphytically through most of Brazil except for the southern-most states. It inhabits both the hot humid lowlands and the cooler mountain ranges to moderate elevations.

The flattened, more or less zigzag stems are usually less than 30 cm long, but sometimes reach 75 cm. They may grow in large masses, which are often only precariously attached to the host by a few of the many aerial roots produced along the stems. The stiff 3–13 cm-long leaves are up to 2.5 cm wide with obtuse or unequally bilobed apices. They are arranged alternately in two rows. The lower leaves become deciduous with age. Flower spikes, 2–6.5 cm long, appear, usually in autumn, from the stem just beneath each root. Each spike carries up to thirty tiny flowers in two rows. The very narrow tapering tepals spread only slightly above the middle. They are 0.35–0.45 cm long, and may be white, cream or pale green. The sessile lip is more or less decurved near the middle and forms a curved 0.3–0.4 cm-long spur at the base. The tiny more or less oblong lateral lobes clasp the column, while the 0.25 cm-long mid-lobe is somewhat dagger-shaped.

This species needs year-round moisture and does best in a humid intermediate environment. Mount and hang in moderate light.

Actual flower size: approximately 0.5 cm long.

Capanemia superflua (Rchb.(f.)) Garay

First described as *Oncidium superfluum* in 1864 by Reichenbach, based on material supplied by Widgren, this species was transferred by Garay in 1967 to *Capanemia*, a genus created by Barbosa Rodrígues in 1877. *Capanemia uliginosa*, *C. juergensiana* and *Rodriguezia anomala* are conspecific with this species. It occurs in the cooler mountains from Minas Gerais and Espírito Santo to Rio Grande do Sul, and also in Argentina, growing on slender twigs with mosses and lichens at altitudes above 500 m.

The clustered cylindrical pseudobulbs are 1.5–3.0 cm long, but very narrow. Covered with papery bracts, they bear a single terete leaf 5–10 cm long, with a single furrow on the upper surface, and tapering to a narrow point. Arching spikes appear from the base of the pseudobulbs in spring or summer with about twelve delicate flowers which last well. Each flower is up to 1 cm long with sparkling white tepals which may have a pinkish stripe on the back. The dorsal sepal is rather concave, the petals point forward, and the oblong lateral sepals are spreading. The fiddle-shaped lip is about 0.6 cm long and has two clear yellow calli at the base.

This very attractive little species will grow well in cool to intermediate conditions and semi-shade. It does nicely for us when mounted on a small treefern slab or a small branch. It prefers year-round moisture, but should be allowed to dry out between waterings, especially in winter.

Actual flower size: approximately 1 cm long.

Catasetum barbatum (Ldl.) Lindley

Discovered in Guyana by Henchman, *C. barbatum* first flowered in England in 1835. Lindley described it as *Myanthus barbatus* in 1836, based only on male flowers. In 1844, knowing by then that *Catasetum* species produce both male and female flowers, Lindley reclassified the species, giving it its present name. Synonyms include *C. spinosum* and *C. polydactylon*. In Brazil it grows epiphytically in the hot lowlands of Pará, Amazonas, Mato Grosso, Minas Gerais and Goiás. It also occurs in Peru and Boliva, as well as northern South American countries.

The spindle-shaped pseudobulbs are 8–15 cm long and have several pleated leaves 20–45 cm long and 3–8 cm wide. They are deciduous and have three prominent veins. Flowers are borne from spring to autumn on pendulous spikes up to 45 cm long from the base of the pseudobulbs. The variable fragrant male flowers have narrow lanceolate tepals about 2.6 cm long. They are yellowish-green with many purple-black markings. The narrow, oblong 1.5 cm–long lip, which is held lowermost, is greenish-white edged with very fleshy 'hairs' or 'fingers'. It is concave, with a tiny conical pouch and usually a large, white horn-like protuberance. Two parallel antennae point downward from the middle of the column. As with all catasetums, the female flowers are much plainer than the male. In this species they are green, with reflexed tepals and a 2 cm sac-like lip which is held uppermost.

C. barbatum may be mounted or potted in a coarse mixture. Give moderately bright light, high humidity, intermediate to warm temperatures and a dry rest in winter.

Actual flower size: approximately 4 cm long.

Catasetum fimbriatum (Morr.) Lindley

This species was introduced into cultivation by de Jonghe in 1847 following its discovery in São Paulo. Morren described it, based on male flowers, as *Myanthus fimbriatus* in 1848, and Lindley transferred it to *Catasetum* in 1850. Synonyms include *C. cogniauxii* and *C. ornithorrhyncum*. It occurs in Venezuela, Argentina, Paraguay and Bolivia as well as Brazil, where it is found in the hot lowlands and savannah country below 800 m in Amazonas, Pará, Mato Grosso, Minas Gerais, São Paulo and the southern states.

The spindle-shaped pseudobulbs are 12–30 cm tall and 3–5 cm in diameter. Each bears about five pleated deciduous leaves 30–55 cm long and 6–10 cm wide. In spring or summer an arching spike up to 45 cm long carries seven to fifteen variable flowers. The fragrant male flowers are usually pale green or yellowish green with many red-purple markings. The 2.8–3.8 cm-long sepals are 0.9–1.4 cm wide, while the petals are slightly shorter. The deeply fringed lip, which is greenish-yellow with red spots at the base, is held lowermost. About 3 cm long and 4 cm wide, it is somewhat fan-shaped with a small sac-like depression near the base. Two parallel antennae hang from the column. The resupinate female flowers are yellow-green with reflexed oblong tepals and a deep pouch-like lip with slightly reflexed edges.

C. fimbriatum may be mounted or potted in a freely draining medium. It needs a warm to intermediate environment with moderate to bright light and good air movement. Give plenty of water when in growth and a decided long dry rest in the cool season.

Actual flower size: 6–7 cm long.

Catasetum gnomus Linden & Reichenbach (f.)

Discovered by Wallis along the Rio Negro in Amazonas, this species was sent to Linden who, together with Reichenbach, described it in 1874. *C. heteranthum*, *C. quornus*, *C. huebneri*, *C. negrense* and *C. mocuranum* are all synonyms. Confined to the lowlands of Amazonas, Pará and Bahia, *C. gnomus* grows epiphytically on trees near watercourses.

The slightly compressed pseudobulbs are 11–16 cm long and 3–4 cm wide. They bear three erect to spreading leaves 20–25 cm long and up to 4 cm wide. The deciduous lanceolate leaves have recurved apices. Flowers are borne in summer on a more or less erect spike up to 60 cm long. The tepals of the male flowers are green with maroon-purple suffusions and mottling, with the spreading lateral sepals almost completely maroon on the inside. The margins of the 5 cm-long sepals are more or less rolled inwards. The dorsal sepal overlaps the shorter and narrower petals. The 2 cm-long pouch-like lip, which is held uppermost, is creamy white or green with many small purple spots. It has a wide white margin which is irregularly toothed, undulating, and turned back. A pair of crossed 2 cm-long antennae is attached to the column. The tepals of the non-resupinate female flowers are green spotted with purple, while the large pouch-like lip is pale green with a yellow toothed margin. Hermaphroditic flowers are known to occur.

C. gnomus needs a warm humid environment with plenty of bright light. Sudden temperature variations should be avoided. Plants may be mounted or potted. A dry winter rest is not essential for this species.

Actual flower size: approximately 10 cm across.

Catasetum pileatum Reichenbach (f.)

Introduced into cultivation from Venezuela by Linden in 1882, this species was described soon after by Reichenbach. Until 1921 it was the national flower of Venezuela. *C. bungerothii* (actually a variety of *C. pileatum*) and *C. imperiale* are conspecific. Apart from Venezuela, this epiphyte also occurs in Ecuador, Colombia and in Brazil, where it is confined to the hot lowlands of Pará and Amazonas.

The oval to spindle-shaped pseudobulbs are 15–30 cm long and up to 7.5 cm in diameter. They become furrowed with age, and each bears several lanceolate plicate deciduous leaves 20–35 cm long and 4–7 cm wide. They are grey-green with several prominent veins. From four to ten long-lasting fragrant flowers are produced in autumn on an arching spike 30–40 cm long which rises from the base of the pseudobulb. The fleshy male flowers are produced in several colour varieties, but are typically pure white to yellowish-green, more or less suffused or spotted with purple. The oblong-lanceolate sepals are 4–7 cm long and 1.4–1.7 cm wide. The dorsal sepal and the wider petals form a hood above the column. The 6–7 cm-wide shell-shaped lip is held lowermost. It has a sac-like pouch near the base and serrated edges. The two antennae are crossed. The non-resupinate female flowers are creamish-green with darker veins on the large pouch-like lip which has irregular margins. These are turned outward and pointed at the apices. The lanceolate tepals are strongly recurved.

C. pileatum appreciates a warm humid environment with bright light and good ventilation. A dry rest is needed only in intermediate conditions.

Actual flower size: 7–10 cm across.

Catasetum saccatum Lindley

Plants of this species were first introduced into cultivation by Loddiges. Lindley described it in 1840. Synonyms include *C. secundum*, *C. incurvum* and *C. colossus*. It occurs in Peru, Guyana, and possibly in Ecuador. In Brazil it is found throughout the Amazon basin, from Acre in the west to Pará in the east, and in Mato Grosso at up to 500 m.

The pseudobulbs are spindle-shaped, slightly compressed, 7–20 cm long and 2–5 cm wide. From five to seven deciduous leaves 20–40 cm long clasp the pseudobulb. Five to eight flowers are borne in summer on an arching spike 25–45 cm long. The male flowers, variable in colour, are typically greenish- or olive-brown with green mottling. The slightly lanceolate sepals are about 6.5 cm long and 0.6–0.9 cm wide, while petals are slightly shorter and narrower. The 2.5–3.0 cm-long lip is held lowermost and is deeply fringed along its somewhat reflexed margins. Three-lobed, with large lateral lobes and a smaller mid-lobe, it is usually greenish-yellow with or without red-brown markings. Towards the base is a conical brownish sac. Two crossed 1.5 cm-long antennae hang from the column. The female flowers have strongly recurved tepals about 3 cm long and a slightly compressed pouch-like lip with irregular toothed edges that are rolled outward.

C. saccatum needs bright light and high humidity in a warm environment. Plants may be potted or mounted. A dry rest in winter is not essential, but is recommended when temperatures drop below 20°C. Avoid sudden temperature fluctuations.

Actual flower size: approximately 13 cm across.

Catasetum saccatum var. *christyanum* (Rchb.(f.)) Mansfeld

This variety, which tends to be more colourful than the type, was introduced into England by Christy, who obtained plants from Brazil. Reichenbach described it in 1882 as *C. christyanum*, naming it in Christy's honour. However, it has since proved to be only a colour variation of *C. saccatum.** Mansfeld reduced it to varietal status in 1932.

The pseudobulbs are covered by the bases of the plicate deciduous leaves. The very showy resupinate male flowers are more numerous but smaller than in the type, with six to twelve flowers about 10 cm across borne on an arching spike up to 45 cm long. The lanceolate sepals and petals are yellowish-green with deep red-brown blotches. They are somewhat concave with the dorsal sepal and the petals overlapping to form a hood above the pinkish brown column. The lateral sepals are spreading. The lip is more prominently three-lobed than in the type species, with large rounded ear-like lateral lobes and a smaller rounded mid-lobe. All are more or less strongly reflexed with deep fimbriations. The lip is bright green shaded with purple or pinkish brown. Between the lateral lobes is a conical depression which is outlined in white or red. The female flowers are the same yellowish-green as in the type.

C. saccatum var. *christyanum* requires the same warm humid environment as does the type, with no sudden fluctuations in temperature. Treefern, either as mounts or coarse chunks in a pot, preferably suspended in good light, makes an ideal substrate for both type and variety.

Actual flower size: approximately 10 cm across.

Catasetum spitzii Hoehne

Belonging to the *trulla* alliance, this species, which is rarely seen in collections, is closely related to *C. cernuum*, *C. trulla*, *C. vinaceum* etc., all of which have an almost flat lip with no pouch. Discovered at Campinas, Gioás, in 1936, *C. spitzii* was described by Hoehne and named in honour of the Brazilian naturalist, Spitz. The species is endemic to the state of Gioás, including the Distrito Federal around Brasília, where it grows on trees at elevations up to 800 m. In this area hot conditions prevail for much of the year, with a very dry period usually from June to September.

The clustered, club-shaped pseudobulbs are about 15 cm long and bear three to five fairly long deciduous leaves which are jointed at the base. A more or less horizontal spike is produced from the base of the pseudobulb and carries from three to twelve yellowish-green flowers in autumn. In the male flower the tepals are 3.0–4.5 cm long. The dorsal sepal is 1.2 cm wide and together with the narrow petals curves over the column. The wider lateral sepals are oblong to triangular with their margins rolled inward at the apex. The somewhat triangular lip is fleshy with a rounded apex. From 4.0–4.5 cm wide, it is green with yellow at the base. Its edges are reflexed and fringed basally. Two parallel antennae are attached to the column. The female flowers are green with short tepals and a large pouch-like lip.

Because of its horizontal spike, *C. spitzii* is best mounted or grown in baskets or suspended pots. It needs bright light, warmth and humidity, plenty of water when in growth, and a dry winter rest.

Actual flower size: 6–8 cm across.

Cattleya aclandiae Lindley

An early introduction to horticulture, this beautiful species was first flowered in Sir Thomas Acland's collection in 1840, a year after it was introduced by its discoverer, Lieutenant James. Lady Acland illustrated the plant for Lindley, who named it in her honour. Confined to the north-eastern state of Bahia, this species grows between 100–400 m above sea level and occurs up to 100 km inland from Salvador. Now quite rare in its habitat, it generally grows 3–6 m above the ground in broken shade on rough-barked trees scattered across the hot dry caatinga. However, it usually receives sea breezes and night-time dew.

The slender pseudobulbs are only 5–12 cm tall, but grow into large clumps in nature with extensive root systems which are often covered with tillandsias. Each pseudobulb has two or occasionally three oval horizontally spreading leaves 2–9 cm long. These leaves are fleshy and more or less suffused or spotted with dark reddish brown, depending on light intensity. This species flowers from spring to summer and sometimes again six months later. The spike has no sheath, but is enclosed within the leaves of the developing pseudobulb. It bears one or two long-lasting waxy flowers from 6–8 cm across, which have a faint spicy fragrance. The colour of the flower varies, with green or yellowish tepals covered with dark red-brown, or sometimes almost black, blotches. Lip colour ranges from creamy-white to magenta, streaked and suffused with darker veins.

Slabs of cork seem to suit this species in cultivation. It may be watered all year round, but prefers to dry out quickly. Intermediate conditions suit it, with as much light as possible short of burning.
Actual flower size: 6–8 cm across.

Cattleya amethystoglossa Linden & Reichenbach (f.) ex Warner

In 1856–57 Linden of Brussels received plants of this species, and sent a flower (in poor condition) to Reichenbach in Vienna. Reichenbach thought it was *C. porphyroglossa,** but mistakenly told Linden that it was *C. amethystoglossa*. Warner described it in 1862, recognising the differences from *C. porphyroglossa*. Synonyms include *C. guttata* var. *prinzii* and *C. purpurina*. It is found in coastal Espírito Santo and Bahia, in inland Bahia up to 450 m, and has also been reported from Pernambuco and Minas Gerais. Once plentiful on rocks, it is now almost always found growing epiphytically.

Pseudobulbs are typically 25–60 cm tall, but may exceed 1 m. They bear two fleshy leaves 14–25 cm long and 5–7 cm wide. These may be oblong to lanceolate or narrowly elliptic. Flowers are produced in late winter to spring, or occasionally in autumn, on spikes 7–18 cm long from the apex of the pseudobulb. There are usually four to eight flowers, but up to twenty is not uncommon. The tepals are pure white to pale pink with purple or magenta spots. The dorsal sepal is 3.8–4.5 cm long and 1.4–1.7 cm wide, while the slightly falcate lateral sepals are up to 4 cm long. The wider, 3.5–4.5 cm-long petals have undulating margins. The 3–4 cm-long lip has large white to pale pink lateral lobes, which have a few amethyst warty ridges on the recurved apices. The kidney-shaped apical lobe, which is covered with warty ridges and has wavy edges, is bright amethyst. There are several longitudinal ridges in the throat.

For cultural advice, see following entry.
Actual flower size: 7–9 cm across.

Cattleya amethystoglossa varieties

Although *C. amethystoglossa* has only a few validly described varieties, Brazilian growers recognise several others, among them the var. *salmonea* with salmon-coloured flowers and var. *coerulea* with a blue lip and a few spots.

Like the type species, all have furrowed pseudobulbs which are slightly compressed, 25 cm–1 m or more long, and up to 2.5 cm across near the apex. All bear two leathery leaves and very fleshy flowers. *C. amethystoglossa* var. *rosea* — pictured here — was described by Rolfe in 1892, as having 'flowers suffused with rose'. The tepals of the pictured clone, which flowers in autumn, are completely pink with heavy amethyst spotting and blotching. The oblong to lanceolate dorsal sepal and the more rhomboidal petals, which have coarsely undulating margins, are longer than the falcate lateral sepals. The large lateral lobes of the lip, which meet above the column to conceal it, are pink on the outside and paler within, with amethyst warty ridges at the apex. The very crisped apical lobe is bright amethyst and covered with many minute glands. There are several longitudinal keels in the paler throat of the lip. *C. amethystina* var. *lilacina* (Rchb.(f.)) Fowlie was described by Reichenbach in 1881 as *C. guttata* var. *lilacina*, with Fowlie recognising it as a variety of *C. amethystoglossa* in 1977. The tepals are a pale lilac with darker spots concentrated mainly on the edges of the segments.

All varieties, like the type, are easily cultivated in intermediate to warm conditions. They should be given bright light and high humidity with a dry winter rest.

Actual flower size: approximately 8 cm across.

Cattleya araguaiensis Pabst

Described by Pabst in 1967, this unusual cattleya is restricted to the state of Gioás at about 400–600 m along the banks of the Rio Araguaia and its tributaries. It grows low down on thin tree branches, usually in shady positions. This region experiences a hot wet season from November to April, when temperatures may reach 42°C, followed by a cool dry season when temperatures may fall to 8°C.

The clustered pseudobulbs are 5–12 cm long and up to 0.6 cm in diameter near the apex. Each bears a single fleshy leaf, which may be elliptic or linear-oblong, and usually 7–10 cm long and 1.7–3.0 cm wide. A single starry flower is borne from autumn to spring on a spike up to 6 cm long. The narrow tepals are greenish, and almost completely suffused, blotched or striped with red-brown. The oblong to lanceolate sepals are 5.5–7.0 cm long, while the petals are slightly shorter. The 5 cm-long lip is vaguely three-lobed with more or less triangular lateral lobes, which wrap around the column to form a tube. The rounded to triangular apical lobe is greenish-brown with a transverse red stripe at its base, or completely reddish. There is a large brown-red to purple-red blotch in the throat.

C. araguaiensis does best in intermediate to warm conditions in partial shade. It needs plenty of water during growth, and a drier winter rest. It does best for us when mounted on treefern slabs or thin branches of rough-barked trees. Good ventilation or air movement is required, particularly around flowering time, when buds may be subject to fungal attack if plants are kept too moist.

Actual flower size: approximately 10 cm across.

Cattleya bicolor Lindley

Lindley based his 1836 description of this species on a drawing by Descourtilz, who had depicted a plant from São Paulo and had tentatively named it *Epidendrum iridee*. Plants of the species were introduced into England by Loddiges in 1837–38. *C. grossii* and *Epidendrum bicolor* are conspecific. *C. bicolor* grows in gallery forests near watercourses at 600–1,200 m, and occasionally on mossy rocks. It is found in the states of Rio de Janeiro, São Paulo, Minas Gerais and Goiás.

It is a very variable species, both in plant form and flower, with grooved pseudobulbs usually 25–90 cm tall, but occasionally to 1.3 m. The fleshy elliptic leaves are 10–25 cm long and 2.5–7.0 cm wide. From two to ten faintly fragrant flowers, which last for several weeks, are borne in late summer or autumn on an apical spike 10–35 cm long. The fleshy tepals range from clear green to coppery brown or dark chestnut with or without lavender or purple-brown spots. The oblong to lanceolate dorsal sepal is 5.5–6.5 cm long and up to 2 cm wide, while the falcate lateral sepals are slightly shorter. The normally wider petals are narrow at the base and have much crisped margins. The pale rose to amethyst-purple lip is 3.5 cm long, strongly deflexed, with the fan-shaped apical lobe often edged with white. The lip is oblong to wedge-shaped at the base with a central groove and numerous minute projections giving it a velvety texture.

C. bicolor grows well mounted or potted in intermediate conditions. It appreciates a short drier rest in winter, but should not be allowed to remain completely dry for long periods.

Actual flower size: 7.5–10 cm across.

Cattleya dormaniana (Rchb.(f.)) Reichenbach

Discovered by Blunt in 1879, plants of this species were sent by him to Low & Co. in England. The first flowering occurred in the collection of Charles Dorman, for whom Reichenbach named the species *Laelia dormaniana* in 1880. In 1882 he transferred it to the genus *Cattleya*. *C. dormaniana* is endemic to a small area of the Organ Mountains in the state of Rio de Janeiro, growing mostly on dead or rotting trees at 600–1,000 m above sea level.

The 8–30 cm pseudobulbs are narrow at the base and only 0.8–1.0 cm wide near the apex, where two lanceolate to elliptic leaves are borne. These are 8–14 cm long, 3–6 cm wide, fleshy, stiff, and tinged with maroon-purple when young. This species flowers predominantly in autumn, with one or two starry flowers on a spike up to 9 cm long. The tepals are usually olive-green with reddish-bronze margins or maroon blotches. The slightly concave sepals are 3.5–4.5 cm long and 1.0–1.6 cm wide. The petals are narrow, recurved, and have slightly wavy margins. The lip is 3.2–3.8 cm long and 2.3–2.8 cm across the amethyst-purple mid-lobe. The large lateral lobes are pale mauve. There is a white longitudinal band down the centre of the lip.

C. dormaniana, although not a robust plant, is relatively easy to cultivate. We grow our plants mounted on treefern slabs. A cool to intermediate environment is ideal, with moderately bright light. In winter, when watering is reduced, plants appreciate misting on warmer days, which will prevent undue shrivelling of the pseudobulbs.

Actual flower size: approximately 8 cm across.

Cattleya forbesii Lindley

The Brazilian botanist Vellozo first described this species in 1790 as *Epidendrum pauper*. This appellation was overlooked until Stellfield rediscovered it in 1945 and Lindley's name, from his 1823 description, remains the generally accepted one. Lindley named the species in honour of Forbes, who had sent plants from Rio to London. This charming species inhabits swampy areas and forested riverbanks where it grows, mostly on trees but occasionally on rocks, up to 200 m above sea level. It occurs in a narrow band almost parallel to the coast from the state of Rio de Janeiro south to Santa Catarina. It is often found growing alongside *Cattleya guttata,** *Oncidium flexuosum,** and *Bifrenaria inodora*, etc.

The slender pseudobulbs are typically 10–15 cm tall, but may be slightly taller. We have had plants flower on 4 cm pseudobulbs. The two leathery leaves are 6–15 cm long with a rounded apex. The two to five long-lasting flowers are borne on a 9–15 cm spike in late spring or summer. The flowers are apple-green to greenish-yellow or bronzy-tan, from about 6–11 cm wide. The long tubular lip curls round the fleshy column, concealing it. The exterior of the lip is pinkish-white, while the interior has a central yellow-gold stripe and is streaked with reddish-brown. The lip on some forms may be golden yellow.

This is a very adaptable species, growing and flowering in unheated greenhouses with temperatures as low as –2°C in winter. Intermediate conditions suit it best, however, with warm humid summer conditions. Pot plants in coarse well-drained material, or mount on slabs of cork, etc.

Actual flower size: 6–11 cm across.

Cattleya granulosa Lindley

Closely related to *C. schofieldiana,** this species was discovered in 1840 by Hartweg, who sent plants to England. Lindley described the species in 1842 and, as plants had arrived in England with a consignment of Guatemalan plants, believed that it was a native of Guatemala. It is, however, endemic to Brazil. *Epidendrum granulosum* is conspecific. It occurs predominantly in the hot humid lowlands of Pernambuco, Paraíba and Ceará, and possibly also in Piauí, Rio Grande do Norte and Bahia.

The pseudobulbs are 25–60 cm tall and 0.6–1.0 cm in diameter. They bear two spreading, oblong to lanceolate leathery leaves 7–18 cm long and 3–9 cm wide.

From one to nine fleshy flowers are borne on a 15–25 cm-long spike in spring, autumn, or early winter. The fragrant flowers have typically olive-green tepals with amethyst spots. The 4.0–6.5 cm-long dorsal sepal is 1.4–2.0 cm wide, somewhat elliptic, with an acute apex. The slightly shorter lateral sepals are falcate. The 3.5–5.0 cm-long petals have very crisped, more or less reflexed, margins. They are narrow at the base and 2.5–4.0 cm wide near the apex. The 3.0–4.5 cm-long lip is white, usually with yellow-orange on the basal half. The mid-lobe is covered with tiny amethyst glands. It is narrow at the base, with an irregularly toothed apical half, comprising two rounded lobes. The large lateral lobes curve over the column, are white outside and pale yellow inside.

C. granulosa needs a warm humid environment with fairly bright light, good air movement and plenty of water when in growth.

Actual flower size: 8–10 cm across.

Cattleya guttata Lindley

Introduced into cultivation by Gordon, who sent plants to London from Rio de Janeiro in about 1827, this species was described by Lindley in 1831. Synonyms include *C. elatior*, *C. sphenophora* and possibly *C. tigrina*, which Withner considers closer to this species than to *C. leopoldii*,* the species considered by Braem to be synonymous with *C. tigrina*. *C. guttata* occurs in Espírito Santo, Minas Gerais, Rio de Janeiro, São Paulo and Paraná, usually growing in full sun at 160–600 m on rocks or on trees overhanging waterways.

The cylindrical pseudobulbs are typically 18–75 cm tall, but may reach 1.5 m. The two or three stiff fleshy leaves are 15–25 cm long and up to 7 cm wide. They are broadly lanceolate to elliptic. From three to twenty or more fragrant flowers are borne on a spike 7–30 cm long, commonly in summer or autumn. However, northern populations tend to flower in winter. The tepals are usually yellow-green to olive-green with dark purple-maroon blotches. The dorsal sepal is 3.7–5.0 cm long and up to 1.4 cm wide, while the falcate lateral sepals are shorter. The more or less elliptic petals are similar in size, but have wavy margins. The 2.7–3.5 cm-long lip has large wing-like lateral lobes, which are white to pale pink and enclose the column. The mid-lobe is suffused with yellow at the base, then becomes pink on the narrow isthmus. The bright magenta apical portion is covered with shallow ridges of tiny warts. There are also about six warty ridges in the throat and on the isthmus.

This species prefers bright intermediate to warm conditions, lots of water when in growth, and a distinct dry winter rest.
Actual flower size: 5–8 cm across.

Cattleya harrisoniana Bateman ex Lindley

Introduced into England in 1836 by Harrison, after whom it was named, *C. harrisoniana* was often regarded as a variety of *C. loddigesii*.* Lindley described it in 1836 using material supplied by Bateman. Synonyms include *Epidendrum harrisonianum* and *C. papeiansiana*. It occurs in Rio de Janeiro, Espírito Santo, Minas Gerais and São Paulo from sea level to 800 m, frequently in humid swampy situations.

The laterally compressed pseudobulbs are typically 12–30 cm tall, but may be taller, and 0.6–1.0 cm across near the apex. Each bears two, or occasionally three, elliptic leaves 7–12 cm long and up to 5 cm wide. In late spring or summer one or two bright mid- to dark-lavender flowers are produced on a 7–10 cm spike. The lanceolate dorsal sepal and the decidedly falcate laterals are 6.0–6.5 cm long and about 1.5 cm wide. The 5.0–5.5 cm-long petals have slightly undulating margins and are up to 2.2 cm wide. The 4–5 cm-long lip is lavender on the outside. The large lateral lobes, which are folded over the column, are lavender with creamy yellow crisped edges. They also have several prominent yellow ridges, which are absent in *C. loddigesii*. The strongly crisped mid-lobe is cream with a thickened bright yellow-orange callus, which is strongly ridged, and about seven keels running from the base to near the bilobed apex.

This species is most adaptable, doing well in warm to cool, even cold, conditions, with lots of water when in growth, high summer humidity, and a dry winter rest. Bright light tends to intensify the colour of the flowers.
Actual flower size: approximately 10 cm across.

Cattleya harrisoniana varieties

As with many *Cattleya* species, *C. harrisoniana* exhibits a certain amount of floral variation. We have a number of clones in our collection, and no two are identical, even if variation is sometimes not great. One clone has very pale pink-mauve sepals and petals, another has tepals which are very dark pinkish-purple; one has no pink inside the lip, others have predominantly pink lips with yellow in the centre. We have one in which, uncharacteristically, the lateral lobes do not envelop the column. Considering the fairly wide variation found in this beautiful and easily grown species, it is surprising that there are few described varieties. Published varieties include var. *alba*, which was described by Beer in 1854 and has pure creamy-white flowers with a yellow blotch at the base of the lip, and var. *violacea* (Williams, 1888), which has extremely dark violet flowers. The lip is violet, too, with yellow longitudinal ridges on the mid-lobe. We call the clone pictured here *C. harrisoniana* 'Speckled Lip'. It has an excellent shape, without the very falcate lateral sepals which tend to give the flowers of some clones a rather untidy appearance. The lip is very pale pink on the outside, while the inside is mainly creamy-white with just the merest hint of pink on the lateral lobes. What makes this clone rather unusual are the purplish veins on the apical section of the lateral lobes and on the basal edges of the apical lobe.

Like our other plants of this species, it grows well either mounted or potted in coarse chunks of treefern fibre.

Actual flower size: approximately 10 cm across.

Cattleya intermedia Graham ex Hooker

This species was introduced into cultivation in 1824 by Graham, who brought plants from Rio de Janeiro to Glasgow, where they first flowered in 1826. Hooker described it in 1828, using information supplied by Graham. Synonyms include *C. ovata* and *C. amabilis*. Found also in Paraguay and Uruguay, *C. intermedia* occurs in Rio de Janeiro, São Paulo, and other southern Brazilian states, including several nearby islands. Predominantly an epiphyte, it is sometimes found growing amid accumulated detritus on rocks. It favours coastal or stream-side swamps from sea level to 300 m, growing often in full sun.

The cylindrical pseudobulbs are 7–50 cm tall and up to 1.5 cm wide at the apex. The two or three fleshy leaves, which are 7–15 cm long and 3–7 cm wide, are elliptic to oblong-ovate. From two to nine fragrant flowers are borne primarily in spring and early summer on spikes 7–25 cm long. The tepals are typically pale rosy-pink, occasionally spotted with purple on the outer half. The erect oblong dorsal sepal is up to 7.8 cm long and 1.5 cm wide, while the falcate laterals are shorter. The curved petals are slightly shorter, but up to 2 cm wide. The 5.0–6.5 cm-long lip is pink with an undulating amethyst apical lobe. The large, curved lateral lobes meet above the column, but are reflexed at the wavy apex. Six ridges run from the base of the lip to the base of the apical lobe.

C. intermedia requires bright light and high humidity, with a dry winter rest. An intermediate to warm environment is ideal, although plants will tolerate quite low winter temperatures.

Actual flower size: 10–13 cm across.

Cattleya intermedia var. *alba* & other varieties

Pure white varieties of all species have always been very popular with orchid growers, and the elegant *C. intermedia* var. *alba* is no exception. Although said to exist only among the southern populations of *C. intermedia*, the *alba* variety was reported as early as 1909 by Keevil on the island of Santo Amaro in the state of São Paulo. The clone pictured here has pseudobulbs about 45 cm long and leaves up to 15 cm long. It flowers in spring with several flowers which are pure white except for a greenish tinge on the tips of the tepals. About 12 cm across, the flowers are rather fleshy and last reasonably well.

C. intermedia is the symbol of several of the orchid societies in Brazil, with some societies dedicated solely to the species and its many varieties. Many of these are horticultural varieties which have never been scientifically described, and some confusion and duplication exists. The var. *punctatissima*, however, was described by Sander in 1892. In this variety the sepals and petals are finely sprinkled with small red spots. Several *semi-albas* are in cultivation, including var. *semi-alba* 'Irrorata', which is white with a pale mauve-pink band about the apical and lateral edges of the mid-lobe of the lip. The var. *semi-alba* 'Sonia' is white with a dark red blotch in the throat. Other *semi-alba* varieties include 'Fantasia', a pure white form with amethyst in the throat and an amethyst blotch on either side of the apical lobe of the lip; and 'Venosa', which has dark lilac-pink veins on the lip.

Actual flower size: approximately 12 cm across.

Cattleya intermedia var. *amethystina* (Morren ex Lemaire) Fowlie

This is one of the better-known varieties of *C. intermedia*, and was first described as *C. amethystina* in 1848 by Morren. Five years later Lemaire reclassified it as a variety of *C. loddigesii*.* In 1909 Rolfe described it as *C. intermedia* var. *coerulea*, using dried flowers received from Graciano de Azambuja who collected them near his native town of Porto Alegre in Rio Grande do Sul. Rolfe's description indicates a pure white flower with violet-blue on the apical lobe of the lip and the front edges of the lateral lobes. In 1977 Fowlie recognised Lemaire's *C. loddigesii* var. *amethystina* as identical with Rolfe's description. Lemaire's varietal epithet predated Rolfe's var. *coerulea*, and so the taxon took its present name. This variety is found amongst the southern populations of *C. intermedia*.

Its habit is similar to that of the type species; ours has pseudobulbs 15–25 cm tall with more or less horizontally held leaves 7.5–12.0 cm long. The 10–12 cm-wide flowers have white petals and sepals which occasionally have the faintest hint of pink. The sepals have green tips, with the erect to recurved dorsal sepal about 6 cm long, and the somewhat falcate lateral sepals about 5 cm long. The petals have slightly undulating margins. The apical lobe of the lip varies from bluish-purple to amethyst-violet, and this colour, which may or may not extend to the apex of the lateral lobes, is also found between the white keels at the base of the mid-lobe.

Cultivation for this variety is as for the species.

Actual flower size: approximately 11 cm across.

Cattleya intermedia var. *aquinii* (Barb. Rod.) Rolfe

Probably the most widely known variety of *C. intermedia*, this taxon first appeared in 1874–75 in the collection of da Silva Valadares, a resident of Porto Alegre in Rio Grande do Sul. He gave a piece to his friend Francisco d'Aquino, who subsequently propagated it and sold a plant to Thomas de Oliveira e Silva in Rio de Janeiro. The latter forwarded the plant to Barbosa Rodrígues, who believed it was a new species and described it in 1891 as *C. aquinii*, naming it for d'Aquino. In 1900 Rolfe recognised that it was simply a variety of *C. intermedia*. It soon became keenly sought, and was first exhibited in England in 1902. Since its original discovery, several other clones have been found, some of quite inferior quality.

C. intermedia var. *aquinii* is an aberrant form of the species in that it has labelloid petals, i.e. petals which have taken on, in varying degrees, the colour and form of the lip. These petals are usually almost rhomboidal and much wider than in the type species. They have more strongly crisped margins and a blunt and irregular apex, with the apical portion coloured like the apical lobe of the lip. A central longitudinal groove is also present. The sepals are identical with those of the type species. The gene which causes this unusual feature is a dominant one, and usually imparts the labelloid characteristic to its progeny. Because of this, *C. intermedia* var. *aquinii* has been much used in hybridising to produce 'splash' petals.

Cultural requirements are as for the type species.

Actual flower size: 10–13 cm across.

Cattleya intermedia var. *vinicolor* (hort.) & other varieties

As mentioned in the entry for *C. intermedia* var. *alba*, many cultivated clones of this species carry horticultural varietal appellations which lack uniform acceptance and vary from one locality to another. Add to this the large number of cultivar names, and we have a seemingly infinite number of *Cattleya intermedias*. One variety, however, which has universal recognition is var. *vinicolor*, which is really a *semi-alba* with pure white petals and sepals. The apical lobe of the lip is a rich velvety wine-red. Sometimes there are creamy patches near the recurved apices of the lateral lobes. This variety is divided further, with the var. *vinicolor-escuro* having an even darker lip.

Sometimes the tepals carry tiny red spots, as in the clone pictured here, when it is known as var. *vinicolor-punctata*. There are also a number of published varieties of *C. intermedia* with quite different coloration. The var. *gibeziae* was described by Linden and Rodigas in 1887, and has pure creamy-white tepals with three faint pink veins in the throat of the lip, merging to form a pale pink flush at the base of the apical lobe. The var. *picturata*, which was described by Rolfe in 1893, has rosy streaks and splashes on the pale pink tepals, and the lateral lobes of the lip are heavily flushed and striped with bright amethyst. In 1877 Barbosa Rodrígues described a variety with a very large flower and abnormally large lip as var. *macrochila*. This may be identical to what some Brazilian nurseries call var. *gigantea*.

Actual flower size: approximately 11 cm across.

Cattleya labiata Lindley

This species was first sent to England by Swainson, and used by Lindley as the type for the genus *Cattleya*. Synonyms include *C. warocqueana*, and perhaps *C. warneri*,* although this is usually treated as a separate species. *C. labiata* grows epiphytically in the mountains of Ceará, Pernambuco, Paráiba and Alagoas.

The heavy club-like pseudobulbs are 10–30 cm long and 2–3 cm wide. They are slightly compressed and strongly furrowed. Each bears a single very stiff leaf 14–30 cm long and up to 8 cm wide. These oblong to oval leaves are erect to arching with recurved apices. From autumn to winter, two to five fragrant flowers 12–17 cm across are carried on a 12–15 cm spike, which is enveloped by a single or double sheath. The flowers are very variable, with light to very dark lilac-rose tepals from 7.0–9.5 cm long. The lanceolate dorsal sepal, whose basal margins are deflexed, and the keeled slightly falcate lateral sepals, are 2.0–2.5 cm wide with recurved apices. The rhomboidal petals are 5–6 cm wide and have irregular margins which are usually very much crisped. The obscurely three-lobed lip is 7 cm long and 4 cm across the frilly mid-lobe. The mauve lateral lobes meet above the column. The basal half of the lip between the mid-lobes is orange-brown. There is often a central white to yellow band, while the bilobed bright amethyst apical area of the lip is edged in mauve.

C. labiata does very well mounted or grown in baskets of chopped treefern fibre. It appreciates an intermediate to warm environment with high humidity and a drier, cooler winter rest.

Actual flower size: 12–17 cm across.

Cattleya labiata — aberrant forms

An extremely variable species — it is difficult to find two clones with absolutely identical flowers — *C. labiata* continues to be the subject of a great deal of study. The petals vary slightly, usually in width and in the degree to which they possess undulating margins. However, the lip is much the most variable feature of the flower. It is an extremely popular species in Brazil, and aficionados there have for generations recognised numerous varieties and cultivars, often making little or no allowance for normal and minor variation. There have, however, been few validly published descriptions and much confusion until 1987 when Lou C. Menezes published a monograph in the *Orchid Digest* (Vol. 51, No. 3) which provided much-needed clarification. This monograph, profusely illustrated, includes several unusual or aberrant forms, among them *C. labiata* f. *labelloid*, a form which itself exhibits some variation. The dorsal sepal may be shaped like the petals, but is generally only slightly larger than usual, while the lateral sepals are often streaked like the lip. It is more often the petals which more or less resemble the lip. When the resemblance is strong — as in clone pictured here, where the petals are much crisped and shaped like the lip — then the taxon is referred to as *C. labiata* f. *peloric*. The peloric form often, though not necessarily, shows the colouring of the lip towards the apices of the petals. In *C. labiata* f. *trilabelliae*, as the name indicates, the aberrance is so strong that the flower appears to have two extra lips, but without extra columns.

Actual flower size: approximately 12 cm across.

Cattleya labiata var. *venosa* (hort.) ex Menezes & other varieties

One of many varieties described by Menezes in 1987, *C. labiata* var. *venosa* has beautiful rose-coloured sepals and petals, with the same colour around the edge of the frilly lip. The remainder of the lip is paler with a yellow blotch, partly suffused with purple, in the throat. This variety is distinguished by the presence of several radiating maroon to purple central veins which fuse at the base to form a blotch.

It is frequently confused with the variety *purpureo-striata* (Cogn.) Menezes, often known simply as var. *striata*. Originally described in 1897 as a form of *C. labiata* by Cogniaux, it was elevated to varietal status by Menezes in 1987. It is similar to var. *venosa*, but has reddish-purple stripes in the centre of the lip which do not follow the veins. There is a variety *alba* of the species, described by Linden and Rodigas in 1892. The flower is white except for a yellow, or occasionally green, patch in the throat. There are also several *semi-alba* cultivars, with white tepals and a reddish-purple blotch in the centre of the lip, and yellow, sometimes with purple streaking, in the throat. Other varieties include var. *coerulea*, which has very pale lilac flowers with bluish-violet to greyish-blue markings on the apical half of the lip; and var. *rubra*, with dark rosy-crimson tepals with an even darker lip, and yellow veins in the throat.

Actual flower size: approximately 12 cm across.

Cattleya leopoldii Verschaffelt ex Lemaire

Lemaire described this species in 1855, soon after it was introduced into cultivation by Verschaffelt of Belgium, who named it for the Belgian king, Leopold I. It is often known as *C. guttata* var. *leopoldii*. Some authors believe that Richard's *C. tigrina* of 1848 refers to this species, while others consider it to be closer to *C. guttata.** C. leopoldii* once inhabited the coastal strip from Espírito Santo to Rio Grande do Sul, but is now probably extinct in the southern part of its range. It prefers humid swampy areas, growing on trees up to 100 m above sea level.

The pseudobulbs, 36 cm–1.2 m or more in length, have two or three oblong to elliptic leathery leaves up to 22 cm long and 6 cm wide. Typically three to fifteen or more fragrant flowers are produced in spring or summer, but occasionally also in autumn. The sepals are light to dark brown, sometimes suffused with pink, and more or less heavily spotted with maroon-purple. The lanceolate dorsal sepal and the falcate laterals are 5–6.5 cm long and up to 2 cm wide, while the undulating petals are 4–5 cm long. The 4.5 cm lip is deeply tri-lobed, so that the column is visible from the side, although the whitish, triangular lateral lobes meet above it. There are several longitudinal ridges on the basal half of the mid-lobe, which is white to pale pink merging into rich rose-purple on the warty-veined broad apical lobe.

We grow our plants in suspended pots or baskets of coarsely chopped treefern fibre. *C. leopoldii* prefers bright light and high humidity in intermediate to warm conditions.

Actual flower size: 7–10 cm across.

Cattleya leopoldii varieties

There are several described varieties of this species, all with glossy, rather fleshy flowers. *C. leopoldii* var. *alba* — pictured here — was originally described by Bracey as *C. guttata* var. *alba*, but reclassified by Fowlie in 1964. Unlike most *albas*, this variety does not have white flowers; in this instance the epithet merely indicates that red pigmentation is lacking in the flowers. The petals and sepals, which have no spots, are yellow-green to apple-green, while the broad lip is pure white.

The variety *leopardina* was first described as *C. guttata* var. *leopardina* by L. Linden and Rodigas in 1885, with Fowlie reclassifying it in 1964. It is still sometimes known as *C. guttata* var. *flava* by Brazilian growers. The tepals are yellow-orange to tan with 0.1–0.3 cm-wide chocolate-brown to blood-red spots. The lip is white at the base with a red-amethyst apical lobe. *C. leopoldii* var. *williamsiana* was described by Reichenbach (f.) in 1884 as a variety of *C. guttata*,* and reclassified by Fowlie in 1964. The sepals and petals are said to be dull creamish-purple with purple spotting or, according to Reichenbach, 'faintly striped towards the margins'. The pale lip has a darker apical lobe. *C. leopoldii* var. *pabstia*, described by Braem as *C. tigrina* var. *pabstia* (see entry for *C. guttata* for discussion on *C. tigrina*) is a relatively recently described variety. Named to honour the Brazilian botanist Guido Pabst, it is a peloric form, with petals resembling the lip.

Cultivation of these varieties is as for the type — bright light, high humidity and intermediate to warm temperatures.
Actual flower size: 7–10 cm across.

Cattleya loddigesii Lindley

Probably introduced into England about 1810 by Woodroofe, this species was first known as *Epidendrum violaceum* (1819). Lindley transferred it to the genus *Cattleya* in 1823, but found that the epithet *violacea* was a homonym, and renamed the taxon *C. loddigesii*. Other synonyms include *C. arembergii* and *C. maritima*. Often confused with *C. harrisoniana*,* it inhabits coastal ridges and sub-tropical rainforests of the interior at 500–900 m in the states of Rio de Janeiro, São Paulo and Minas Gerais.

The slightly compressed pseudobulbs are 13–40 cm tall and up to 1.5 cm wide at the apex. Each bears two stiff elliptic to oval leaves 6.5–16 cm long and up to 7 cm wide. From two to nine light lavender to pale pink flowers appear in autumn, early winter, or sometimes in early spring, on a 10–15 cm spike. The sheath from which the spike is produced is usually dry when the flowers open. The tepals normally have some dark lavender spots. The lanceolate 4.5–6.5 cm-long dorsal sepal is 1.4–2.0 cm wide, as are the vaguely falcate shorter lateral sepals. The wider petals have finely undulating margins. The outside of the lip is creamy-white with lilac-lavender on the large lateral lobes, which form a broad tube around the column. Inside there is a narrow, pale yellow band on the front of the lateral lobes and across the short wide mid-lobe, which is pale amethyst-purple to white with crisped edges. The lip has a faint yellow blotch at the base and six ridges only 0.1 cm high.

C. loddigesii prefers a humid, intermediate to cool environment with partial shade and a distinct dry rest in winter.
Actual flower size: 8–11 cm across.

Cattleya loddigesii var. *alba* (hort.) 'San Carlos'

The correct name for this variety may possibly be *C. loddigesii* var. *candida* Reichenbach (f.), described in 1886. But there are enough discrepancies between the clone illustrated and Reichenbach's description to persuade us to retain the var. *alba* appellation. Reichenbach's description, as cited by Fowlie, states that flowers are 'snow white with green tips of sepals and green middle lines on them outside'. While the flowers of the pictured clone do have green-tipped sepals, they have no green lines and, except for some yellow-green on the column, are otherwise pure white. Reichenbach's description also states that 'There is a certain aetherial lightest hue of lightest purple on the petals'. Further, Williams' description of *C. candida*, which is synonymous with

C. loddigesii var. *candida*, says that the sepals and petals are 'delicate white, slightly shaded with pink'.

Like the type species, the var. *alba* grows in shady or exposed conditions in areas of relatively high humidity, often in trees in swamps or along river banks. In its natural habitat it experiences warm wet summers and cool, dry winters. We obtained the beautiful 'San Carlos' clone from the Florália nursery in Niteroi, near Rio de Janeiro.

The pseudobulbs of this plant stand 14–24 cm high with two very leathery spreading leaves 6.5–9.0 cm long. It flowers for us in late autumn to winter.

Cultivation is as for the type. We grow our plants in baskets of chopped treefern fibre or on treefern mounts. Like the type, and unlike *C. harrisoniana*, this variety blooms best for us if moved into a shady position when buds appear.

Actual flower size: 8–9 cm across.

Cattleya loddigesii 'Pink Pearl'

This species has very few named varieties. The one pictured here which is the result of selfing a white clone, has delicate mauve-pink colouring and the broader segments and fuller shape favoured by breeders. As mentioned in the introduction to this listing, there has been much confusion regarding the status of *C. loddigesii* and *C. harrisoniana*.* Treated in the past as a variety of *C. loddigesii*, *C. harrisoniana* is now generally accepted as a separate species. These notes assist in distinguishing one from the other.

C. harrisoniana is said to have more slender pseudobulbs and narrower leaves than *C. loddigesii*. However, the vegetative differences are not consistent, and it is best

to look to floral characteristics for distinguishing features. *C. harrisoniana* flowers from mid-spring to summer with a green sheath at the base of the spike, whereas *C. loddigesii* usually flowers in autumn or early winter, with some clones flowering in spring. Regardless of flowering time, the sheath at the base of the spike of *C. loddigesii* is normally dry when the flowers open. *C. harrisoniana* flowers are generally darker than those of *C. loddigesii*, with more falcate lateral sepals. The lip of *C. loddigesii* is broader at the opening and not as crisped or recurved as that of *C. harrisoniana*. In *C. harrisoniana* the wavy yellow keels run almost the entire length of the lip, while the straight low keels of *C. loddigesii* end near the base of the apical lobe. Also, *C. harrisoniana* has raised veins from the base to the edge of the lateral lobes, a feature absent in *C. loddigesii*.

Actual flower size: 8–10 cm across.

Cattleya luteola Lindley

From the Amazon Basin, this variable species extends beyond the borders of Brazil into Peru, Ecuador, Colombia, Venezuela and Bolivia. It was described by Lindley in 1853, based on plants from Amazonian Brazil. Synonyms include *C. meyeri*, *C. flavida*, *C. sulphurea* and *Epidendrum luteolum*. It is found there in Amazonas and Pará, growing at altitudes of up to 600 m. In Peru it has been reported at altitudes up to 2,000 m. In both Brazil and Peru, where the major populations are found, its habitats are subject to long hot periods followed by heavy seasonal rains.

The pseudobulbs are furrowed, flattened, and closely set on a stout rhizome. They are sometimes tinged with reddish-brown and are commonly 5–15 cm tall, although Peruvian plants are sometimes larger. The single stiff leaf is 6–17 cm long. Brazilian plants tend to an average of about 15 cm tall *in toto*. The four to six flowers are borne on a terminal spike from summer to autumn. They are among the smallest of the genus, seldom more than 5 cm across. Their colour is typically pale yellow, but may be apple-green or greenish-yellow. The tubular 2.8 cm lip is generally bright yellow inside, spotted or streaked with crimson and white along the frilled edges.

This species does best for us when mounted, placed in a bright humid environment with intermediate conditions, and given plenty of water in the growing season, followed by a dry rest in winter.

Actual flower size: approximately 5 cm across.

Cattleya porphyroglossa Linden & Reichenbach (f.)

Reichenbach described this species, which is closely related to *C. granulosa*,* in 1856, having received material from Linden in Brussels. *C. dijanceana* and *Epidendrum porphyroglossum* are later synonyms. Rare now in nature, *C. porphyroglossa* is restricted to a few small areas of Rio de Janeiro, Minas Gerais and Espírito Santo. In Rio de Janeiro it occurs predominantly on low trees in coastal swamps, along the Rio Paraíba and on its islands.

The slender pseudobulbs are typically 12–30 cm long, but may reach 60 cm or more. Each bears two elliptic leaves 7–15 cm long and up to 5 cm wide. From three to eight fragrant flowers, which do not open fully, are borne on a spike up to 10 cm long in spring or summer. The tepals range from yellow-brown to orange-brown, and may have slightly darker veins. The oblong to lanceolate dorsal sepal and the falcate laterals are 4–5 cm long and 1.5 cm wide. The almost rhomboidal to spathulate petals are shorter but wider with rounded apices and wavy margins. The large lateral lobes of the 3.0–3.5 cm-long lip, which curve over the column, are white outside, but are suffused with yellow on the inside and have purple veins and lavender apices. The mid-lobe is yellow at the base with the apical portion shading from lavender to reddish-purple. Both the long narrow isthmus and the apical lobe are covered with granular protuberances.

C. porphyroglossa requires a warm humid environment with partial shade to moderately bright light. Plants may be potted or mounted. A distinct resting period is not essential for this species.

Actual flower size: approximately 7 cm across.

Cattleya schilleriana Reichenbach (f.)

This species, described by Reichenbach in 1857, was named in honour of Consul Schiller of Hamburg, in whose collection it had recently flowered. *Epidendrum schillerianum* is synonymous, as is *C. regnellii*, which refers to the blue-lipped form, *C. schilleriana* var. *lowii*. This species is endemic to Espírito Santo, where it grows on mossy trees and moss-covered cliffs and boulders from sea level to 800 m. The area has a humid climate with heavy night-time dews during the drier summer months.

The compressed, furrowed, club-shaped pseudobulbs are typically 9–15 cm tall and up to 1.5 cm across at the apex. They are often tinged with red-purple, as are the two leaves, which are elliptic to oblong, 6–10 cm long and 3–5 cm wide. Up to five glossy fragrant long-lasting flowers are borne on a 6–15 cm spike in late spring or summer, although some plants may flower twice a year. The olive-brown or red-brown to yellow-green tepals are more or less densely spotted with dark maroon to chestnut brown. The oblong to lanceolate dorsal sepal, which is 5–6 cm long and 2 cm wide, has slightly undulating margins, as do the shorter slightly falcate laterals. The narrower petals have recurved, very wavy margins. The 4.5–5.5 cm-long lip is typically whitish streaked with amethyst-purple. The lateral lobes meet above the column. The yellow disc has five furrows extending on to the kidney-shaped apical lobe, which is minutely fringed.

C. schilleriana does best mounted on treefern or in suspended pots or baskets. It needs an intermediate humid environment with fairly bright light and good ventilation.

Actual flower size: 7–10 cm across.

Cattleya schofieldiana Reichenbach (f.)

Closely related to *C. granulosa** and *C. porphyroglossa*,* this species flowered for the first time in England in 1882 in Schofield's collection. He sent a sketch to Reichenbach, who described it later that year. *C. granulosa* var. *schofieldiana* is conspecific. A native of Espírito Santo at 300–700 m, this species grows epiphytically, often on moss- or lichen-covered trees on almost vertical cliff faces.

The pseudobulbs are up to 1 m tall and 1.5 cm wide near the apex. The two or three leathery leaves are elliptic to oblong, 8–15 cm long and 3.5–5.0 cm wide. Up to five glossy flowers 10–15 cm across are borne on a short spike in summer or early autumn. The tepals are light greenish-yellow to bronze-brown, more or less densely spotted with maroon to purple. The sub-erect dorsal sepal is lanceolate, while the falcate laterals may point inward towards each other. The undulating petals are very narrow at the base and have a broad blunt apical section with reflexed margins at the base. The large, more or less triangular lateral lobes of the lip are creamy-white on the exterior and yellow inside. The mid-lobe is oblong for about half its length, with a fan-shaped apical section, which is finely and irregularly fringed and may be notched. The apical lobe is whitish with many magenta to purple hair-like ornaments.

C. schofieldiana likes humid intermediate conditions with moderately bright light and plenty of air movement. It may be potted or mounted, and does not require a distinct resting period.

Actual flower size: 10–15 cm across.

Cattleya velutina Reichenbach (f.)

This species was described by Reichenbach in 1870, and is conspecific with Barbosa Rodrígues' *C. fragrans* and *C. alutacoa* var. *velutina*. A native of Espírito Santo, Rio de Janeiro and São Paulo at 400–800 m above sea level, it favours moss-covered trees in riverside forests and swampy areas. In Espírito Santo it is found in association with *C. schofieldiana** and *C. schilleriana.**

The grooved pseudobulbs are 20–50 cm tall and 0.4–1.2 cm in diameter near the apex. The two or three elliptic to strap-like leaves are 10–15 cm long and up to 3.5 cm wide. From one to eight very fragrant fleshy flowers are borne from late spring to autumn on a spike 4–8 cm long from the apex of the newest pseudobulb. All segments have undulating margins and are recurved at the apex. The tepals may be bright orange, orange-yellow, golden brown or greenish-brown, more or less densely spotted with dark purple to dark red. The oblong to lanceolate dorsal sepal, which is 5.4–6.6 cm long and about 1.5 cm wide, is longer than the somewhat falcate laterals and the narrowly elliptic wider petals. The 4–5 cm-long fiddle-shaped lip is whitish with a yellow blotch in the throat, a yellow to brown band around the edge of the mid-lobe, and several reddish-purple veins. The very small lateral lobes meet above the column. There are several shallow ridges on the fleshy disc.

Some growers report difficulty with this species. The essential requirements seem to be bright indirect light, high humidity and very good drainage, whether mounted or potted. An intermediate environment suits the species best.

Actual flower size: 6–9 cm across.

Cattleya x *venosa* Rolfe

This natural hybrid between *C. forbesii** and *C. harrisoniana** was described by Rolfe, the founder of the British *Orchid Review*. It is found where the two parent species intergrade in Espírito Santo and Rio de Janeiro, growing epiphytically in coastal swamps which are flooded during the rainy season.

The furrowed pseudobulbs are 8–20 cm tall, covered with white bracts and slightly compressed. There are one or two, rarely three, stiff fleshy leaves at the apex. These are oblong to narrowly elliptic, with an obtuse apex and a prominent keel below. In spring, summer or early autumn one or two flowers are produced on a 4–9 cm spike. The flowers usually resemble those of *C. harrisoniana*, but with the venation of *C. forbesii* on the lip. The mauve-pink tepals have a satiny texture and green tips. The concave lanceolate dorsal sepal is 4.2–4.8 cm long and 1.2–1.5 cm wide. The more or less falcate lateral sepals are 3.5–4.0 cm long, as are the 1.3–2.2 cm-wide petals, which are elliptic to rhomboidal, and have irregular slightly undulating margins. The 3.5 cm-long lip is white to pale pink. The large rounded lateral lobes meet above the column, which is clearly visible, and are more or less covered with pink-purple veins on the inside. The somewhat rounded mid-lobe has a yellow-orange blotch in the centre, with purple veins on either side. It has crisped margins and a notched apex. Near the base are six keels, which continue to the centre of the mid-lobe in two thick raised ridges.

Despite its hot humid habitat, *C. x venosa* will grow in cool conditions, with bright light and a cool rest after flowering.

Actual flower size: 7–8 cm across.

Cattleya violacea (HBK) Rolfe

The original description of this epiphyte as *Cymbidium violaceum* was published in 1815 by von Humboldt, Bonpland and Kunth, based on plants collected from the Rio Orinoco on the border between Colombia and Venezuela. Rolfe transferred it to *Cattleya* in 1889. Synonyms include *C. superba* and *C. schomburgkii*. *C. violacea* inhabits the Amazon Basin, occurring in eastern Colombia, southern Venezuela, Guyana, eastern Peru and Brazil, where it is found in Amazonas, Pará and northern Mato Grosso along waterways at 150–500 m.

The clustered pseudobulbs are club-like to cylindrical, 10–30 cm long and 1.7–2.5 cm wide near the apex. The two oblong-elliptic to oblong-ovoid leaves are 6–16 cm long and up to 8.5 cm wide. From two to eight fragrant long-lasting flowers are borne on spikes up to 30 cm long in spring or autumn, and occasionally in summer. The tepals are rose-purple to bright pink. The narrowly elliptic dorsal sepal is 4.5–7.0 cm long and 1.0–1.5 cm wide, while the somewhat falcate laterals are slightly shorter and wider. The almost rhomboidal petals are 4.5–6.5 cm long and up to 3.5 cm wide, with slightly undulating margins. The 4.0–5.5 cm-long lip is deep maroon-purple with white to mauve on the inside of the large lateral lobes. The undulating margin of the recurved mid-lobe is finely irregular. Several yellow ridges run down the centre of the lip.

C. violacea should be mounted or grown in a well-drained pot or basket as it does not like 'wet feet'. A warm, humid environment is preferred, with moderate to bright light. It needs no definite resting period.

Actual flower size: 7.5–10 cm across.

Cattleya walkeriana Gardner

Closely related to *C. nobilior*, but with smaller flowers, this species was discovered by Gardner in 1839 and described by him in 1843. *C. walkeriana* was named after Gardner's assistant in Brazil. Synonyms include *C. princeps*, *C. bulbosa* and *C. gardneriana*. Endemic to Brazil, this species has a variety of habitats at elevations to 2,000 m in Minas Gerais, Goiás, São Paulo, and Mato Grosso. It grows on large trees on rocky limestone plateaux, smaller rough-barked trees and granite cliffs. It is often exposed to full sun and high temperatures, moderated on occasion by low cloud and mist.

The club-shaped pseudobulbs, 3–12 cm tall, and well spaced on a stout rhizome, may be green or reddish-purple. Each bears a single leathery leaf (rarely two) from 4–12 cm long, often tinged with red. The flowers, which last about six weeks, are borne, up to three to a spike, in autumn or spring. The spikes rise usually from the base of the pseudobulb, but sometimes from the apex in what is sometimes termed the variety *walkeriana*. Braem contends that this variety is probably a natural hybrid between *C. walkeriana* and *C. loddigesii*.* The pale to dark rosy-pink flowers are 8–10 cm across. The narrow pointed sepals contrast nicely with the almost diamond-shaped petals. The three-lobed lip is up to 4.5 cm long with a deeper colouring and veins on the mid-lobe, and a pale yellow or white disc streaked with purple.

This species is very adaptable, and grows well on treefern or cork mounts or in suspended pots in bright light and intermediate to cool conditions. Give plenty of water when in growth.

Actual flower size: 8–10 cm across.

Cattleya warneri Moore

Still usually treated as a separate species, *C. warneri* is closely related to *C. labiata** and is considered by some authors — including Pabst — to be synonymous with it. Moore described it in the early 1860s, naming it for Warner, in whose collection it first flowered. *C. trilabiata* and *C. labiata* var. *warneri* are conspecific. *C. warneri* grows epiphytically (or, rarely, on rocks) at 200–800 m above sea level in Bahia, Espírito Santo, Minas Gerais, and possibly in eastern Rio de Janeiro.

The club-like ridged pseudobulbs are compressed, 9–25 cm tall and 2–3 cm wide. They are sometimes tinged with red, as is the reverse of the single leathery leaf, which is 12–30 cm long, 4–8 cm wide, and recurved at the apex. From two to six fragrant flowers are produced in spring. (Those of *C. labiata* appear from late summer to autumn.) The 8–11 cm-long tepals are usually light to dark rose-lilac. The erect lanceolate dorsal sepal and the somewhat falcate lateral sepals are 2.0–2.5 cm wide, while the rhomboidal petals, which often droop more than those of *C. labiata*, are 5–7 cm wide with irregular wavy margins. The obscurely three-lobed lip is about 7 cm long, and coloured on the outside like the tepals. The very frilly apical lobe has a rich lilac-purple blotch, while the lateral lobes are white, edged with pink-purple and sometimes suffused with mauve. The yellow throat is usually shaded with purple and marked with cream to bright yellow veins.

C. warneri requires a humid, intermediate to warm environment with moderately bright light and a cooler drier winter rest. *Actual flower size: 15–22 cm across.*

Caularthron bicornutum (Hook.) Rafinesque-Schmaltz

First described in 1834 by Hooker as *Epidendrum bicornutum*, this species was transferred in 1836 by Rafinesque-Schmaltz to the genus *Caularthron*. For many years, however, it has been better known by Bentham's 1881 name, *Diacrium bicornutum*. *D. amazonicum* is also synonymous. It is a common species in Trinidad and Tobago and its range extends to Venezuela, Colombia, Guyana and Brazil, where it inhabits the inland forests of Amazonas, Rondônia and Roraima.

The clustered, spindle-shaped pseudobulbs are usually 9–20 cm tall, although most of the plants we have seen are quite short. They produce two to three stiff leathery leaves 7–20 cm long. An erect spike carries three to twenty flowers in spring. This spike, 15–30 cm long, rises from between the leaves. The closely set fragrant flowers are up to 6 cm across and last for two to three weeks. The sepals and the broader petals are pointed at the apex. The more or less concave sepals are sometimes marked with lavender on the backs and at the tips. The three-lobed lip and the column are spotted and streaked with purple. The pointed mid-lobe is about 2.5 cm long with a central yellow area. Near the base there is a fleshy crest with two prominent yellow ridges.

This species, which rather resents division, enjoys warm to intermediate conditions with bright light and good ventilation. It does well for us in a suspended pot in a mixture of treefern chunks, broken brick and coarse bark. Keep on the dry side during winter dormancy. *Actual flower size: approximately 5 cm across.*

Chytroglossa marileoniae Reichenbach (f.)

Rarely seen in collections, this charming miniature deserves to be more widely grown. Related to *Ornithocephalus*, the genus *Chytroglossa* contains only three species, all natives of southern Brazil. *C. marileoniae*, the best known of the genus was described by Reichenbach in the latter half of the nineteenth century. It grows epiphytically in mountainous areas in the states of Rio de Janeiro and São Paulo, where rain is common throughout the year and cooling mists form late each day as warm air rises from the valleys.

The olive-green leaves form fan-like growths. The narrow pointed leaves are 3–4 cm long, with a slightly reflexed apex. Four to six flowers, each about 2 cm long, are borne in spring on a wiry pendent spike about 5 cm long. The sepals and petals are apple-green to yellow, while the lip is white at the base with dark red-brown blotches providing a focus. The almost erect dorsal sepal and rounded petals are curved inward at the tip. The lateral sepals are virtually hidden by the lip, which is minutely serrated, as are the petals near the tips. The lip has two calli at the base and an upturned mid-lobe.

This species prefers a fibrous mount such as treefern and cool to intermediate conditions with year-round humidity. It needs semi-shade to full shade, regular watering, and — most importantly — good air movement.

Actual flower size: approximately 2 cm long.

Cirrhaea dependens (Lodd.) Reichenbach (f.)

Originally described in 1825 by Loddiges as *Cymbidium dependens*, this epiphyte was transferred to the genus *Cirrhaea* in 1863 by Reichenbach. Its many synonyms include *Gongora viridipurpurea*, *Sarcoglossum suavolens* and *Cirrhaea livida*. It inhabits the cooler mountains of Rio de Janeiro, São Paulo, Paraná and Santa Catarina.

The strongly ridged dull green pseudobulbs are ovoid to conical, 4–7.5 cm tall and approximately 2–3 cm wide. The single more or less lanceolate pleated leaf is 20–30 cm long and about 4 cm wide. It has three to five prominent veins beneath and a very sharply tapering apex. Up to twenty long-lasting flowers are borne in summer on a pendulous spike up to 45 cm long from the base of the pseudobulb. Colour is variable, with the tepals ranging from apple-green to yellowish- or dark brownish-red, with or without red-brown to maroon-purple spots and bars. The narrow linear petals are usually more or less heavily marked, so that they are sometimes almost completely red-purple in colour. The 2.5–3.0 cm-long sepals are oblong to lanceolate and up to 0.9 cm wide, with more or less deflexed margins. The complex fleshy lip, which is held uppermost, is white to pale purple, with the long tapering apical section usually barred with red-purple. The concave central section and the very narrow basal claw may be blotched or spotted. The arching column is white to reddish-purple.

C. dependens, whether potted or mounted, should be suspended so that the pendulous spikes may develop and hang freely. A fairly humid intermediate environment with partial shade is recommended.

Actual flower size: approximately 5 cm across.

Cochleanthes candida (Ldl.) Schultes & Garay

Lindley described this species, which was introduced into cultivation by Morel of France, as *Warrea candida* in 1851. Schultes and Garay transferred it to *Cochleanthes* in about 1959. *Zygopetalum candidum*, *Warscewiczella candida* and *Huntleya radicans* are conspecific. It grows epiphytically or among decomposing vegetation on the ground in both the cooler mountains and the hot lowlands of Rio de Janeiro, Espírito Santo, Minas Gerais and Bahia.

The plants, lacking pseudobulbs, comprise fan-like clumps of leaves. Each growth has several pale green equitant leaves up to about 20 cm long and 2–5 cm wide with a reflexed acute apex. A single perfumed flower is borne on a short spike in late autumn or early winter. The tepals are white. The oval to lanceolate dorsal sepal is 2.0–2.2 cm long and 1.0–1.2 cm wide, while the laterals, which are concave and overlap at the base to form a short chin, are slightly longer. The oval to oblong petals are recurved at the acute apices. The obscurely three-lobed lip is about 2.5 cm long and almost as wide across the mid-lobe. The lateral lobes, which are curved towards the column, are white with mauve on the front edges. The squarish mid-lobe is slightly rounded in the two-lobed apical section. It may be white with purple in the middle or completely rose-purple. The crest comprises a fleshy plate about 1 cm long, which is five-toothed along the front and joined only to the lateral lobes by an additional section on each side.

C. candida prefers an intermediate to warm environment with high humidity, moderate shade and year-round moisture.

Actual flower size: approximately 4.5 cm across.

Comparettia coccinea Lindley

The plantsman and botanical writer Conrad Loddiges first imported this species into England in 1837, and it was described by Lindley a year later. It was then lost to cultivation until reintroduced in 1865. It is limited to the states of Espírito Santo, São Paulo, Rio de Janeiro, Paraná and Minas Gerais, where it grows either epiphytically or lithophytically in cooler areas.

The clustered pseudobulbs are rather compressed and tinged with red. They are usually 1.5–3.0 cm tall and bear a single fleshy leaf at the apex. This narrow leaf is 5–15 cm long, pointed, dark green above and purplish beneath. The arching, often branched, spike, may appear at any time between summer and winter. From 15–22 cm long, it carries three to ten flowers, each about 2 cm long, towards its apex. The sepals and petals are usually yellow-orange shaded with red. The 0.8 cm dorsal sepal and petals hide the column, while the joined lateral sepals are obscured by the lip, except for the curved 1.0–1.5 cm spur formed at their base. The wide lip is bright scarlet with two yellow keels and two thread-like projections from the base. The latter are hidden within the spur. The lip has wavy edges and is bent slightly outwards.

This species does best when mounted, but may be potted in a coarse well-drained mixture. It likes intermediate to cool temperatures in semi-shade to moderately bright light. Give plenty of water when in active growth, followed by a drier rest in mid-winter.

Actual flower size: approximately 2 cm across.

Comparettia falcata Poeppig & Endlicher

Discovered by Poeppig in Peru, and described in 1836, this is the species on which the genus *Comparettia* was based. Lindley's *C. rosea* is conspecific. It is the most widespread of the comparettias, extending from Mexico through Central America and the West Indies, as far south as Bolivia and Brazil. (Schweinfurth says it occurs in Brazil, Pabst disagrees.) It grows usually on trees and shrubs in humid forest up to an altitude of 1,800 m above sea level. Not surprisingly in view of its extensive distribution it is a variable species.

The clustered pseudobulbs are from 1–4 cm tall, compressed, and bear a single leaf 3–18 cm long. This leaf is oblong, fleshy, and folded inward at the base, and is often suffused with red-purple. Flower spikes, from 6–90 cm long, may appear at any time of the year. Sometimes branched, they carry anything from two to thirty flowers about 2 cm long. These are a deep rosy-pink, paler towards the centre and with darker veining. The concave dorsal sepal and slightly broader spreading petals are arranged round the column, while the joined lateral sepals, which form a slender slightly compressed spur, are hidden behind the large three-lobed lip. Two slender appendages at the base of the lip are small, while the kidney-shaped mid-lobe is large, with undulating edges. It may have a white central keel at the base.

This species prefers to be mounted, and likes intermediate to cool conditions with semi-shade to moderate light. Fairly high humidity is desirable, with year-round watering and good air movement.

Actual flower size: approximately 2 cm long.

Cycnoches pentadactylon Lindley

This species was discovered in 1841 by Lobb, and described by Lindley in 1843. *C. amesianum*, *C. cooperi* and *C. espiritosantense* are conspecific. It is reported from Peru and from Brazil, where it is found growing epiphytically in the hot humid lowlands of Amazonas and Espírito Santo, and at higher altitudes in the Distrito Federal around Brasília.

The oblong to spindle-shaped pseudobulbs are 10–45 cm long and bear several pleated lanceolate leaves 15–35 cm long and up to 7 cm wide. Non-respunate male and female flowers are borne on separate spikes from near the apex of the pseudobulb — or, very rarely, on the same spike — in spring or summer. Male flowers are white or yellow-green, spotted and barred with chestnut brown or red. The lanceolate dorsal sepal, which is 3–5 cm long and about 1 cm wide, and the shorter sub-falcate to oblong lateral sepals are more or less reflexed, as are the 3.5–4.0 cm-long petals. The fleshy complex lip has a 1.5 cm-long greenish claw adorned with a curved horn. The four-lobed white mid-section is spotted, as is the acute yellowish apex, which is usually recurved. The long slender column measures about 3.5 cm. Female flowers have similar colouring but shorter tepals. The ovate to oblong lip is white with a yellow claw, a sharp point at the apex, and two calli at the base. The shorter yellow-green column has purple-red spots.

C. pentadactylon prefers a warm humid environment with bright indirect light and plenty of water while in growth, followed by a slightly drier resting period.

Actual flower size: approximately 7.5 cm long.

Cyrtopodium andersonii (Lambert ex Andrews) R. Brown

Using material supplied by Lambert, Andrews described this species in 1811 as *Cymbidium andersonii* to honour Anderson, who had discovered it on St Vincent in the West Indies. In 1813, R. Brown used it as the type for his new genus, *Cyrtopodium*. Synonyms include *Epidendrum polyphyllum* and *Cyrtopodium glutiniferum*. Native to northern South America, Cuba, the West Indies, and possibly Florida, *C. andersonii* grows epiphytically and amid humus on rocks in a variety of habitats in the Brazilian states of Roraima, Rondônia, Pará, Amapá Pernambuco, Rio de Janeiro, Santa Catarina and Minas Gerais.

The erect clustered pseudobulbs are spindle-shaped to cylindrical, 60 cm–1.2 m tall and up to 5 cm in diameter. The upper section bears several deciduous leaves 30–75 cm long and 2–5 cm wide. In spring an erect, predominantly branched, spike up to 1.8 m long carries many long lasting waxy, fragrant flowers. The vaguely undulate sepals, which are ovate to elliptic, are yellowish-green to pale green, 1.8–2.2 cm long and up to 1.7 cm wide. The similarly sized petals are lemon-yellow with green at the apex. The waxy yellow lip has erect rounded lateral lobes and an irregular more or less oblong mid-lobe which is concave in the apical half. At the base is a thickened grooved callus, which is orange-yellow, densely spotted with red.

C. andersonii prefers intermediate to warm conditions with moderately bright light. It needs a well-drained medium and should be given plenty of water when in growth, followed by a drier cooler resting period during dormancy.

Actual flower size: approximately 5 cm across.

Cyrtopodium palmifrons Reichenbach (f.) & Warming ex Reichenbach

This species was studied by both Reichenbach and the Danish botanist Warming, and was validly described by Reichenbach in 1881. *C. palmifrons* inhabits the cooler mountains of São Paulo, Paraná, Santa Catarina and Rio Grande do Sul, and also the savannahs of Minas Gerais, where it experiences a continental climate. It also occurs in Argentina.

The erect, spindle-shaped pseudobulbs are up to 1.2 m tall, but usually much shorter, and up to 5 cm in diameter. The upper part of the pseudobulb has several alternating deciduous leaves up to 75 cm long. These are sub-erect to arching, pleated, and have several prominent veins. Many fragrant flowers about 3 cm wide are borne in autumn or winter on a branched spike up to 1.5 cm tall. The spike carries large spotted bracts, mostly at the base of each branch. The 1.0–1.5 cm-long sepals are yellow-green with reddish blotches. They have very wavy margins and are oval to rounded. The yellow petals may have a few spots, and are also rounded. The lip is yellow, suffused and blotched with red. The large rounded erect lateral lobes are narrow at the base. The mid-lobe, which is bilobed at the apex, is often edged with red and has strongly deflexed lateral margins. At the base is a yellow warty callus marked with red.

C. palmifrons prefers an intermediate environment with moderately bright light and good air movement. Pots of coarsely chopped treefern fibre or bark are suitable media. Give plenty of water when in growth, followed by a cool dry winter rest.

Actual flower size: approximately 3 cm across.

Dipteranthus duchii Pabst

Described by the late Guido Pabst, the well-known Brazilian taxonomist, this pretty miniature belongs to a small and little-known genus. The genus was established by Barbosa Rodrígues, and is closely related to *Ornithocephalus*, *Zygostates* and *Capanemia*. It is endemic to Brazil, and originates from the hot humid lowlands of Pernambuco in the north-east. It is a rather delicate species, and grows predominantly on the outer twigs of trees overhanging rivers or streams, or in clearings. It is thus provided with good air movement, which is essential in an environment where temperatures are high for most of the year, with only humidity fluctuating.

The tiny clustered pseudobulbs are almost obscured by the bases of the 2–5 cm-long leaves, which are acute and have a prominent keel below. Spikes are produced from the base of the pseudobulbs, are up to 5 cm long, and bear several flowers. The 0.7 cm sepals are bright apple-green and swept backward. The edges are sparsely toothed, and the apex is rounded. The 0.3 cm petals are white and project forward on either side of the column. The almost circular lip is 0.5 cm across and has a horseshoe-shaped callus at the base. The lip is a translucent white with orange-yellow markings in the centre.

We have found that plants of this species prefer small mounts — pieces of cork, twigs or small branches of paperbark, etc. — with their roots exposed to the freely moving air. A humid semi-shaded spot in an intermediate to warm environment suits them best.

Actual flower size: approximately 1 cm long.

Dipteranthus grandiflorus (Ldl.) Pabst

Discovered in the Organ Mountains near Rio de Janeiro by Gardner in 1837, this epiphyte was described as *Ornithocephalus grandiflorus* in 1840 by Lindley. More than a century later, Pabst transferred it to the genus *Dipteranthus*. *Zygostates grandiflorus* is conspecific. Found in Espírito Santo and Rio de Janeiro, *D. grandiflorus* grows in the cool mountain regions which are generally damp all year round and experience nightly dews.

The largest of the genus, this species comprises a loose 'fan' of four to six quite fleshy leaves 7–15 cm long and up to 2.5 cm wide. Folded only at the base, these are mid- to dark green with an obtuse apex. Twenty to thirty flowers are borne on an arching spike up to 22 cm long which rises from the leaf axil in late spring or summer. The tepals are white with bright to dull green at the base of the fan-shaped 1 cm-long petals, which are occasionally also marked with yellow on the narrow claw. The sepals are more or less ovoid with the 0.8–1.0 cm-long dorsal slightly larger than the laterals. The apical halves of the dorsal sepal and of the petals curve inward. The concave white lip is about 1 cm long with a green horseshoe-shaped callus, which sometimes has a yellow patch in the centre. The column has a long thread-like appendage between the stigma and the stamen.

D. grandiflorus does well when mounted on small pieces of treefern or cork or potted in coarse treefern fibre. It prefers intermediate to cool conditions with high humidity, partial shade and good ventilation, and needs year-round moisture.

Actual flower size: approximately 1.5 cm across.

Dipteranthus pustulatus (Krzl.) Pabst

This charming miniature was originally described by Kraenzlin late in the nineteenth century as *Ornithocephalus pustulatus*. Pabst later transferred it to the genus *Dipteranthus*, although it is sometimes sold by Brazilian nurseries as *Zygostates pustulatus*. Endemic to Brazil, it inhabits cool moist mountain areas in the southern states of Paraná and Santa Catarina, which experience year-round rain. The forests of these areas are bathed each evening with mist which forms as warm air rises from the base of the mountains. This species grows on small lichen-encrusted twigs in shaded positions.

The tightly clustered pseudobulbs are almost egg-shaped, 0.5–0.8 cm tall, and are at first glossy pale green, later turning duller and darker. A single 2–6 cm leaf rises from the apex of the pseudobulb, and several pairs of leaves clasp the base. The more or less erect spikes, 5–10 cm long, rise from the base of the pseudobulb in spring. They each carry about fifteen delicate white flowers and present a lovely sight, especially on a specimen plant. The spreading 0.2 cm sepals and 0.4 cm petals are rounded at the apex. The lateral sepals are hidden by the 0.5 cm lip, which is somewhat concave and has a patch of yellow-green in the throat.

This is a particularly easy species to grow — perhaps the easiest of the genus — and is very rewarding in its regularity of flowering. Give it cool to intermediate temperatures and a shady position with year-round moisture. It grows especially well, we find, on small treefern mounts.

Actual flower size: approximately 0.8 cm across.

Dryadella lilliputana (Cogniaux) Luer

Discovered by Edwall in the state of São Paulo, and originally described by Cogniaux in 1906 as *Masdevallia lilliputana*, this tiny species was transferred by Luer in 1978 to the new genus *Dryadella* (named for the mythical wood nymphs) which he created for it and similar species. It grows as an epiphyte in moist rainforests in the states of São Paulo, Rio de Janeiro, Paraná, Santa Catarina and Rio Grande do Sul.

The leaves are quite succulent and grow in tightly clustered clumps 1.2–1.6 cm tall. Minutely dimpled, the leaves are dark green with paler bases. They have a deep channel on the upper surface and a rounded underside. The flowers, which appear in winter, stand just above the leaves, and thus are more easily seen than those of most other species in the genus. The sepals form a very short tube before opening widely. The concave dorsal and the joined lateral sepals are pale cream lightly spotted with crimson, both inside and out. The free parts of the sepals, with narrow to slender tails about 0.4 cm long, are about 0.3 cm wide. The yellow, spotted lip and erect petals are very small.

This species seems to be the most difficult of the genus to maintain in cultivation. It needs cool to intermediate conditions with fairly high humidity and really excellent ventilation or air movement. It should be kept moist but not wet. Use a small pot and ensure adequate drainage.

Actual flower size: approximately 1 cm long.

Dryadella zebrina (Porsch) Luer

First collected at the beginning of the twentieth century by von Wettstein and sent by him to the Botanical Gardens of Vienna, this species was studied and described soon after by Porsch as *Masdevallia zebrina*. Luer transferred it to his new genus *Dryadella* in 1978. It inhabits areas of temperate climate in the states of São Paulo, Santa Catarina and Rio Grande do Sul, which receive abundant rainfall as well as mist and fog, which often occur late in the day.

The plant has stiff pointed leaves 5–6 cm long and 0.5–1.0 cm wide with a central keel. The leaves are sometimes reddish-purple towards the apex. The plant usually forms small dense clumps. Very short spikes are produced in winter, each bearing a single flower which may be hidden by the foliage. The greenish-yellow flowers have variable crimson spots, blotches and stripes, with only the tails being unmarked. The flowers, produced in some profusion, are about 1.5 cm in diameter across the tips of the tails. The dorsal sepal is hooded so that its tail points forward. The lateral sepals are free except for the very short tube and often have a central yellow vein. The tiny tongue-like lip may be orange or yellow with deep red blotches.

This species should be grown in a cool humid situation in semi-shade and kept moist. It may be mounted or potted in a fibrous well-drained mixture.

Actual flower size: approximately 1.5 cm across.

Encyclia amicta (Ldl. & Rchb.(f.)) Schlechter

Lindley and Reichenbach first described this species over one hundred years ago as *Epidendrum amictum*. Schlechter later transferred it to the genus *Encyclia*. Synonyms include *Encyclia linearifolioides* and *E. bicornuta*. It inhabits the warm lowlands in the central Brazilian states of Pará, Alagoas, Minas Gerais, Goiás and Mato Grosso, where the vast expanses of tropical forest create a very humid atmosphere. Short violent storms are followed by relatively dry days. Many of the epiphytic orchids of this region, like *E. amicta*, seek out for their hosts trees on open slopes, along stream beds and in clearings where air movement is good.

E. amicta has clustered egg-shaped pseudobulbs 1.0–2.5 cm tall which bear one or two very narrow arching leaves from 10–23 cm long. Arching spikes to about 16 cm, each with a few flowers, rise from the apex of the pseudobulbs from late spring to winter. The pointed sepals and petals are 1.4–2.0 cm long, and are yellow-green to green, more or less suffused or blotched with purple-brown, sometimes only on the reverse. The 1.0–1.5 cm-long lip is three-lobed; the white lateral lobes are triangular, while the amethyst mid-lobe is rounded. The central callus has two keels.

This species is a relatively easy grower in intermediate to warm conditions and moderately bright light. It is a compact species, and will grow happily for many years on a mount no bigger than 8 x 10 cm. It may be potted, but does best for us on treefern mounts.

Actual flower size: 2.5–3 cm across.

Encyclia dichroma (Ldl.) Schlechter

In 1843 the French Consul, Quesnel, introduced this species into cultivation in Europe with plants collected in Pernambuco. Later that year Lindley described it as *Epidendrum dichromum*. Schlechter transferred it to the genus *Encyclia* in 1914. Synonyms include *Epidendrum guesnelianum* and *Epidendrum conspicuum*. Also occurring in Suriname, *E. dichroma* inhabits the cooler mountains and savannahs in Pernambuco, Minas Gerais and Bahia. It usually grows epiphytically, but in the savannahs is often found growing in sand deposits between rocks in exposed positions at 700–900 m above sea level.

The cylindrical to conical pseudobulbs are 7–15 cm tall with two or three leathery strap-like leaves at the apex. The leaves are 15–30 cm long and up to 3 cm wide.

Several fragrant long-lasting flowers are borne on an erect to arching spike up to 60 cm long usually in autumn or early winter. The 2 cm-long tepals may be almost white, pinkish-red or mauve, usually with a darker network of veins, particularly on the petals, which are oval to rhomboidal with a narrow claw at the base. The sepals are elliptic to spoon-shaped. The lip is heavily streaked and suffused with red to purple. The more or less oblong lateral lobes curl up beside the column and are reflexed at the apex. The lateral margins of the mid-lobe are strongly recurved. There are two fleshy plates on the disc. The column has two short wings.

E. dichroma prefers a moderately bright intermediate to warm environment, and plenty of water when in growth, followed by a definite dry winter resting period. It may be mounted or potted in any well-drained mixture.

Actual flower size: 3.5–5 cm across.

Encyclia fausta (Rchb. (f.) ex Cogn.) Pabst

Described by Cogniaux in the late nineteenth century as *Epidendrum faustum*, a name by which it is still sometimes known, this species was transferred to the genus *Encyclia* in the second half of the twentieth century by the late Guido Pabst, the eminent Brazilian taxonomist and founder of the Herbarium Bradeanum in Rio de Janeiro. This species is endemic to Brazil, being found only in the southern states of Rio de Janeiro, Paraná, Santa Catarina and Rio Grande do Sul. The areas which it inhabits are characterised by chains of wooded hills subjected to almost daily mist and light rain. Humidity is mostly high, though less so in winter when temperatures drop.

The spindle-shaped pale green pseudobulbs, set at intervals of 1.0–1.5 cm on the rhizome, are 5–11 cm tall, and each bears a pair of narrow strap-like leaves at the apex. Leaves are 8–12 cm long. The short erect inflorescence rises from the apex of the pseudobulb in summer to autumn. About 12 cm long, it typically bears four to ten starry white flowers with a pleasant astringent fragrance. The acute sepals and petals are reflexed. Sepals are about 3 cm by 0.7 cm, the petals 2.8 cm by 1.0 cm. The pointed lip, which is held uppermost, is 2.2 cm long with turned-down sides and purple streaking.

This species grows quite happily either mounted or in baskets of coarsely chopped treefern and sphagnum moss. It likes a cool to intermediate environment and moderately bright light, and prefers a slightly dry rest in winter.

Actual flower size: approximately 5 cm across.

Encyclia fragrans (Sw.) Lemée

This 'cockle-shell' encyclia was described as *Epidendrum fragrans* in 1788 by Swartz, and only tranferred to *Encyclia* in 1955 by Lemée. One of the first epiphytic orchids to be successfully cultivated, its synonyms include *Epidendrum lineatum* and *Epidendrum aemulum*. It occurs throughout the Americas from Mexico to Bolivia and Brazil. In Brazil it inhabits the hot humid lowlands from Amazonas and Pará in the north to Santa Catarina and Rio Grande do Sul in the south. In other countries it is found at up to 1,800 m above sea level.

Set 1–2 cm apart, the elliptic to spindle-shaped slightly compressed pseudobulbs are 4.5–13.0 cm long and 1–3 cm wide. There is typically a single strap-like apical leaf 9–35 cm long and up to 4.8 cm wide. In winter or spring two to six fleshy fragrant flowers are borne on a 5–17 cm-long spike from the apex of the pseudobulb. The spreading, more or less reflexed tepals may be white, greenish or yellowish. The linear to lanceolate sepals are 1.5–3.5 cm long and 0.4–0.9 cm wide, while the shorter petals are up to 1.2 cm wide. The lip, which is held uppermost, is whitish with purple stripes and is joined to the column for half the length of the latter. The rounded apical portion of the lip is concave and has a sharply pointed apex. The fleshy disc has an oblong callus with a deep central furrow.

E. fragrans is reasonably tolerant of a range of temperatures and grows well mounted or potted in a well-drained medium such as coarsely chopped treefern. It likes bright indirect light and plenty of water when in active growth.

Actual flower size: 4–6 cm across.

Encyclia oncidioides (Ldl.) Schlechter

Lindley described this epiphyte as *Epidendrum oncidioides* in 1833, and Schlechter transferred it to *Encyclia* in 1914. Several Central American species have at times been mistaken for this species, which is actually endemic to South America. Pabst's *Encyclia vellozoana* is conspecific. Found in northern South America, Brazil and Peru, *E. oncidioides* inhabits both the hot humid lowlands and cooler mountains. It occurs in the Brazilian states of Amazonas, Amapá, Pará, Pernambuco, Sergipe, Espírito Santo, Rio de Janeiro, Paraná and Santa Catarina.

The more or less conical to ovoid pseudobulbs are 3–6 cm tall and bear two or three strap-like leaves from 12–50 cm long. From late spring to early summer many flowers, about 3–4 cm across, are carried on a spike from 50 cm to 1.5 m or more long. The spreading 1.5–2.0 cm tepals are yellowish-brown or greenish-yellow, heavily suffused with brown. The sepals are more or less lanceolate, while the rounded petals are narrow at the base. The prominently three-lobed lip is white, cream or yellow, marked with red-purple or dull brown. It is 1.3–1.7 cm long, with the large more or less oblong lateral lobes curved up on either side of the column. The mid-lobe is rounded, with a pointed apex and undulating edges, or more or less rhomboidal. The disc has a diamond-shaped callus, while there are several raised veins on the mid-lobe.

E. oncidioides prefers intermediate to warm conditions, but will tolerate cooler temperatures provided it is kept drier in winter. It needs moderately bright light and high humidity.

Actual flower size: 3–4 cm across.

Encyclia patens Hooker

Better known as Lindley's *Epidendrum odoratissimum* (1831), which was later transferred to *Encyclia* by Schlechter, *Encyclia patens* was described by Hooker in 1830. Synonyms include *Encyclia serroniana*. It occurs in the cool and moist mountain areas of Pernambuco, Minas Gerais, Rio de Janeiro, São Paulo, Paraná, Santa Catarina and Rio Grande do Sul.

The clustered pseudobulbs are more or less conical, 3.5–6.5 cm tall, and up to 2.5 cm wide. Each carries two fleshy strap-like apical leaves 20–30 cm long and 1.3–2.0 cm wide with a prominent mid-vein beneath. From five to fifteen fragrant flowers are borne in winter on a spike up to about 30 cm long. The fleshy well-spaced flowers have green spreading tepals, with or without brownish streaks and suf-fusions. The lanceolate sepals are 1.3–1.6 cm long and 0.4 cm wide. The erect dorsal sepal is obtuse at the apex, while the lateral sepals, which are slightly concave near the base, are acute. The somewhat spathulate petals are slightly wider, have a short sharp point at the apex, and curve slightly inward. The 1.5 cm-long lip is creamish, with more or less oblong lateral lobes which are greenish at the base and streaked with red. They stand erect on either side of the column before recurving slightly at the rounded apex. The roundish mid-lobe, which has several raised veins, may have a small point at the apex and reddish streaks. At the base is a diamond-shaped concave crest.

E. patens is an easy plant in cultivation, tolerating diverse conditions, and does well in a humid, intermediate to cool environment with bright indirect light.

Actual flower size: 2–3 cm across.

Encyclia randii (Barb. Rodr.) Pôrto & Brade

Barbosa Rodrígues described this little-known encyclia as *Epidendrum randii* in 1891, naming it in honour of its discoverer, Rand, whose book, *Flowers for the Parlor and Garden*, was popular at the time. In 1935, Campos Pôrto, grandson of Barbosa Rodrígues, and Brade transferred this species to the genus *Encyclia*. *E. randii* is found in the hot lowlands of Amazonas, Pernambuco and Mato Grosso.

The clustered pseudobulbs are ovoid to conical, 2.5–6.0 cm tall, and 2–4 cm wide near the base. They are greenish to dark red or brownish-purple and bear two stiff strap-like leaves at the apex. These leaves, 23–50 cm long and 1–2 cm wide, are folded at the base, have a prominent keel and an acute to obtuse apex. They are often suffused with dark purple. In late spring or early summer a reddish-purple spike, 30 cm or more long, rises from the apex of the pseudobulb. It carries several faintly perfumed flowers 5–6 cm across. The spreading tepals, which are 3 cm long and 1 cm wide, are brown with several darker veins and have yellow-green edges and bases. The petals have undulating margins. The 3 cm-long lip is white with many amethyst markings on the rounded mid-lobe, which is 2.5 cm wide and thickened at the basal claw. The 1.5 cm lateral lobes are oblong, rounded at the apex, and suf-fused with green at the base.

Like most Brazilian encyclias, *E. randii* is a relatively easy and rewarding species in cultivation. A humid, warm to intermediate environment with fairly bright light suits it well. Give plenty of water when in growth, and a resting period only if grown in cooler conditions.

Actual flower size: 5–6 cm across.

Encyclia vespa (Vell.) Dressler

One of the most widespread American species, *E. vespa* was described by Velloso in 1827 as *Epidendrum vespa* and was transferred to the genus *Encyclia* by Dressler in 1971. Its many synonyms include *Epidendrum crassilabium*, *Epidendrum variegatum* and *Epidendrum tigrinum*. It occurs throughout Central America, the West Indies and northern South America, south to Brazil and Peru. It is found in almost all Brazilian states, inhabiting the cool mountain regions, the hot lowlands and the inland savannahs.

The pseudobulbs are cylindrical to spindle-shaped, 6–38 cm tall and 0.5–2.5 cm in diameter. Each bears one to four strap-like leaves near the apex. From 8–40 cm long and 1.8–6.5 cm wide, these leaves are folded near the base and have a sharp point at the obtuse apex. From six to thirteen fleshy flowers are borne in summer on a spike 6–35 cm long. Flowers are long-lasting and vanilla-scented. The more or less lanceolate sepals and spoon-shaped petals are white, green or yellowish with reddish-brown markings on the inside. They curve inward at the apex. The sepals are 0.7–1.7 cm long and up to 0.6 cm wide, with the dorsal curved forward. The petals are slightly shorter and narrower. The trowel-like lip, which is held uppermost, is joined to the column at the base. It is creamish with a maroon-purple blotch at the base. Two fleshy ridges, which are rounded at the front, form a very fleshy callus.

E. vespa tolerates a wide range of conditions from cool to warm. It needs moderately bright indirect light and plenty of water when in active growth.

Actual flower size: 1.5–3 cm across.

Encyclia widgrenii Lindley

Restricted to the state of Minas Gerais, this charming epiphytic species was described by Lindley and named in honour of Widgren, who collected plants between 1841 and 1847. The topography of Minas Gerais is characterised largely by savannah country and the flat-topped hills of the cerrado. It is an area of temperature extremes with hot dry days and very cool nights when temperatures can fall as low as 0°C in winter. Humidity ranges from 20–60 per cent. Here, epiphytes are restricted to the narrow stretches of woodland — usually small trees and stunted scrub — along rivers and around lakes.

The pale green to yellowish pseudobulbs are spindle-shaped and somewhat flattened. Covered with light-brown bracts when young, they are 5–9 cm tall and 0.7–1.2 cm across, set at intervals of 1.5–2.5 cm on a creeping rhizome. Each pseudobulb bears two narrow leaves 8–9.5 cm long near the apex. In winter and early spring the erect inflorescence rises from the top of the pseudobulb with two or more very fragrant flowers about 5 cm long. They are glistening white to cream and non-resupinate, holding the 2 cm-long lip uppermost. Streaked with purple near the base, the lip has two calli on the section obscured by the column. The sepals and petals are slightly reflexed, with a prominent mid-vein.

This species does well in pots of chopped treefern chunks in a moderately bright position with intermediate to cool conditions and a dry winter rest.

Actual flower size: approximately 5 cm long.

Epidendrum ciliare Linnaeus

Described by Linnaeus in 1759, *E. ciliare* was purportedly introduced into Britain from the West Indies in 1790 *E. cuspidatum* is a later synonym. Widespread from Mexico to Peru and Brazil, *E. ciliare* grows as an epiphyte or lithophyte. In some countries it occurs up to 2,000 m above sea level; in Brazil it is restricted to the hot humid lowlands of Amazonas, Amapá, Pará and Ceará.

The more or less club-like to cylindrical pseudobulbs are set 1–3 cm apart on a stout rhizome. Slightly compressed, the pseudobulbs are 5–22 cm tall and 1.5–2.5 cm wide. They have one or, sometimes, two very stiff fleshy leaves at the apex. From 8–28 cm long and 2.5–8.0 cm wide, these are elliptic to oblong–lanceolate. The plants greatly resemble unifoliate cattleyas. In summer or early autumn, a few to several fragrant flowers are borne on an erect spike up to 47 cm long from the apex of the pseudobulb. The fleshy linear to lanceolate tepals, which may be pale green, whitish or pale yellow, are 3.5–9.0 cm long and 0.4–0.8 cm wide with long tapering apices. The white lip is joined by a grooved claw to the basal half of the column, which is irregularly toothed at the apex. The 1.7–4.0 cm-long lateral lobes are deeply fringed on the outer edge, which often curls upward. The stiff linear mid-lobe is very narrow and up to 6 cm long. There are two thick yellow calli at the base of the mid-lobe.

E. ciliare does well mounted or potted. While it prefers humid, intermediate to warm conditions, it will tolerate cooler temperatures. Bright light and a dry winter rest are recommended.

Actual flower size: 10–14 cm across.

Epidendrum difforme Jacquin

Jacquin described this epiphyte in 1760, using material from the Caribbean island of Martinique. Although Pabst renamed it *Neolehmannia difformis* in 1978, this reclassification has been accepted by few taxonomists, and the taxon remains generally known by its original name. Synonyms include *Amphiglottis difformis*, *Auliza difformis* and *Epidendrum umbellatum*. *E. difforme* is widespread from southern Florida and Mexico to Brazil in the south, where it occurs through most of the country, from the hot humid lowlands to the cool moist mountain areas and inland savannahs, which experience a continental climate.

E. difforme is a 'reed-stem' epidendrum, with stems typically up to 30 cm tall, but occasionally longer. Covered with persistent sheaths, they are terete at the base and flattened above. The alternating fleshy leaves are elliptic to oblong, 1.5–12.0 cm long and 0.5–3.5 cm wide. Flowering is typically in late summer to autumn with a cluster of up to twenty flowers from the apex of the pseudobulb. Each fleshy flower has a long stalk and is usually yellowish to pale green, with a more or less translucent glossy lip. The margins of the 1.1–3.5 cm-long sepals and the slightly shorter and narrower petals are recurved. The clawed, deflexed lip is joined to the column for the length of the latter, and has several thickened veins. From 0.7–2.0 cm long and up to 3.4 cm wide, the lip has two erect calli at the base.

E. difforme is reasonably temperature tolerant, but probably does best in intermediate to warm conditions with semi-shade to bright indirect light.

Actual flower size: 2–3 cm across.

Epidendrum latilabre Lindley

One of several species often reduced to synonymy with *Epidendrum difforme*,* E. latilabre* was described by Lindley in the nineteenth century. *E. radiatum*, *E. uniflorum*, *E. arachnoideum* and *E. althausenii* are all later synonyms. *E. latilabre* grows epiphytically in either the cool mountains or the hot humid lowlands. It occurs in Amazonas, Pará, Pernambuco, Espírito Santo, Minas Gerais, Rio de Janeiro, São Paulo and the southern states.

The flattened, sometimes zigzag, stems are up to about 30 cm long and covered with sheaths. The stiff fleshy leaves clasp the stem. Up to 12 cm long and about 3 cm wide, they are alternating, more or less elliptic, and bilobed at the apex. *E. latilabre* has fewer flowers than *E. difforme*, often only one or two, on short stalks from the apex of the pseudobulb. The flowers are usually green with several visible veins, especially on the sepals and lip. The lanceolate sepals are about 2.3 cm long, 0.6 cm wide, and have recurved margins at the base. The narrow 1.9 cm-long petals are recurved, rather than more or less straight as in *E. difforme*. The lip, which is joined to the column, is vaguely four-lobed and up to 3.5 cm wide when flattened. It is deflexed at the sides and bent downward at the front. There are two erect calli at the base, and a darker stripe down the middle.

E. latilabre does well when mounted or potted in a freely draining mixture. It will tolerate temperatures ranging from cool to warm. It needs fairly high humidity, plenty of water when in growth, and a short dry rest in winter.

Actual flower size: approximately 3.5 cm across.

Epidendrum nocturnum Jacquin

This species, whose synonyms include *E. longicolle* and *E. tridens*, was originally described by Jacquin in 1760. Growing as an epiphyte or lithophyte, this 'reed-stemmed' epidendrum is found from Florida and Mexico in the north to Brazil, Peru and Bolivia in the south. Occurring throughout most of Brazil, it experiences widely varying climatic conditions over the range of its habitats — cool mountains, hot lowlands and inland savannahs.

The stems of this species are almost terete near the slender base, but are strongly flattened above, and typically 20–60 cm tall (occasionally to 1 m) and 0.5–1.5 cm across at the apex. Some clones are no more than 12 cm tall. Covered by brown sheaths, the stems bear several leathery leaves in two alternating rows, mostly on the upper part. The 5–18 cm-long leaves are 0.8–6.5 cm wide. Very short spikes are produced in winter with usually one or two flowers open at once. From 5–9 cm or more across, the flowers have narrow linear to lanceolate tepals 3–9 cm long with rolled-back margins. They may be greenish-white, yellow-green, occasionally pinkish, or bronze-green. The white lip has a narrow claw and is joined to the column for the entire length of the latter. The 1–4 cm-long lateral lobes are fan-shaped and joined to the tapering thread-like midlobe only at the base. The 2.2–5.7 cm-long mid-lobe has two parallel yellow keels at the base.

E. nocturnum is a very adaptable species in cultivation, although best results are probably obtained when the plant is given humid intermediate to warm conditions.

Actual flower size: 5–9 cm across.

Epidendrum paniculosum Barbosa Rodrígues

Barbosa Rodrígues described this species towards the end of the nineteenth century. Endemic to Brazil, it inhabits the warm humid lowlands of Rio de Janeiro and São Paulo, growing as an epiphyte, often on trees in coastal swamps.

The clustered stem-like pseudobulbs are typically 30–47 cm tall, but only 0.4–0.6 cm in diameter. Each has several internodes, is covered with white papery bracts, and becomes furrowed with age. There are three to five apical leaves 7–11 cm long and up to 2.5 cm wide. These slightly fleshy leaves are more or less oblong, but taper at both ends. In autumn, arching to pendulous spikes approximately 15–20 cm long are produced from the apex of the leafed, but often immature, pseudsobulbs. Each sparsely branched spike bears about twenty to thirty flowers about 1 cm wide in panicles of six to ten. The tepals are pale green with a few darker veins. The sepals are 0.7–1.5 cm long and approximately 0.3 cm wide. The oblong to lanceolate dorsal sepal curves forward over the column and the oval to elliptic lateral sepals are spreading. The very narrow petals are held forward. The very fleshy lip is fused to the column. More or less heart-shaped, the lip is very glossy and has a large maroon-purple blotch at the base. There is also a form with a plain green lip. There are three keels on the lip; two short ones at the base, and a central one running the length of the lip. The anther cap is purple.

E. paniculosum, because of its flowering habit, is best grown mounted or in a suspended container. It needs a humid, intermediate to warm environment with bright indirect light.

Actual flower size: approximately 1.5 cm long.

Galeandra devoniana Schomburgk ex Lindley

Schomburgk discovered this species near Barcelos on the Rio Negro and named it to honour the Duke of Devonshire. Lindley received details of the species from Schomburgk and described it in 1838. Also found in Venezuela and Guyana, it inhabits the hot lowlands of Amazonas and Pará in Brazil, growing on trees along watercourses or on flood plains and as a terrestrial in rotting vegetable matter.

The spindle-shaped to cylindrical pseudobulbs may reach 1.8 m tall, but in cultivation are typically 40–75 cm. They bear many deciduous plicate leaves. These are 12–30 cm long, 1–3 cm wide, and linear to lanceolate. The fragrant long-lasting flowers are usually borne in summer on a terminal spike. The 4–5 cm-long lanceolate tepals vary in colour from brownish-green striped with pale green-brown or tinged and veined with maroon to dark purple-brown edged with green. The obscurely three-lobed lip is up to 5 cm long, with the large lateral lobes curled over the column. The throat may be tinged with yellow-green. At the base of the lip is a 1.5 cm-long greenish spur, with or without maroon stripes. The white apical lobe is deflexed and has purple-red veins. The basal half of the lip carries two longitudinal ridges.

G. devoniana requires a warm humid environment with bright indirect light. It may be mounted or grown in well-drained pots of treefern fibre or bark and leaf mould. Plenty of water is necessary when the plant is in growth, followed by a slightly cooler resting period. Humidity should be high all year round.

Actual flower size: 6–10 cm across.

Gomesa crispa (Ldl.) Klotzsch & Reichenbach (f.)

This epiphyte was originally described by Lindley in 1839 as *Rodriguezia crispa*. Klotzsch and Reichenbach transferred it to the genus *Gomesa* in 1852. *G. undulata*, *G. polymorpha* and *Odontoglossum crispulum* are all conspecific. *G. crispa* grows at moderate elevations in the cool damp mountains of Rio de Janeiro, São Paulo, Paraná, Santa Catarina, Rio Grande do Sul and Minas Gerais.

The clustered, oblong to tapering pseudobulbs are yellow-green to olive-green, compressed, 4–10 cm tall and up to 2.5 cm wide. There are several papery bracts at the base, and two erect to spreading leaves at the apex. From 9–28 cm long and 2.0–3.5 cm wide, these leaves are folded at the base and have a sharp tapering point at the apex. An arching to pendulous spike 10–22 cm long rises from the base of the pseudobulb in winter, bearing many yellow-green to yellow flowers. The undulating tepals are oblong to lanceolate, 0.8–1.0 cm long and up to 0.35 cm wide. The lateral sepals may overlap at the base, but are not joined. The 0.6–0.8 cm-long lip is joined to the column at the base by two irregularly toothed column wings. It is obscurely three-lobed with tiny rounded lateral lobes and a strongly deflexed midlobe. This is rounded, with a short point at the apex. At the base are two parallel ridges. The column is whitish with the stigmatic cavity more or less outlined in red.

G. crispa does well in cool to intermediate conditions, either mounted or in pots. It requires moderate shade, relatively high humidity, and sufficient year-round moisture to prevent shrivelling.

Actual flower size: approximately 2 cm long.

Gomesa recurva R. Brown

Brown used this species as the type for his new genus, *Gomesa*, in 1815. It is closely related to *G. planifolia* and *G. fischeri*, etc., with *G. densiflora* and *Odontoglossum recurvum* being later synonyms. *G. recurva* grows as an epiphyte in the cool moist mountain regions of Minas Gerais, Espírito Santo, Rio de Janeiro, São Paulo, Paraná and Santa Catarina.

The clustered mid-green pseudobulbs are oblong to ovoid and compressed. From 4.0–7.5 cm tall and 2.0–3.5 cm wide, each bears two or three oblong to lanceolate leaves 15–30 cm long and up to 3 cm wide with an acute apex. In winter an arching spike 20–35 cm long rises from the base of the pseudobulb and bears many fragrant yellow-green flowers. The more or less oblong tepals are 0.9–1.2 cm long, about 0.4 cm wide, and may have deflexed margins. The sepals are pointed at the apex, with the dorsal curving forward near the apex and the laterals joined for at least half their length. The flat to slightly wavy petals are rounded, or have a small point at the apex. They also curve slightly forward. The 0.9–1.1 cm-long lip, which is strongly recurved at the mid-point, is ovate with a rounded apex which may have a short point in the centre. There are two parallel keels on the crest. There is a red mark below the stigma which contrasts strongly with the overall flower colour.

G. recurva is an easily grown species which flowers regularly in cultivation. It may be mounted or potted, and needs a moderately shady position. Intermediate to cool conditions suit it, with fairly high humidity and year-round moisture, with a slight reduction in winter.

Actual flower size: approximately 2 cm long.

Gomesa species — *recurva* alliance

This species belongs to the *recurva* alliance of the genus *Gomesa*, which is endemic to Brazil. All members of the *recurva* alliance have pseudobulbs which are closely set on the rhizome and lateral sepals which are more or less connate. We have no direct knowledge of the habitat of this species, but have little doubt that it comes from the cooler mountain areas at moderate elevations in the southern states.

The strongly compressed pseudobulbs are dull olive- to dark green. About 2.5–7.5 cm tall, they are up to 2.5 cm wide at the swollen base, tapering to about 0.5 cm at the apex. At the base are a few papery bracts, while the apex has two erect to spreading leaves up to about 20 cm long and 2.0–3.5 cm wide. An arching to pendent spike about 10–20 cm long bears up to twenty or more greyish-green to greyish-buff flowers. The sepals are oblong, with the apical half of the 1 cm-long dorsal sepal curved forward. The longer lateral sepals, which are joined for about half their length and have blunt apices, project backward towards the spike. The spreading petals have slightly reflexed margins and are more or less oblong with a knob-like apical section. The white lip is very strongly bent backward at the centre, so that the apical half is held horizontal to the ovary. At the base are two raised keels which extend for at least half the length of the lip.

Like most *Gomesa* species, this is an easy subject in cultivation. It does very well when mounted on a treefern slab and grown in a moist, intermediate to cool environment with light to moderate shade and year-round moisture.

Actual flower size: 2–2.5 cm long.

Gongora bufonia Lindley

First described by Lindley in 1841, this species is regarded by some as conspecific with *G. quinquinervis.** However, Pabst and Dungs consider it a separate species. Their opinion is based on the lack of appendages at the base of the lip, a feature present in *G. quinquinervis*. Synonyms include *G. irrorata* and *G. minax* (Hoehne & Schlechter, not Reichenbach (f.)). *G. bufonia* grows on trees in the lowlands of São Paulo, Rio de Janeiro, Santa Catarina, Paraná and Pernambuco.

The strongly ribbed pseudobulbs are typically 3–6 cm tall and 2.5–3.0 cm across. There are two pleated leaves at the apex. They are more or less elliptic, up to 45 cm long and up to 6 cm wide, with an acute tapering apex. In autumn or winter a pendulous spike up to 90 cm long bears several to many flowers about 5 cm long. All segments are cream, buff-coloured or pale pink, with reddish blotches. The more or less oblong dorsal sepal, which is about 2 cm long, and the larger triangular to oblong lateral sepals, have recurved margins. The narrow strap-like petals are partly fused to the column. The fleshy 2.5 cm-long lip is held uppermost and is more or less concave with two armlike projections on the apical section.

G. bufonia does best when mounted or grown in hanging baskets of treefern chunks or similar material, owing to the pendent nature of the inflorescence. A humid, intermediate to warm environment is preferred, with moderate shade to indirect bright light. Plants need copious water when in growth, with a reduction in winter.

Actual flower size: approximately 5 cm long.

Gongora quinquinervis Ruíz & Pavón

Ruíz & Pavón described this species in 1798 using material they had collected in Peru. Its many synonyms include *G. maculata*, *G. retrorsa* and *G. quinquivulneris*. Widespread from Mexico to Peru and Brazil, *G. quinquinervis* grows epiphytically at elevations up to 1,400 m in humid forests in Central America, while in Brazil it inhabits the lowlands of Amazonas, Pará, Maranhão and Ceará. According to Pabst and Dungs, it is also found in the cooler mountains of Paraná.

The clustered pseudobulbs are oblong to conical, strongly ridged, 4–12 cm tall and up to 4 cm wide. Each has two pleated lanceolate to elliptic leaves at the apex. They are 15–60 cm long with wavy edges and five prominent veins beneath (thus the specific epithet). Several non-resupinate flowers are borne in autumn on a pendulous spike 30–90 cm long from the base of the pseudobulb. The tepals may be reddish with yellow or white markings, or yellow with maroon spotting. The lanceolate dorsal sepal is 1.5–2.3 cm long and 0.8–1.2 cm wide with recurved margins. The strongly reflexed laterals are triangular to ovate-lanceolate, and 2–3 cm long. The shorter linear to lanceolate petals are joined to the side of the column in their basal half. The fleshy yellow-cream lip is 2–3 cm long. The triangular lateral lobes have an erect protuberance at the base, and the mid-lobe is spear-shaped.

G. quinquinervis prefers a humid, intermediate to warm environment, with moderate to bright indirect light to semi-shade. Give plenty of water when in growth and less in winter. It grows well mounted or in a hanging basket.

Actual flower size: 4.5–6 cm long.

Grobya amherstiae Lindley

This species is the type for Lindley's genus *Grobya*, established in 1835. The specific epithet honoured the Countess Amherst, to whom Hayne sent a plant from Brazil. *G. amherstiae* grows epiphytically at 600–900 m above sea level in the Serra do Mar, Serra da Mantiqueira and the Serra dos Orgãos in south-eastern Brazil.

The dark green ovate to globose pseudobulbs are 2.5–3.5 cm tall and are covered with whitish fibrous leaf bracts when young. Each bears four to six erect to arching leaves up to 40 cm long and 1.0–1.6 cm wide. Up to ten flowers are borne in winter on erect to arching spikes up to 15 cm long which emerge from the base of the mature pseudobulbs. The 2 cm-long and 0.7 cm-wide sepals are pale green to yellow, tinged or striped with reddish-purple. The much wider petals, which are curved inward at the obtuse apex, are translucent with longitudinal rows of small reddish blotches. The dorsal sepal curves forward, while the oblong to lanceolate lateral sepals, joined at the base, curl and twist downward. The sub-erect lip is yellow, with large rounded lateral lobes. The tiny mid-lobe has about seven parallel ridges. Two narrow dull reddish to purple plates, with a short sharp point between, project over the mid-lobe. The pale yellow to white column has reddish-purple markings.

G. amherstiae enjoys intermediate humid conditions with moderate shade and plenty of water when in growth, followed by a cooler, drier resting period. It may be potted or mounted, and grows well on treefern slabs.

Actual flower size: approximately 4 cm long.

Huntleya meleagris Lindley

Discovered by Descourtilz in Minas Gerais early in the nineteenth century, this epiphyte was described by Lindley in 1837. Synonyms include *Batemania meleagris* and *Huntleya burtii*. The latter, which is sometimes treated as a variety of *H. meleagris*, has bright purple markings at the base of each petal, and occurs in Central America, Ecuador and Colombia. The Brazilian populations of *H. meleagris* inhabit damp woods along watercourses in Bahia, Minas Gerais, Espírito Santo, Rio de Janeiro, Paraná, Santa Catarina and Rio Grande do Sul. The species is also found in Venezuela.

Without pseudobulbs, *H. meleagris* comprises a fan of several alternating leaves 10–45 cm long and 2.5–5.0 cm wide. These are linear to lanceolate, with several prominent veins and a sharp tapering apex. Single glossy flowers are borne from mid-summer to autumn on a short spike rising from the leaf axil. The bases of the tepals are usually white grading to yellow, with the apical two-thirds yellow-brown to dark purplish-red more or less tesselated with yellow-orange. The 4–6 cm-long dorsal sepal and the laterals, which are joined at the base, are up to 2.5 cm wide, while the shorter petals are slightly wider. The obscurely three-lobed lip, 2.5–3.5 cm long, is yellowish or white at the base with the acute recurved apex the same colour as the tepals. The short claw has a thick white crest which is toothed.

H. meleagris does best for us when potted in a freely draining medium. It likes a humid semi-shaded position with good ventilation in an intermediate to cool environment. Give year-round moisture.

Actual flower size: approximately 7.5 cm across.

Ionopsis utricularioides (Swartz) Lindley

A species with an extremely wide range, from Florida in the north to Brazil and Paraguay in the south, *Ionopsis utricularioides* was first described by Swartz in 1788 as *Epidendrum utricularioides*, based on a plant from Jamaica. Lindley transferred it to the genus *Ionopsis* in the 1820s. It grows almost throughout Brazil from sea level to about 1,000 m, and is common in areas with very dry winters, such as deciduous lowland forests. It also occurs in more humid forests and commonly grows into large clumps.

The 2–3 cm pseudobulbs are almost obscured by the two to four sheathing leaves, each 5–17 cm long, stiff and leathery, and often reddish on the undersides. Flower spikes are produced from late winter to summer from the base of the pseudobulbs. Typically about 40 cm long, but occasionally up to 70 cm, each spike carries three to many delicate flowers. These are variable in colour and may be white, pale rose or red-rose, usually with darker veins and a magenta blotch on the 0.7–1.6 cm lip, which dominates the flower. The sepals and petals are 0.3–0.6 cm long, with recurved ends. The dorsal sepal and the petals hide the tiny column, while the lateral sepals form a small sac. The bilobed lip has wavy edges and two small thin calli at the base.

This species prefers warm to intermediate conditions and a semi-shaded position. It should be mounted on twigs, cork, or paperbark. While plenty of water may be given in the growing season, plants should be kept drier in winter, and perhaps a little cooler. Humidity should be moderately high.

Actual flower size: approximately 1–2 cm long.

Isabelia pulchella (Krzl.) Senghas & Teuscher

Endemic to Brazil, this pretty miniature was originally described by Kraenzlin as *Neolauchia pulchella*, a name still in common use for this species. Recently, however, Senghas and Teuscher transferred it to *Isabelia*, a genus created by Barbosa Rodrígues to honour Princess Isabel de Alcantara, who was a contemporary patron of horticulture. Porsch's *Meiracyllium wettsteinii* is conspecific. This species grows in the cool damp mountain areas of the southern states of Rio de Janeiro, São Paulo, Paraná, Santa Catarina and Rio Grande do Sul at moderate elevations.

Pseudobulbs are borne 1–3 cm apart on a flexible, freely branching rhizome which often outgrows its mount and hangs freely in the air with no apparent harm. The 0.6–1.0 cm conical pseudobulbs are often flushed with reddish-purple and are covered at their bases with fibrous sheaths. The single grassy leaf is 5–11 cm long, 0.3 cm wide and acutely pointed. The threadlike spike rises from the apex of the pseudobulb in autumn to winter, and bears a single rosy-pink to bright magenta flower 1.5–2.0 cm across, which does not open widely. The oblong petals are slightly longer than the 1 cm sepals, which form a rounded spur at the base, concealing the chin formed by the lip and column foot. The outer lobe of the lip is almost circular with toothed edges and darker veins.

Because of its rambling habit, this species is best mounted on treefern or similar material. It should be placed in moderate shade in intermediate to cool conditions and kept moderately damp.

Actual flower size: 1.5–2 cm across.

Isabelia virginalis Barbosa Rodrígues

The original member of this genus of only two species, *I. virginalis* was described by Barbosa Rodrígues late in the nineteenth century. Frequently sharing its habitat with orchid species such as *Capanemia superflua*,* *Encyclia patens** and *Laelia lundii*,* this charming and easily grown miniature comes from the coastal mountains of São Paulo, Rio de Janeiro, Paraná, and Minas Gerais. It grows on small twigs and branches in the cool misty forests.

The 0.7–1.0 cm-long pseudobulbs, which are egg-shaped and almost obscured by a regular network of yellow to brown fibres like miniature baskets, are closely set on a creeping rhizome and, in time, form dense mats. Each pseudobulb has a single needle-like leaf from 2.5–7.5 cm long with a single narrow groove. The 1 cm-wide flowers are borne singly on short spikes from the apex of the pseudobulb. The tepals are white, sometimes flushed with pink or mauve. This flushing is usually restricted to the sepals, which are oblong with rounded ends. The narrow petals are curved forward. The lateral sepals form a spur with the base of the broad rounded lip, which is pure white. The white column is marked with amethyst and has an anther cap of the same colour. Flowering is mainly in late autumn to spring, but can occur intermittently through the year.

I. virginalis may be grown on small rough-barked branches or treefern slabs. Intermediate to cool conditions suit it best, with moderate shade, year-round moisture and good air movement.

Actual flower size: approximately 1 cm across.

Isochilus linearis (Jacq.) R. Brown

Described by Jacquin in 1763 as *Epidendrum lineare*, this species was used as the type for Brown's genus *Isochilus* in 1813. Its many synonyms include *I. brasiliensis* and *I. pauciflorus*. It occurs from Mexico to Brazil and Argentina. In Brazil, it ranges from the hot lowlands to cooler mountain areas and savannah country and is found in Minas Gerais, the Distrito Federal, Rio de Janeiro, São Paulo and the southern states. It grows on trees, or rocks, and as a terrestrial.

The 0.1–0.2 cm-thick stems, which are 20–60 cm long, are covered with leaf sheaths. The alternating linear leaves are jointed at the base, 2.0–6.5 cm long, about 2.5 cm wide and bilobed at the apex. One or more small flowers, which do not open widely, are borne on a short terminal spike at any time during the year. Flowers range in colour from white through orange-yellow to dark reddish-purple, but are commonly pale to dark pink-purple. The narrow lanceolate sepals are 0.8–1.2 cm long, with the laterals joined for about half their length to form a short chin at the base. The more or less rhomboidal petals are shorter but wider, with recurved apices. The narrowly fiddle-shaped lip is joined to the base of the column by a short claw. The apex of the lip is deflexed.

I. linearis is tolerant of a wide range of temperatures, from warm to cool. It may be mounted, but does well for us when grown in suspended pots of freely draining but moisture-retentive material. It prefers moderate shade and year-round moisture. *Actual flower size: 0.8–1.2 cm long.*

Laelia angereri Pabst

Closely related to *L. cinnabarina*,* this species was discovered in 1971 in the Serra do Mané Pinheiro in Minas Gerais by Angerer, after whom Pabst named it in 1975. *L. angereri* appears to be restricted to the north-east of Minas Gerais, where it grows on rocks amid shrubby vegetation at 1,000–1,300 m above sea level. The area experiences hot summers and cold nights during the dry winters, when dews provide sufficient moisture to sustain the plants.

The elongated tapering pseudobulbs are 20–35 cm tall, and are often suffused with reddish-purple, as are the 15–30 cm-long succulent leaves. These leaves are about 3 cm wide and have a roughened surface. In winter or spring a spike 30–40 cm or more long bears five to twenty brick-red to orange-red flowers, which are set close together at the apex of the spike. All flowers are open more or less at the same time. The lanceolate dorsal sepal is 1.4–2.2 cm long and about 0.5 cm wide, while the narrowly elliptic petals are slightly longer. The lateral sepals are very slightly falcate. The throat of the 2 cm-long lip is white to yellow with red veining. The recurved frilled apical lobe is similarly veined. The lateral lobes, which curl up to enclose the column, are rounded with a more or less triangular apex.

L. angereri does well in indirect bright light in an intermediate to cool environment. It requires a dry winter rest, with only light misting to simulate the dew it experiences in its native habitat. Good ventilation is essential. We find that it grows well in rather small pots of broken sandstone pieces and chopped treefern fibre. *Actual flower size: approximately 4 cm across.*

Laelia bahiensis Schlechter

Schlechter described this species in 1921. Originally discovered in the Serra da Sincora, it is endemic to the state of Bahia at elevations of 1,000–1,200 m. It has now also been found in the Serra do Calabocária and the Serra do Capa-Bode, the only yellow-flowered rupicolous laelia found in this area. Often growing in association with *Laelia pfisteri*,* it clings to rocks amid lichens and mosses in areas of low stunted scrub and tall grasses. This is a region of extremes of temperature with a long dry season.

This species has conical, reddish-brown pseudobulbs from 7–10 cm long, bearing a single leathery curved leaf 9–15 cm long. From late spring to autumn erect apical spikes 30–50 cm long carry five to ten or more flowers which open successively over a short period so that most are open together. The buttercup-yellow flowers are 3–4 cm across with pointed sepals and blunter, slightly narrower petals about 2 cm long. These are narrow at the base and often recurved. The pale yellow lip is veined with reddish-brown and has three lobes. The lateral lobes are curled over the column to form a narrow tube. About 1.5 cm long, the lip has a very frilly burnt-orange mid-lobe.

L. bahiensis needs a very freely draining medium, as its roots rot easily, a problem for many rupicolous laelias in cultivation. A horizontal slab of treefern makes a good mount. For potting, a mix of coarse gravel and bark is suggested. The medium or slab should be allowed to dry out between waterings. Intermediate to cool conditions are preferred, with bright light, good air movement and a dry winter rest.

Actual flower size: 3–4 cm across.

Laelia blumenscheinii Pabst

Discovered by Baron Anton Ghillany, this species was described in 1975 by Guido Pabst. He named it to honour the scholar Blumenschein. Often confused with *L. gracilis*,* which has reddish-purple pseudobulbs and leaves and an arching spike, *L. blumenscheinii* inhabits rocky outcrops at about 1,200 m in Espírito Santo.

The clustered green pseudobulbs are 8–15 cm tall and about 2 cm wide near the base. Each has a single more or less erect leaf which is green, sometimes with the slightest hint of red. The lanceolate leaf has a roughened surface, is keeled below, up to 17 cm long and 2–3 cm wide. From four to thirteen flowers are usually produced in autumn to early winter on an erect spike up to 40 cm or more long. The pale yellow flowers, which have a sparkling crystalline texture, are reasonably well spaced on the apical portion of the spike. The lanceolate dorsal sepal and petals and the somewhat falcate lateral sepals are up to 2 cm long and about 0.5 cm wide. The 1.5 cm-long lip has several reddish-brown veins. It is strongly three-lobed, with large lateral lobes enclosing the column. The front edge of the lateral lobes and the apical lobe, which has a short stalk at the base, are very wavy. The base of the mid-lobe has four keels and the apex is recurved.

L. blumenscheinii requires an intermediate to cool environment with moderately bright light. It grows best in pots of some coarse freely draining material. Give plenty of water while plants are in growth, followed by a drier winter rest.

Actual flower size: approximately 4 cm across.

Laelia briegeri Blumenschein

Blumenschein described this rupicolous laelia in 1960, naming it in honour of the well-known orchidologist Brieger. It is found in Minas Gerais at 980–1,400 m above sea level, growing on sandstone with its roots protected by mosses, lichens and other low vegetation, and also around *Vellozia* shrubs. The diurnal temperature range is high, although strong winds help to moderate day temperatures. Dews are frequent.

The light green pseudobulbs of this species may be short and squat or more or less cylindrical. From 3–10 cm tall and 0.6–1.6 cm wide, they bear a single sub-erect to arching leaf 3–11 cm long and up to 2 cm wide. These very fleshy leaves are channelled above and lightly keeled below. Flower spikes are typically 10–20 cm long, but may reach 40 cm, and bear three to five flowers (occasionally more) near the apex in spring or early summer. These yellow flowers open together and last reasonably well. The ovate to lanceolate dorsal sepal and the ovate to elliptic petals are 2.3–3.0 cm long and about 1 cm wide, while the broadly falcate lateral sepals are slightly shorter. The recurved lip is about 1.7 cm long, with its lateral lobes meeting above the column. The mid-lobe has two keels for most of its length and very frilly margins.

L. briegeri is reasonably temperature tolerant, but requires bright light, good ventilation or air movement and a freely draining potting mix. We use broken sandstone pieces mixed with chopped treefern fibre. To flower well it needs a dry winter rest with just enough misting to prevent undue shrivelling of the plant.
Actual flower size: 4–5.5 cm across.

Laelia cinnabarina Bateman ex Lindley

This species was introduced into England in 1836, and flowered the following year in Young's collection at Epsom. Lindley described it in 1838, using information from Bateman. Synonyms include *Bletia cinnabarina* and *Cattleya cinnabarina*. *L. cinnabarina* grows on rocky slopes and in crevices amid tall grasses and shrubby vegetation in Rio de Janeiro, São Paulo and Minas Gerais at elevations of 700–1,500 m.

The 12–25 cm-tall pseudobulbs are cylindrical to tapering and are tinged with purple. Each usually has a single sub-erect to spreading leaf 12.5–30.0 cm long and about 3 cm wide. The leaf is more or less oblong, and also tinged with purple. In winter or spring ten to fifteen starry flowers open over an extended period on a spike up to 50 cm or more long. The solid orange to cinnabar-red tepals are linear to lanceolate. The dorsal sepal and petals are 3.5–5.0 cm long and about 0.7 cm wide, while the lateral sepals are slightly shorter. The 2.0–3.5 cm-long lip has more or less triangular lateral lobes which meet above the column. They are orange, veined with red and slightly recurved at the acute apex. The strongly recurved mid-lobe has a narrow isthmus and a rounded very frilly apical lobe, which is dark orange-red. The base of the mid-lobe is white to yellow, streaked with red. Yellow and red forms are known to exist.

L. cinnabarina grows well potted. It needs a freely draining medium, good ventilation, bright light and intermediate to cool conditions. It should be given a dry winter rest, with only sufficient moisture to prevent undue shrivelling of the plant.
Actual flower size: 6–9 cm across.

Laelia crispa (Ldl.) Reichenbach (f.)

So called because of its much-crisped segments, especially petals and lip, *Laelia crispa* was introduced into England in 1826 by Sir Henry Chamberlain. Lindley described it as *Cattleya crispa* in 1828, and Reichenbach transferred it to the genus *Laelia* in 1853. *Bletia crispa* and *Cattleya reflexa* are synonyms. *L. crispa* grows in bright light on the upper branches of tall trees or occasionally on rocky outcrops at 800–1,150 m above sea level in Espírito Santo, Rio de Janeiro and Minas Gerais.

The club-like pseudobulbs are 18–30 cm tall, and each bears a fleshy, oblong to lanceolate leaf which is 15–30 cm long and about 5 cm wide. In late spring or summer up to ten fragrant flowers are borne on a spike up to 30 cm long. Flowers are typically white to light pink with yellow or orange at the base of the lip, and a dark maroon-purple apical lobe. The 6.0–7.5 cm-long sepals are 1.5 cm wide with an acute apex and reflexed lateral margins. The very crisped petals are about 2.5 cm wide, but the edges are often reflexed or rolled back. The lateral lobes of the 5 cm-long lip meet above the column with flared wavy apices. The apical lobe is frequently reflexed and twisted. The exceptional clone of *L. crispa* var. *concolor*, pictured here, is completely pink but for a hint of yellow in the throat. It has flatter segments than usual, giving the flower a generally more pleasing appearance.

L. crispa, although not common in collections, is an easily grown species. Mounted or potted, it requires a bright position in a humid intermediate environment, good drainage and a winter rest.
Actual flower size: 10–15 cm across.

Laelia crispata (Thunb.) Garay

Probably better known as *Laelia rupestris*, this species was originally described by Thunberg in 1818 as *Cymbidium crispatum*. In 1974 Garay resurrected Thunberg's epithet, and transferred the species to the genus *Laelia*. Some authors treat this species as conspecific with *L. tereticaulis.** *L. crispata* is one of the most widely distributed of the rupicolous laelias, ranging 500 km from Belo Horizonte to Montes Claros in Minas Gerais. It favours exposed, almost horizontal ledges at 400–800 m above sea level, and is protected by *Vellozia* bushes and other stunted vegetation.

The almost terete pseudobulbs are 4–22 cm tall and 1.0–1.5 cm in diameter. Each bears a single fleshy leaf up to 20 cm long and 1.5–3.2 cm wide. This oblong leaf is channelled above and covered by a protective layer of greyish powder. From mid-winter to early spring, three to five or, occasionally, more flowers are crowded near the apex of the spike, which is longer than the leaf. The flat to slightly recurved tepals are rosy-pink to dark lavender, usually with white at the base. The sepals are about 2 cm long and 0.7 cm wide, while the petals are slightly longer. The pink lip is white to yellow in the throat and on the basal half of the ovate, very crisped apical lobe. The lateral lobes meet above the column, but leave it exposed at the base. From two to four keels run almost the complete length of the lip.

Like most of the rupicolous laelias, *L. crispata* is an easy subject once established. It does well in pots of well-drained material, and needs intermediate conditions with bright indirect light and a dry winter rest.
Actual flower size: 4–5 cm across.

Laelia crispilabia A. Richard ex Warner

Described in 1865 by Warner, using information from Richard, this species is often confused with *L. mantiquierae*.* However, *L. crispilabia* is the only purple-flowered rupicolous laelia whose mid-lobe has a very long stalk. Veitch called it *L. cinnabarina* var. *crispilabia*. Synonyms include *Laelia lawrenceana* (Hort.) and *Bletia crispilabia*. It grows usually in full sun on iron ore ledges — occasionally on granite — around Belo Horizonte in Minas Gerais at 1,000–1,200 m above sea level.

The clustered green pseudobulbs may be short and squat with tapering necks, or somewhat elongated with swollen bases. From 3.5–7.0 cm tall, they are about 1.5 cm in diameter, and bear one or two almost flat, green leathery leaves 5–10 cm long and 2 cm wide. A tallish spike carries two to six starry flowers in late autumn or winter. The tepals have recurved apices, and are about 2–3 cm long and 0.6 cm wide. The lanceolate dorsal sepal is longer than the petals and the slightly falcate lateral sepals. Tepals are typically pink to mauve. The paler pink clone pictured is probably not typical. White clones have been reported, as have white ones with bluish-purple on the lip. The strongly three-lobed lip is 1.5–2.0 cm long, white in the throat, with large lateral lobes which form a tube around the column. The long recurved mid-lobe is strongly crisped.

L. crispilabia, like most rupicolous laelias, grows well when potted in a freely draining material. It needs bright light, cool to intermediate conditions, and a dry rest in winter with only occasional misting. *Actual flower size: 4.5–5.5 cm across.*

Laelia dayana Reichenbach (f.)

Originally imported into England by Low and Co. as *Laelia pumila*,* this species is still regarded by a number of Brazilian nursery operators as a variety of *L. pumila*. It is closely related to the latter species, and to *L. spectabilis*.* *L. dayana* was discovered by Boxall and described by Reichenbach in 1876, using material supplied by Day, for whom the species was named. The exact location of its native habitat was something of a mystery for many years. It appears now that the species is restricted to the state of Rio de Janeiro at 900–1,300 m. Its range extends from the Organ Mountains near Rio to the Serra do Rio Preto. It prefers to grow in indirect light on lichen-encrusted trees along river banks.

The cylindrical pseudobulbs are 3–7 cm long with extensive white sheaths. They bear a single fleshy leaf up to 10 cm long. Single flowers are borne on 3 cm spikes from summer to autumn, with occasional flowers appearing in spring. The rosy-pink to dark mauve flowers are about 4.5 cm across with strongly reflexed sepals and petals. The large trumpet-shaped lip is obscurely three-lobed, with the lateral lobes meeting above the column. The edges of the lip are frilled, and turn outward. The throat is white with a few obscure calli and several prominent velvety red-purple veins. The rest of the lip is dark rose-purple.

This species will grow in suspended baskets or pots of coarse medium, but does exceptionally well for us when mounted on fairly large treefern slabs. It prefers bright light and intermediate conditions, and a dry rest in winter. *Actual flower size: approximately 4.5 cm across.*

Laelia endsfeldzii Pabst

This is a relatively new species, and was only described in 1975 during Pabst's study of the rupicolous laelias. It is an endemic species, being restricted to a small area near Itutinga in Minas Gerais at 900 m above sea level. This area experiences a continental climate, with wide variations in temperature between day and night. The vegetation provides little shade as it comprises mostly tall grasses, *Vellozia* bushes and other low shrubs. Cold dry seasons may last for up to six months.

L. *endsfeldzii* has clustered pseudobulbs from 5–12 cm long, tapering in their upper half, and tinged with purple. The more or less erect leaves are usually less than 10 cm long, but may reach 17 cm. They are reddish-purple beneath and along the upper margins. The upper surfaces are rough, and have central channels and a network of transverse wrinkles. Flower spikes from 40–50 cm long are produced in autumn and winter, carrying several well-spaced flowers which open in succession. The starry pale yellow flowers are 3–4 cm across, with dagger-shaped sepals and petals about 2 cm long. The lateral lobes of the 1.3 cm lip meet above the column, while the mid-lobe is recurved and crisped.

This species grows well when potted in a well-drained mix. Chopped treefern chunks are satisfactory, but must be allowed to dry out completely between waterings. A bright intermediate environment is ideal, with plenty of water in the growing season and a fairly long dry resting period in winter with no more than occasional misting. *Actual flower size: 3–4 cm across.*

Laelia esalqueana Blumenschein

In 1960 Blumenschein described this species, using as its specific name the acronym for the Escola Superior de Agricultura 'Luiz de Queiroz', an institution in the state of São Paulo. The species was then lost to horticulture until it was later rediscovered by Dr Jack Fowlie. L. *esalqueana* is confined to an area south-west of Datas on the Rio São Francisco at 1,100–1,200 m above sea level in Minas Gerais. It is found growing on rocks or in rocky crevices with its roots protected from the sun and drying winds by mosses and lichens, etc.

The clustered pseudobulbs are cylindrical to tapering, 2.5–4.5 cm tall and about 1 cm in diameter. Each has an erect to arching leaf 2–8 cm long and 1–2 cm wide. This very succulent leaf, which is channelled above, may be boat-shaped or lanceolate. Flowering is in late spring to early summer on spikes which are only slightly longer than the leaf. It carries two to four buttercup-yellow flowers which all open at the same time. The elliptic to lanceolate dorsal sepal is 1.2–1.7 cm long and up to 0.5 cm wide, while the slightly falcate lateral sepals are shorter. The petals are elliptic to almost round. The 0.8–1.0 cm-long lip has large rounded lateral lobes which have warty obtuse apices and meet above the column. The rounded mid-lobe has very wavy margins.

L. *esalqueana* should be grown in moderately bright light, in intermediate to cool conditions. It needs a dry winter rest when only an occasional misting is required to prevent undue shrivelling of the plant. *Actual flower size: approximately 3 cm across.*

Laelia flava Lindley

Introduced into cultivation by Sir Charles Lemon, *L. flava* was probably discovered by Gardner. Lindley described it in 1839. Synonyms include *Bletia flava*, *L. fulva* and *Cattleya lutea*. Endemic to Minas Gerais at 800–1,500 m above sea level, including the Serra do Frio and the Serra da Piedade, *L. flava* is the most widespread of the yellow-flowered rupicolous laelias, and the only one found on the iron ore mountains around Belo Horizonte.

The somewhat conical pseudobulbs are 4–20 cm tall, up to 2 cm wide at the base, and more or less strongly suffused with purple. Each has a lanceolate, 10–19 cm-long leaf, about 3 cm wide, very leathery, dark green above and purple beneath. The leaf is arching, with a rough upper surface and a keel below. From five to ten yellow flowers, which may have faint reddish veining and which open together, are carried near the apex of a 30–60 cm spike, usually in mid-winter to early spring. The oblong to lanceolate petals and dorsal sepal are 2.0–3.5 cm long, while the somewhat falcate lateral sepals are shorter. The 2.4–3.0 cm long lip has semi-ovate lateral lobes which hide the column, while the oblong mid-lobe is strongly recurved, with very crisped margins and two to four ridges down the middle. White varieties occur, as does the rare orange-flowered var. *aurantiaca*.

L. flava requires fairly bright light and an intermediate to cool environment with good air movement. It does well when potted in a freely draining material such as chopped treefern fibre. Plants should be given a dry winter rest with only occasional light mistings.

Actual flower size: 4–6 cm across.

Laelia x *gerhard-santosii* Pabst

Pabst described this natural hybrid between *L. harpophylla** and *L. kautskyana** in 1975, naming it in honour of the Governor of Espírito Santo, Arthur Carlos Gerhard Santos, who was keenly interested in preserving the orchids of that state. *L.* x *gerhard-santosii* occurs, along with its parents, at about 600 m above sea level, growing on trees in humid shady forests in Espírito Santo. Its habit resembles that of its parents, and the three are so similar in appearance as to be indistinguishable, one from another, when not in flower.

The slender terete pseudobulbs are 10–50 cm long with faint grooves. Each bears a single almost flat leaf with a prominent mid-vein and a long tapering apex. The lanceolate leaves may be up to 30 cm long and approximately 2.5 cm wide. In winter or spring apical spikes, which are shorter than the leaves, carry three to ten orange flowers about 6 cm across. The lanceolate dorsal sepal and petals are approximately 3 cm long and 0.8 cm wide, while the somewhat falcate lateral sepals are slightly shorter. The shape of the 2 cm-long lip is intermediate between that of the parent species, with a relatively short mid-lobe about 0.5 cm wide. The recurved mid-lobe, which is creamy-yellow to pale orange, is rounded with crisped margins. The 1.2 cm-long lateral lobes are curved on the upper edges and meet above the more or less straight column.

L. x *gerhard-santosii* prefers in intermediate to cool environment with light shade. It may be potted or mounted. Although it has no true resting period, watering should be reduced in winter.

Actual flower size: 5–6 cm across.

Laelia ghillanyi Pabst

This species was described in 1973 by Pabst, who named it in honour of its discoverer, Baron Anton Ghillany, a well-known Brazilian orchid collector and nurseryman. *Laelia ghillanyi* has been found only near the Serra do Cipó in Minas Gerais. It grows on volcanic rock and in sandy soil amid tall grasses and stunted shrubs.

The clustered pseudobulbs taper from a swollen base and are usually tinged with maroon-purple. They are 5–7 cm tall and about 2.5 cm wide near the base. The single stiff leaf is very fleshy. From 8–15 cm long, the boat-like leaves are often edged with maroon and have an acute apex. In spring two to seven rose-pink to dark lavender flowers are borne on an erect spike which is just a little longer than the leaves. In some clones — as in the one pictured — the tepals have darker 'flares' towards the apex. The lanceolate to almost elliptic dorsal sepal and petals are about 1.6–2.0 cm long, while the vaguely falcate lateral sepals are shorter. The lip is white to yellow in the throat, and this coloration extends on to the deflexed frilly apical lobe. The roundish lateral lobes meet above the column, which is much wider at the base than at the tip — a distinctive feature of this species, as are the four keels in the throat.

L. ghillanyi does well when potted in a well-drained medium such as chopped treefern fibre with the addition of some broken sandstone, granite or brick. It prefers fairly bright light in intermediate to cool conditions. Water copiously when the plant is in growth, and follow with a drier winter rest.

Actual flower size: 3.5–4 cm across.

Laelia gracilis Pabst

Often confused with *L. blumenscheinii*,* to which it is closely related, this species was described in 1979 by Pabst. Its specific name alludes to its gracefully arching spike, which contrasts with the erect spike of *L. blumenscheinii*. *L. gracilis* is confined to the Serra do Cipó in Minas Gerais, where it grows on rocks amid stunted vegetation. The plants are usually quite tall, although shorter forms do exist.

The clustered cylindrical pseudobulbs are reddish-purple and become wrinkled with age. Up to 30 cm tall, each carries a single stiff leathery leaf, which is purple below. The lanceolate leaves are spreading, with a keel below and a channel above. Up to seven starry flowers are borne in spring on a slender spike about 35 cm long. The yellow flowers have several slightly darker veins on their tepals. The erect dorsal sepal is lanceolate, 1.6–1.7 cm long and about 0.5 cm wide, while the vaguely falcate lateral sepals are slightly shorter. The petals are usually lanceolate to elliptic, 1.6–1.8 cm long and about 1.6 cm wide. The clone pictured here has slightly wider petals than is usual. The 1.3–1.5 cm-long lip has large, almost semi-circular lateral lobes which meet above the column. The recurved apical lobe has a short stalk at the base and is very frilly. There are four visible veins on the disc.

L. gracilis does best in an intermediate to cool environment with fairly bright light. It needs a fairly coarse potting medium, such as chopped treefern with a little broken sandstone added. Give plenty of water in the growing season, followed by a drier rest.

Actual flower size: approximately 4.5 cm across.

Laelia grandis Lindley

Introduced into cultivation by Morel in France, who received plants from Pinel in 1849, this species was described by Lindley in 1850, using material received from Morel. Along with species such as *L. lobata** and *L. tenebrosa*, it belongs to the section *Cattleyodes* of the genus. *L. grandis* is endemic, occurring only in the Serra da Onça, in the south of Bahia, at about 160 m above sea level, where it grows in the upper branches of tall trees. Its habitat is shrinking, and it is now a species under some threat.

The compressed pseudobulbs are club-like to spindle-shaped, about 22 cm tall and 3.5 cm wide. Each one bears a single oblong to lanceolate leaf 20–35 cm long. It is stiff, leathery, and about 4.5 cm wide. The showy flowers, which last for about two weeks, are borne in spring or early summer on a spike up to 25 cm long. There are usually two to six flowers up to 14 cm across on each spike. The greenish-yellow to bronze- or coppery-yellow tepals have very wavy margins and are usually twisted or reflexed along the mid-rib. The elliptic to lanceolate sepals are 6–7 cm long and about 1.4 cm wide, while the somewhat ovate petals are wider. The 6 cm-long lip is white, more or less strongly veined with pale to dark rose-purple. The lateral lobes meet above the column, while the very frilly mid-lobe may be suffused with lilac-rose.

A much sought-after species, *L. grandis* requires bright light and a warm humid environment. It may be mounted — preferably on cork or paperbark — or grown in hanging baskets of some freely draining material. Water should be given all year round.

Actual flower size: 10–14 cm across.

Laelia harpophylla Reichenbach (f.)

Although this very popular species first flowered in cultivation in 1867, Reichenbach did not describe it until 1873. *L. geraensis*, *Bletia harpophylla* and *Hoffmannseggella harpophylla* are conspecific. *L. harpophylla* grows as an epiphyte in humid somewhat shady forests at 500–900 m above sea level in Minas Gerais and Espírito Santo.

While the flowers are similar to those of *L. cinnabarina*,* there is no mistaking the plant itself with its thin terete pseudobulbs, 10–50 cm tall and only 0.3–0.7 cm in diameter. They are faintly grooved and each bears a single lanceolate leaf with a long tapering apex. From 14–30 cm long and up to 2.5 cm wide, the leathery leaves are more or less flat, sometimes with recurved margins. From five to fifteen starry flowers are borne on a spike about 17 cm long in winter or spring. The tepals are pale to dark orange. The somewhat lanceolate petals and obtuse dorsal sepal are up to 4 cm long, while the slightly falcate lateral sepals are a little shorter. The 2.5–3.0 cm-long lip has large lateral lobes, which have acute apices and form an arching tube around the column. The lateral lobes are orange with darker veins, while the very narrow mid-lobe is creamy-white to pale orange, with usually two wavy keels, much crisped irregular margins and an acute recurved apex.

L. harpophylla does well mounted or potted in chopped treefern fibre, with moderate light and a humid intermediate to cool environment. Although it has no distinct resting period, watering should be reduced in winter, when misting is preferable. Do not allow plants to shrivel unduly.

Actual flower size: 5–7.5 cm across.

Laelia itambana Pabst

Endemic to Brazil and found only in eastern Minas Gerais, this species was described by Pabst in 1973. It grows among mosses, lichens and leaf litter in the crevices of sandstone outcrops on Pico da Itambé at elevations of 2,000–2,300 m. The area of its habitat is subjected to climatic extremes, and the vegetation is mainly low scrub. During the long dry period plants are sustained by nightly dews.

The tightly clustered pseudobulbs are cylindrical and 2.5–6.0 cm tall. The boat-shaped leaves are succulent and very stiff. Erect or arching, they are 2.5–6.0 cm long and occasionally tinged with purple. One or two flowers are borne in late spring or summer on an erect spike up to 10 cm long which rises from the apex of the pseudobulb. The very open yellow flowers are 3.5–4.0 cm across. The sepals are an elongated oval with blunt apices, with the laterals slightly shorter than the 2.0–2.5 cm dorsal. The petals are shaped like elongated diamonds, with a very narrow base. The three-lobed lip is 1.1–1.5 cm long with a small recurved and crisped mid-lobe. The lateral lobes scarcely meet above the column.

This species grows well in intermediate to cool conditions with plenty of bright light and good air movement. A dry winter rest should be given after growth and flowering have finished. Treefern mounts seem to retain too much moisture for this species, and we recommend potting material such as broken sandstone and coarse leaf mould. We hang our potted plants for maximum light and air movement.
Actual flower size: 3.5–4 cm across.

Laelia jongheana Reichenbach (f.)

This much-sought species was discovered about 1854 by Libon, who sent plants to de Jonghe of Brussels. Reichenbach described it in 1872, based on material supplied by Lueddemann, and named the species after de Jonghe at Libon's request. Unfortunately this species is nearing extinction in its limited habitat in central Minas Gerais, where it grows at 1,300–1,600 m in medium-sized forests close to the summits of the few mountain ranges in the area.

The slightly compressed pseudobulbs are 3.0–5.5 cm long, up to 1.5 cm wide and up to 1 cm apart on the stout rhizome. They become wrinkled with age. Each one carries a single, very thick, stiff leaf about 7.5–12.0 cm long and 3 cm wide, which has a pointed apex and a shallow v-shaped cross-section. Flowers are produced, usually in pairs, from late winter to early spring on 4 cm spikes. The almost flat flowers are very large for the size of the plant, 10–16 cm across. The sepals and petals range in colour from mid- to dark pink or rose-purple. The sepals taper to a sharp point, while the petals, which are twice as wide, are almost diamond-shaped with wavy edges near the apex. The 5.5 cm tubular lip points downward. It is pale mauve on the outside and golden-orange inside, and edged in cream and mauve. There are seven wavy keels which run almost to the apex of the very frilled mid-lobe.

This is an easy plant to grow in intermediate conditions. It should be given as much light as possible short of burning the leaves. Treefern mounts are ideal. Plenty of water when in growth, and a drier winter rest.
Actual flower size: 10–16 cm across.

Laelia kautskyana Pabst

Closely related to *L. harpophylla*,* this species hybridises with it to create the natural hybrid *L.* x *gerhard-santosii*.* It was described by Pabst in 1974, and named in honour of Kautsky, who supplied him with material of the species. Until then it was known horticulturally as *L. harpophylla* var. *dulcotensis*, or simply as the 'yellow *L. harpophylla*'. The latter is something of a misnomer because, while the flowers open yellow, they soon turn pale orange. *L. kautskyana* grows epiphytically in the shady forests of Espírito Santo at about 600 m above sea level.

The closely set cylindrical pseudobulbs are 10–50 cm tall, but less than 1 cm in diameter. Each bears a single lanceolate leaf, which is more or less flat and 14–30 cm long by about 2.5 cm wide. From three to ten flowers about 6 cm wide are borne on a relatively short spike in winter or early spring. The tepals, which are often recurved, are shorter than those of *L. harpophylla*. The lanceolate dorsal sepal is about 3.5–4.0 cm long and 0.8 cm wide, while the petals and vaguely falcate lateral sepals are 3.0–3.5 cm long and slightly wider. The 2.5 cm-long lip has a few longitudinal keels, and is pale orange inside. The apical lobe is much shorter and about twice as wide as in *L. harpophylla*. It has crisped margins and a recurved pointed apex. The lateral lobes enclose the arched column.

L. kautskyana requires humid, intermediate to cool conditions with partial shade. Treefern makes an ideal mount or potting material. Plants need plenty of water during the growing season, with a reduction in winter.

Actual flower size: 5–6.5 cm across.

Laelia kettieana Pabst

A true miniature, this rupicolous laelia was described in 1975 by Pabst, who named it after its discoverer, Kettie Waras, wife of Eddie Waras, the well-known Danish-born Brazilian orchid collector. Endemic to Minas Gerais, *L. kettieana* was originally collected on the Serra da Moeda near Caeté, but has since been found also on the Serra da Caraça. The area experiences a continental climate, with large diurnal temperature variations and cold dry winters.

The clustered 1.5–4.0 cm-tall pseudobulbs are almost globose to slightly tapering. They are about 1 cm wide and bear a single succulent leaf 2–5 cm long. Leaves are boat-shaped, about 0.5–0.8 cm wide, are channelled above, keeled below, and have acute apices. In spring or summer from one to three glistening mauve-pink flowers are carried on a spike about 2.5–6.0 cm long. The tepals have slightly darker veins and somewhat recurved apices. The lanceolate dorsal sepal is 1.2–1.5 cm long and about 0.4 cm wide, while the petals and somewhat falcate lateral sepals are 1.0–1.2 cm long. The darker, 1 cm-long lip has almost semi-circular lateral lobes which enclose the column and have acute apices. The apical lobe is very frilly. The mid-lobe is very pale to bright yellow with a purple border.

L. kettieana is a trouble-free plant in cultivation once it is established. We grow ours in suspended pots of coarsely chopped treefern fibre and broken sandstone. Fairly bright light and intermediate to cool conditions are ideal. Give plenty of water in the growing season, followed by a decided dry winter resting period.

Actual flower size: approximately 3 cm across.

Laelia lilliputana Pabst

Amongst the smallest of the laelias, this species was discovered by the Brazilian plants-man Ghillany and named by Pabst in 1973 for the fictional land of Lilliput. Restricted to a small area on the Serra do Ouro Branco in Minas Gerais, it grows at about 1,600 m on sloping ledges of granite and gneiss. It is usually found amid lichens and around the roots of *Vellozia* bushes. The area experiences a long dry season relieved only by nightly dews. Plants are subjected to ten hours of direct sunlight each day, but good winds help to moderate temperatures.

The round pseudobulbs are 0.5–1.0 cm in diameter and 0.7–1.5 cm tall. They are tightly clustered and often tinged with pur-ple, as are the succulent boat-shaped leaves, which are stiff and upright and vary from 1–3 cm in length. One or two flowers are produced on spikes from 3–4 cm long in late spring or summer. The widely open-ing flowers are 2–3 cm across, with 1.0–1.7 cm-long tepals. These range in colour from white to pale pink and have a crys-talline texture. The 1.0 cm tubular lip is three-lobed, with the lateral lobes meeting above the column and the much-crisped mid-lobe recurving at the apex. The lip is yellow-orange inside, edged with white or pink.

This species does well in cool to inter-mediate conditions with plenty of light and good ventilation. We grow our plants in small suspended pots of coarse freely draining material. Plants should be given a dry cool rest in winter with only moderate misting.

Actual flower size: 2–3 cm across.

Laelia lobata (Ldl.) Veitch

Discovered by Gard-ner in 1821, this species, which belongs to the section *Cattleyodes*, was not described until 1848, when Lindley named it *Cattleya lobata*. Veitch transferred it to the genus *Laelia* in 1887. Synonyms include *L. boothiana* and *L. riverii*. Once found from the west of Rio de Janeiro almost to Cabo Frio in the east, *L. lobata* is now restricted to almost verti-cal rocky outcrops near the city of Rio de Janeiro at 200–800 m above sea level. It also occasionally inhabits the tops of tall trees.

The pseudobulbs are club-like, 10–20 cm tall and 3.0–3.5 cm wide. Each bears a sin-gle leathery leaf 18–30 cm long and about 4.5 cm wide. In spring or early summer a 30–35 cm spike carries three to six or more fragrant flowers up to 15 cm across. They are typically pale to dark rose or lavender, although white clones are not uncommon. They are similar to the flowers of *L. pur-purata*,* with lanceolate sepals 6.0–7.5 cm long and 2 cm wide which have recurved margins at the base. The slightly shorter petals are 4.0–4.5 cm wide, elliptic to rhomboidal, and have undulating margins. The lateral lobes of the lip, which enclose the pale lilac column and have frilly re-curved apical margins, are marked with yellow and often striped with purple on the inside, as is the throat. The apical lobe is dark pink to amethyst with darker veins.

L. lobata is reputed (with justice, in our experience) to be a shy flowerer, and should be disturbed as little as possible. It is best mounted or grown in baskets or sus-pended pots of any coarse freely draining material. It needs bright light and a warm to intermediate environment, with a slight-ly cooler, drier winter.

Actual flower size: 10–15 cm across.

Laelia lucasiana Rolfe

Rolfe described this species in 1892, and it is conspecific with Hoehne's *L. ostermeyeri*; Garay reduced the latter species to synonymy with *L. lucasiana* about ten years ago. At one stage, *L. lucasiana* was believed to be synonymous with Reichenbach (f.)'s *L. longipes* of 1863, but this is no longer the case. It is found in the mountain ranges from the Serra do Piedade to the Serra da Caraça in eastern Minas Gerais. Growing on rocky outcrops between 1,400–1,700 m above sea level, this species is subjected to a long cold dry season which may last for six months. It grows among lichens in fully exposed positions and is often found in association with *Pleurothallis teres*.*

The clustered pseudobulbs are 1.5–4.0 cm tall, with very succulent pointed leaves 3–8 cm long. They are somewhat boat-shaped with a prominent keel beneath. The entire plant is often tinged with purple, especially when grown in bright light. Plants flower from late spring to summer, with one to three pale to dark pinkish-mauve flowers on erect spikes to 6 cm long. The flowers, which are paler towards the centre, are 3–5 cm across, with rounded tepals 2.0–2.5 cm long. The 1.5 cm lip is bright yellow-orange, with the broad lateral lobes folded over the column. The mid-lobe is much crisped.

This species should be grown in smallish pots of coarse material such as broken rock with some leaf mould added. Bright light in a cool to intermediate environment is best, with good air movement and a dry rest in winter.

Actual flower size: 3–5 cm across.

Laelia lucasiana var. *fournieri* (Cogn.) Pabst

Originally described as *L. longipes* var. *fournieri* by Cogniaux in 1897, and once considered a natural hybrid between *L. longipes* and *L. flava*,* this taxon was later recognised as a variety of *L. lucasiana** by Pabst. Like the type, it occurs in the savannah country of Minas Gerais, where it grows among rocks at 1,400–1,700 m above sea level. This area experiences a continental climate with large diurnal temperature variations.

The mid-green pseudobulbs, which may be almost globose or elongated, are 1–6 cm tall. Each bears a single boat-shaped, very succulent leaf 2.5–9.0 cm long and up to 2 cm across. Flower spikes from 3–5 cm long are produced from the apex of developing pseudobulbs from late spring to early autumn. They carry one to three starry flowers which are sparkling white with a predominantly yellow lip. The 2.0–2.4 cm-long sepals are faintly keeled. The oblong to lanceolate dorsal sepal and the somewhat falcate lateral sepals are 0.3–0.8 cm wide and recurved at the acute apices. The 2.0–2.2 cm-long petals are slightly narrower than the sepals. The gracefully curved lip is about 1.4 cm long and 0.5 cm wide in its natural position. The lateral lobes join above the greenish column to conceal it. They are curved on the upper edges and are pointed at the front edges. About 0.5 cm long, they are white or greenish-white near the base. The very crisped mid-lobe has a few faint keels down the centre.

L. lucasiana var. *fournieri* does well in intermediate to cool conditions with plenty of bright light and a dry rest during the cooler months.

Actual flower size: 2.5–4 cm across.

Laelia lundii Reichenbach (f.)

Johannes Warming, the Danish botanist, discovered this species in Minas Gerais and, with Reichenbach, described it as *Bletia lundii* in 1881. Reichenbach transferred it to *Laelia* later that year, while *L. regnellii* and *L. reichenbachiana* are later synonyms. In Minas Gerais, where it is not common, this species grows on small trees on rocky hills or on the rocks themselves. It is more common in the drier inland areas of São Paulo and Paraná, growing in shady humid positions on forest trees along small rivers.

The glossy pseudobulbs, usually less than 3 cm long, are set up to 5 cm apart on a stout rhizome and are about 1.2 cm in diameter. Unique among Brazilian laelias, it is bifoliate, with two very fleshy erect leaves 6–15 cm long. The leaves are very narrow, with a depressed channel on the upper surface and a rounded underside. One to three flowers appear in winter on short spikes from the developing growth. The starry flowers, which last a little more than a week, are 3–4 cm across. The pointed tepals, about 2 cm long, are white, sometimes tinged with pink, and have several paler veins. The three-lobed lip is tubular at the base where the lateral lobes meet above the column, and broad and frilly at the apex. The lip has several keels in the throat and is veined with rich maroon-purple.

L. lundii may be potted or grown in a basket, but does best for us when mounted, especially on paperbark, and hung in a bright position. An intermediate to cool environment is ideal, with good air movement and fairly high humidity.
Actual flower size: 3–4 cm across.

Laelia mantiqueirae Pabst

Described by Pabst in 1975, this species was named after the Serra da Mantiqueira, one of the ranges in which it occurs. It is another of the distinctive rupicolous laelias and, like so many of them, comes from Minas Gerais. It is a fairly common plant there, occurring in the tableland area bounded by Sao João del Rei, Piedade and Ouro Prêto. This plateau has a continental climate with a wide diurnal temperature range. The hot days, however, are tempered by strong winds, and the cooler nights bring heavy dews. The dry season may be up to six months long, with little or no rain.

This species has clustered conical pseudobulbs from 5–10 cm tall and tinged with purple. Although the leathery leaves may reach 20 cm, they are spreading, so that plant height seldom exceeds 12 cm and may be shorter. The leaves are purple beneath and on the upper edges, and have a prominent keel. Flowering from spring to summer, this species bears seven or more well-spaced flowers, each 4–5 cm across, on tall spikes. The starry flowers are rich rosy-pink, paler at the base, and have a crystalline texture. The tepals are recurved at the pointed apices. The tubular lip is 2 cm long. The side-lobes are veined and edged with dark violet, while the recurved mid-lobe is white in the centre with dark violet ruffled edges.

L mantiqueirae grows well in intermediate conditions with bright light and good air movement. Our plants are hung in baskets of chopped treefern and broken brick. The mixture must be allowed to dry out between waterings, and plants need a dry rest in winter.
Actual flower size: 4–5 cm across.

Laelia milleri Blumenschein

Named to honour Miller, a well-known Brazilian geneticist, this species was described in 1960 by Blumenschein. *L. milleri* is very rare — if not extinct — in nature. It has been reported only from the Serra dos Ingleses at 800–1,300 m above sea level near Itabira in Minas Gerais. It grew on ranges rich in iron ore, but by 1990 mining had confined it to very small areas around *Vellozia* shrubs on steep slopes. These last small populations may now also be gone.

The clustered tapering pseudobulbs are typically 3–8 cm tall, with a swollen base. They are more or less strongly suffused with red or purple, as is the underside of the single stiff fleshy leaf borne at the apex. Up to 10 cm long, the leaves are lanceolate to ovate, flat and spreading. From late spring to early autumn, four to ten starry flowers are carried on an erect spike up to 35 cm tall. Flowers open over an extended period and have dark orange-red to blood-red tepals, which are 0.6–0.8 cm wide. The dorsal sepal, up to 3 cm long, is slightly longer than the lateral sepals and the petals. The 2 cm-long lip is yellow-orange, more or less heavily veined, and edged with red. The rounded lateral lobes form a tube around the column, and have crisped apical edges. The rounded mid-lobe is very frilly.

L. milleri, like most of the rupicolous laelias, is not a difficult subject. It does well when potted in any coarse well-drained medium, and given intermediate to cool conditions, with a dry winter rest. Despite its rarity in nature, *L. milleri* is such an attractive species that, thanks to artificial propagation, it is not uncommon in cultivation.

Actual flower size: 4–5.5 cm across.

Laelia mixta Hoehne ex Ruschi

Hoehne first proposed the name for this species, thinking it might be a natural hybrid between *L. flava** or *L. gloedeniana* and *L. harpophylla**. Ruschi published Hoehne's name with a proper description of the taxon, now considered to be a true species, in 1938. *L. mixta* originally inhabited rocky mountain ranges at 800 m or more above sea level in central Espírito Santo. However, much of its habitat has now been destroyed.

The clustered tapering pseudobulbs are 7–35 cm long, suffused with purple, and covered with papery sheaths. Each bears a single stiff leathery leaf which is more or less erect, lanceolate, 10–20 cm long and about 2.5 cm wide near the base. The leaf is keeled below and minutely wrinkled on the upper surface. It is often suffused with purple beneath and has purple edges above. In spring or summer up to fifteen flowers are borne near the apex of a spike which may reach 65 cm in length, but is often shorter. The flowers open together. The pale yellow tepals have darker veins, which are sometimes almost red. The oblong to lanceolate dorsal sepal and oblong to elliptic petals are about 3 cm long and 0.7 cm wide, while the lateral sepals are slightly shorter. The 2.3 cm-long lip is veined with red. The large lateral lobes form an arching tube, while the recurved apical lobe is very frilly with a more or less rounded apex.

L. mixta grows well for us in suspended pots of coarsely chopped treefern. It prefers moderately bright light and intermediate to cool conditions. It should be given plenty of water when in growth, followed by a drier winter rest.

Actual flower size: 5.5–6 cm across.

Laelia perrinii (Ldl.) Lindley

Lindley first described this species in 1838 as *Cattleya perrinii*, and four years later transferred it to the genus *Laelia*. He named it for the gardener of Harrison, a prominent orchid grower to whom plants had been sent from Rio de Janeiro. *Laelia perrinii* grows on trees on rocky slopes at 400–1,000 m above sea level in Espírito Santo, Rio de Janeiro and Minas Gerais.

The strongly compressed pseudobulbs are 7–25 cm tall, very narrow at the base, and 1.5–3.0 cm wide in the upper section. At the base are several loose bracts, while the apex bears a single leathery leaf, which is suffused or spotted with purple beneath and sometimes mottled above. The leaf is 13–30 cm long, 3.0–4.5 cm wide, and oblong to elliptic. An 8–25 cm spike typically carries two or three flowers (occasionally as many as five) in summer or autumn. The tepals are pale mauve-pink to dark purple. The erect to recurved dorsal sepal is 6.5–8.0 cm long and 1.3–1.5 cm wide. It is faintly keeled and tapers to an obtuse apex. The shorter laterals are falcate and keeled on the reverse. The somewhat rhomboidal petals are 6.5–7.5 cm long and up to 2.5 cm wide. The vaguely three-lobed lip, which is 5 cm long, is creamy-white with a velvety amethyst-purple band around the apical edge and faint purple veins on the lateral lobes. These are more or less triangular and curve up to meet above the column. The mid-lobe is triangular, with an acute apex.

L. perrinii does well when mounted or potted in a coarse freely draining medium. It likes an intermediate environment with moderate to bright light, and reduced watering in winter.

Actual flower size: 10–15 cm across.

Laelia perrinii varieties

The species *L. perrinii* belongs to the section *Cattleyodes*, which includes such laelias as *L. purpurata*,* *L. lobata*,* and *L. grandis*,* all with rather showy flowers. Most are confined to the coastal ranges from southern Bahia to Rio Grande do Sul, and thus make good subjects for intermediate conditions.

There are several named varieties of *L. perrinii*, all with the same elegant shape of the type. The petals, the irregular margins of which may be recurved, are usually held below the horizontal, so that the dorsal sepal stands alone above the other segments. As with the type, the flower spikes of the varieties are protected by large sheaths until buds are well developed. Flowers of all varieties have a sparkling crystalline texture. *L. perrinii* var. *alba*, pictured here, is a pure white variety and was first collected by one of Sander's collectors. It remains a much-sought plant. Another much admired variety is *L. perrinii* var. *coerulea*, which has pale greyish-blue to greyish-purple tepals with a dark slate-blue band on the apical edge of the lip. *L. perrinii* var. *semi-alba* has white petals and sepals, with or without a faint pink tinge, and a dark red-purple blotch at the apex of the mid-lobe. *L. perrinii* var. *concolor* is a very pale uniform pink, while *L. perrinii* var. *amesiana* has white sepals and petals with a light pink lip.

Cultivation of all varieties is as for the type species. An intermediate environment is preferred, with moderately bright light. Plants may be mounted — treefern slabs are ideal — or potted. We grow our plants in suspended pots of coarsely chopped treefern fibre.

Actual flower size: 10–15 cm across.

Laelia pfisteri Pabst & Senghas

Described by Pabst and Senghas in 1975, this species was named in honour of Gerhard Pfister, who was responsible for collecting and introducing many Brazilian species into cultivation in Germany. It is found only around the Serra da Sincorá (home of *Laelia sincorana**) in central Bahia in northeastern Brazil. It grows on the dry rocky hills amid stunted vegetation at 1,100–1,400 m, a habitat it shares with *L. bahiensis.** During the cool dry season, which may last for half the year, the plants are sustained by heavy dews. Plants are usually 15 cm or less in height.

The clustered pseudobulbs are usually 6–7 cm tall, with an enlarged base and a tapering apex. They are reddish-purple and bear a single leathery leaf 5–12 cm long. It is almost flat, recurved, and edged with purple. Flower spikes rise from the apex of the pseudobulb in spring or summer. Up to 1 m tall, they may carry thirty or more well-spaced flowers which open successively so that no more than half the number are open together. The lilac-pink flowers are 3–4 cm across. The 1.5–2.0 cm-long tepals are frequently reflexed. The lip is three-lobed, with the long lateral lobes forming a narrow tube around the column. The mid-lobe is white in the centre and edged with a wide frilly band of dark magenta.

L. pfisteri appreciates bright light. It needs an intermediate environment, plenty of water while in growth, and a dry spell in winter. We hang our plants in pots of coarse material where air movement is good.

Actual flower size: 3–4 cm across.

Laelia pumila (Hook.) Reichenbach (f.)

First described by Hooker in 1839 as *Cattleya pumila*, this species was transferred to the genus *Laelia* by Reichenbach in 1853. *Cattleya marginata* and *C. pinelii* are synonyms. It occurs in the states of Minas Gerais and Espírito Santo, where it grows as an epiphyte in relatively open forest at elevations of 600–1,300 m above sea level. It usually occupies positions low down on trees near watercourses, where the air is relatively cool and fresh. This species is very closely related to *Laelia dayana** and *L. spectabilis;** so much so that plants of the three species are indistinguishable when not in flower.

The 3–8 cm pseudobulbs are set about 1 cm apart on stout rhizomes. They are pencil-shaped and have a single rather fleshy leaf 10–12.5 cm long. One or two showy flowers are borne on short spikes, usually in summer but occasionally at other times of the year. The flat lavender flowers are 7–11 cm across and last well on the plant. The acute sepals and broader petals are 3.5–5.5 cm long. The 4.5 cm lip is white or yellow within the wide tube and has a dark purple band round the undulating edge. There are three to five prominent keels down the centre of the lip.

This species, like *L. dayana*, flowers best if given as much light as possible. We have found that fairly large treefern slabs make the best mounts. *L. pumila* grows fairly quickly into a large plant, so small mounts are not a good idea. Intermediate conditions are ideal, with plenty of water when the plant is in growth, followed by a dry rest in winter.

Actual flower size: 7–11 cm across.

Laelia purpurata Lindley

Discovered in 1846 in Santa Catarina by Devos, this well-known laelia was described by Lindley in 1852 or 1853. Synonyms include *Bletia purpurata* and *Cattleya casperiana*. *L. purpurata* grows on tall trees on rocky hills and in swampy areas near the coast in Rio de Janeiro, São Paulo, Santa Catarina and Rio Grande do Sul. It also occurs on some coastal islands. It is an immensely popular species with Brazilian growers.

The club-like pseudobulbs are 15–28 cm long and 2–3 cm wide. Each bears a single apical fleshy leaf 22–45 cm long and up to 5 cm wide. In late spring or summer a 20–32 cm-long spike carries two to eight (occasionally more) flowers. Typically about 15 cm across, but sometimes reaching 25 cm, the flowers resemble those of *L. lobata*.* The tepals are usually white, white tinged with pale pink, or pink. The 6–12 cm-long sepals are about 1.8 cm wide, with deflexed margins at the base. The elliptic to diamond-shaped petals are normally at least twice as wide, with more or less wavy edges. The lip is obscurely three-lobed, with rounded lateral lobes curling over the column. The lateral lobes are more or less flared at the maroon-purple apex. Together with the throat, they are yellow, veined with purple on the inside. The crisped mid-lobe is typically a deep maroon-purple with darker veins and paler edges.

L. purpurata does well mounted or in baskets or pots of chopped treefern fibre or some similar material. It needs fairly bright light, high humidity and good ventilation in an intermediate to warm environment. It is a much easier species to flower than the closely related *L. lobata*.

Actual flower size: approximately 15 cm across.

Laelia purpurata var. *carnea* & other varieties

The national flower of Brazil and known there as the 'Queen of the Laelias', *L. purpurata** is perhaps the best-known species in the section *Cattleyodes*. It is probably the most widely grown orchid species in Brazil, with more than one hundred colour variations known. In the south there are orchid societies devoted solely to its cultivation, and annual shows — particularly around Santa Catarina and São Paulo — at which no other orchids are displayed.

Most of the colour varieties come from the southern populations in Santa Catarina and Rio Grande do Sul, and are differentiated mainly by the colour and pattern of the apical lobe of the lip. Many are purely horticultural varieties or informally named clones. *L. purpurata* var. *carnea*, also known as var. *semi-alba* subvar. *carnea*, has white petals and sepals and a salmon to flesh-pink-coloured lip with darker veins and yellow in the throat. The clone pictured here was photographed at the Florália nursery in Petropolis during our visit in 1989. This variety is widely used in hybridising. Several other varieties have pink to red colouring in the tepals as well as the lip, including the var. *concolor*, which is pale pink with slightly darker veins on the lip, and var. *rosea* with light rose tepals and a darker lip with no yellow in the throat. The var. *seideliana* has pale pink sepals and petals and a wine-red lip, while the var. *argolão* has pale pink to white flowers with a ring of deep pink around the lip. All are well worth a place in the collection, and no more difficult to flower than the type.

Actual flower size: approximately 15 cm across.

Laelia purpurata var. *coerulea* & other varieties

Blue is a rare coloration in orchid flowers, and blue varieties, even when the blue is only partial, have always been popular. The case of *L. purpurata** is no exception, although here the blue is usually confined to the lip, with only the faintest blue tinge visible in the tepals of some clones. The shade of blue varies from pale sky-blue to bright iris-blue to bluish-purple and blue-black. *L. purpurata* var. *coerulescens* is one variety, however, in which the sepals and petals are light blue, while the lip is darker. Although the term *coerulea* really means sky-blue, it is often applied as a varietal epithet to any clone with white or extremely faint blue sepals and petals, a blue lip, and a yellow throat veined with blue.

The types with different shades of blue are sometimes treated as separate varieties and sometimes only as clones. For example, *L. purpurata* var. *werckhauseri*, pictured here, is often referred to as *L. purpurata* var. *coerulea* 'Werckhauseri', even though the markings on its lip are definitely not sky-blue, but rather indigo or slate-blue with blue-black veins. *L. purpurata* var. *aço* also has blue on the lip, in this case a deep violet-blue. There are several named clones of this variety, including var. *aço* 'Clito' and var. *aço* 'Aurea-violeta'. Other noteworthy varieties include, of course, the var. *alba*, which is typically white with yellow in the throat, although some clones are pure white. The var. *sanguinea* has dark blood-red to red-purple tepals with a darker lip, while the var. *atropurpurea* has dark rose tepals and a magenta-purple lip. *Actual flower size: approximately 15 cm across.*

Laelia purpurata var. *oculata* & other varieties

The varietal epithet *oculata* describes a number of named forms in which the band of colour on the lip is split in two, producing two 'eyes' or blotches, one on either side at the base of the apical lobe and extending on to the flared sections of the lateral lobes.

The sepals and petals are usually white, while the throat of the lip is yellow, more or less veined with the same colour as the eyes. A typical *oculata* variety has magenta to amethyst eyes. It is customary in horticultural circles to use a two-part varietal epithet, the second part indicating the colour of the eyes or blotches. Thus, the pictured plant, photographed at the Florália nursery at Niteroi near Rio de Janeiro, which has salmon to fleshy-

pink eyes, is called var. *oculata-carnea*. Other varieties include the var. *oculata-vinicolor*, which has eyes the colour of port wine; the var. *oculata-coerulea*, with eyes of varying shades of blue; and the var. *oculata-russeliana*, with rosy-lilac or light lavender eyes. There are many more of these horticultural varieties, reflecting both the variability and popularity of *L. purpurata*. The naming process is a fairly informal one in Brazil, and a certain amount of duplication and confusion exists. Two other unusual varieties are *L. purpurata* var. *flammea* and var. *striata*. In the former, the petals have 'flares', i.e. candy-pink veins or suffusions on the outer two-thirds of the petals. The petals of the var. *striata* have pale to dark coloured veins.

Culture in all cases is as for the type, with plenty of water when in growth, followed by a drier cool season.
Actual flower size: approximately 15 cm across.

Laelia reginae var. *alba* Pabst

This species is one of the smallest of the rupicolous laelias. Both the type and the variety *alba*, shown here, were described by Pabst in 1975. The type is named after Regina Angerer, who discovered it in the Serra da Caraça in Minas Gerais. It is found on rocky ledges at 1,200–2,000 m above sea level, growing around the roots of *Vellozia* shrubs which afford it some protection from the harsh conditions — strong drying winds, hot summers and cold dry winters. It has since been reported from near Belo Horizonte.

The tightly clustered pseudobulbs are 1.5–3.5 cm tall and about 1 cm across. Each carries a single apical leaf. This is very fleshy, boat-shaped, 2.5–4.0 cm long and 1.0–1.6 cm wide. The leaves are often tinged with purple below and on the margins. From spring to summer two to six flowers are borne on a 2–5 cm spike. The glistening flowers are often likened to a miniature *L. lucasiana.** Flowers of the type are very light pink to lavender with a pale lip which is golden-yellow inside. The var. *alba* has the golden-yellow lip, but is otherwise white. The more or less lanceolate to oblong tepals are 0.8–1.5 cm long and up to about 0.5 cm wide. The lateral lobes of the 0.8 cm-long lip meet above the column, while the narrow recurved apical lobe has crisped margins. Two parallel ridges run from the base on to the apical lobe.

Both the type and variety require bright indirect light and a well-drained medium. Cool to intermediate conditions are appropriate, with plenty of water in the growing season, followed by a dry winter rest with only occasional misting.

Actual flower size: 1.5–2.5 cm across.

Laelia sanguiloba Withner

Still often sold as *L. sulina*, this rupicolous species from Bahia was known for some time by Pabst's names, *L. flava* var. *micrantha* and *L. flava* var. *sulina*. In 1989 Withner elevated it to specific status, renaming it *L. sanguiloba* in reference to the red lateral lobes of the lip.

The clustered 6–14 cm-long pseudobulbs are elongated and taper gradually towards the apex. They are reddish-purple when grown in bright light. Each has one stiff leaf which has rough edges and some transverse wrinkling above. From 7–17 cm long, the arching lanceolate leaves are heavily suffused with reddish-purple below. Upper surfaces may be lightly suffused. From four to twelve well-spaced dark orange flowers are borne in summer and early autumn on 20–40 cm spikes from the apex of the pseudobulbs. The tepals often have faint red veins. Both the oblong pointed dorsal, which is 3–4 cm long, and the somewhat falcate 2.7–3.0 cm-long lateral sepals are narrow, keeled on the reverse, and slightly recurved at the apex. The more or less oblong petals are 2.7–3.5 cm long and held slightly forward. The lip is strongly three-lobed, with the 1.5–2.2 cm lateral lobes enclosing the reddish column. Joined to the mid-lobe for only half their length, the lateral lobes are semi-circular. The mid-lobe is very strongly crisped and curled under. The recurved section is about 1 cm long and 0.5 cm wide. The base of the mid-lobe is pale, with purple veins, and bears four ridges.

L. sanguiloba prefers an intermediate to warm environment and fairly bright light. It should be permitted to dry out between watering.

Actual flower size: 5–6.5 cm across.

Laelia sincorana Schlechter

Closely related to *Laelia pumila*,* this beautiful species was discovered early this century and described by Schlechter in 1917. *Cattleya grosvenori* is a much later synonym. *L. sincorana* is restricted in nature to the tablelands of the Serra da Sincorá and the Serra do Capa-Bode in Bahia, where it grows at elevations of 1,200–1,500 m on *Vellozia* bushes exposed to full sun, or on rocky ledges. Through the long dry season the sparse vegetation experiences nightly dews.

The clustered pseudobulbs of *L. sincorana* are almost globular when the plant is grown in the bright light of its native habitat, reaching a height of little more than 2 cm. In cultivation, however, with less light, pseudobulbs generally become more elongated and may reach a height of 5 cm. The stiff fleshy leaf is 6–11 cm long, boat-shaped, and protects the emerging flower buds. From mid-spring to summer, one or two, rarely up to four, flowers are borne on a short spike. Usually rose-purple in colour, they are large for the tiny plant — about 7–10 cm across. They have narrow, slightly reflexed sepals and broad rhomboidal petals with wavy edges. The 5 cm lip embraces the column. The exterior is the same colour as the tepals, but the inner surface is yellow in the throat and dark rose-purple on the mid-lobe and around the edges of the lateral lobes. The frilly lip has five central keels.

We find that this species does best when mounted on quick-drying material such as paperbark or natural cork. It needs a bright airy position and intermediate conditions.

Actual flower size: 7–10 cm across.

Laelia spectabilis (Paxt.) Withner

This epiphyte is still generally known and sold as *L. praestans*, Reichenbach (f.)'s 1857 name. In 1990, however, Withner recognised it as being identical with *Cattleya spectabilis* (Paxton, 1850). He therefore resurrected the specific epithet and transferred the species to *Laelia*. Along with *L. dayana*,* it is often still treated as a form of *L. pumila.** *L. spectabilis* grows in the forests of Espírito Santo at 600–1,000 m above sea level. It has also been reported from Minas Gerais, but is all but extinct there.

The spindle-shaped pseudobulbs are typically 3–6 cm long and 0.6–1.0 cm in diameter. Each bears a single leathery lanceolate leaf, 4.5–11.0 cm in length and up to 2.5 cm wide. Flowering is generally in summer or autumn, but the species may flower more than once a year. Single flowers are borne on a short spike from the newest pseudobulb. The sparkling tepals range in colour from rose-pink to dark mauve, and are 4.0–6.5 cm long. The sepals are about 1.5 cm wide and the rounded petals 2.0–2.5 cm. The vaguely three-lobed lip is yellow to dark orange on the basal interior two-thirds, and often on the exterior base. The edges of the lateral lobes and the apical third of the mid-lobe are purple. The lateral lobes are significantly overlapped, forming a horn-like tube. The mid-lobe typically has four keels. A feature distinguishing this species from *L. pumila* is the short wide (as opposed to long narrow) column.

L. spectabilis does well when mounted on a treefern slab and given intermediate to cool conditions, bright indirect light, plenty of water when in growth, and a drier winter rest.

Actual flower size: 8–13 cm across.

Laelia tereticaulis Hoehne

Sometimes regarded as synonymous with *L. crispata*,* this species was discovered about 1947, and described by Hoehne in 1952. *L. tereticaulis* grows amid grasses and sparse vegetation on rocks at about 1,100 m above sea level near Diamantina in Minas Gerais.

The pale to mid-green pseudobulbs are 14–30 cm tall, and up to 2 cm in diameter. Each bears an erect very stiff succulent leaf 14–22 cm long. The grey-green appearance of the leaves is due to a white powdery coating which protects them from the sun's rays. From spring to early summer a spike up to 42 cm long carries usually seven to nine evenly spaced flowers on its upper part. The flowers look rather like those of an untidy *L. crispata*, but with more recurved tepals. These have a sparkling texture and are normally more uniformly coloured than in the one pictured here. They are commonly rose-lilac to violet, with paler areas at the base. The falcate lateral sepals are about 2 cm long and 0.7 cm wide. The lanceolate to elliptic dorsal sepal is about 2.5 cm long, with the petals slightly longer again. The recurved lip is about 1.4 cm long, with its lateral lobes, which are pale at the base and have darker veins, meeting above the upper part of the column. They are rounded with more or less triangular apices. The mid-lobe is cream to yellow, with a very frilly dark red-purple apex. Two main keels run down the centre.

L. tereticaulis does well when potted in a well-drained mixture such as chopped treefern fibre, perhaps with some sandstone or gravel added. It needs fairly bright light, intermediate to cool conditions, and a dry winter.

Actual flower size: approximately 5 cm across.

Laelia virens Lindley

Discovered by Gardner in 1837 in the Serra dos Orgãos near Rio de Janeiro, this species first flowered in England in Loddiges' nursery, and was described by Lindley in 1844. At one time it was considered to be conspecific with *L. xanthina*.* *L. johniana* and *L. goebeliana* are synonyms. (Reichenbach's *L. virens* of 1858 is a varietal form of *L. lobata**). *L. virens* grows mostly on trees in shady forests at 600–1,300 m above sea level in Espírito Santo, Rio de Janeiro, São Paulo and Minas Gerais. However, only a few plants are ever found in any single area.

The plants are typically up to 25 cm tall, but may reach 40 cm. The strongly compressed pseudobulbs are 6–16 cm tall and up to 2.5 cm wide, and become furrowed with age. The single fleshy leaf is more or less oblong, 10–20 cm long and 2.0–3.5 cm wide. From two to ten smallish flowers, which usually open little more than halfway, are borne in autumn or winter on short spikes. The tepals range from an almost translucent pale yellow to greenish-yellow. The lanceolate dorsal sepal is 2.0–2.5 cm long and about 0.7 cm wide, while the somewhat falcate laterals are slightly shorter. The elliptic to rhomboidal petals and the whitish lip, which is about 2 cm long, have slightly undulating margins. The erect lateral lobes of the lip and the deflexed apical lobe are rounded. In the throat are three very shallow ridges.

L. virens does best for us when mounted on cork or paperbark and grown in a semi-shaded position with intermediate conditions. It should be given ample water when in active growth, with a decided reduction in winter.

Actual flower size: 2–3 cm across.

Laelia xanthina Lindley

This species, which belongs to the section *Cattleyodes*, was introduced into cultivation in England by Backhouse and Sons in 1858. Lindley described it a year later. *L. wetmorei*, *Bletia flabellata* and *Bletia xanthina* are later synonyms. *L. xanthina* is found in southern Bahia, where it shares its habitat with *L. tenebrosa* and *L. grandis.** It is also found in shady forest areas in central Espírito Santo at 400–800 m above sea level. The forests of the latter area have been much reduced and are still being destroyed.

L. xanthina is a robust epiphyte with club-like pseudobulbs 15–22 cm tall and 2–3 cm wide. Each carries a single stiff leaf up to about 28 cm long — though often shorter — and 3–8 cm broad. From two to eight greenish-yellow to bright canary-yellow flowers, which last for about two weeks, are borne on an erect spike 10–24 cm long in summer. The oblong to lanceolate tepals usually have recurved lateral margins, but are occasionally flat. The sepals are about 3.0–4.5 cm long and 1–2 cm wide, while the petals are slightly shorter and broader. The obscurely three-lobed lip is white with a large patch of yellow in the throat and extending to the lateral lobes which curl up but do not quite meet above the column. The more or less rounded mid-lobe is somewhat deflexed, is coarsely undulating, and has three or more dark red to purple streaks.

L. xanthina may be mounted or potted in any well-drained medium. It needs humid, warm to intermediate conditions with moderately bright light to partial shade. Watering should be slightly reduced in winter.

Actual flower size: 5–9 cm across.

Laelio–cattleya hybrid (?)

Some years ago we received from Brazil seed of a plant known there as *Laelia dayana* var. *flammea*. A number of the seedlings which we raised have now flowered, and one of the clones is pictured here. We have been unable to identify this taxon, but the flowers show little variation, which suggests a genetically stable population. The plants resemble small-growing bifoliate cattleyas rather than species of the *hadrolaelia* section of *Laelia*, such as *L. dayana,** which, like all Brazilian laelias except *L. lundii,** are unifoliate.

On plants which have flowered for two successive years the pseudobulbs, which become ridged after the first year, are 8.5–10.0 cm tall and about 1 cm wide. In time, of course, the plants may grow larger. The spreading elliptic to lanceolate leaves are leathery with an acute apex. They are 6–10 cm long and 2.5–3.0 cm wide. Single flowers are produced on short spikes in winter. Unable to arrive at any reasonable identification, we sent colour transparencies to Dr J. A. Fowlie in the USA, who has done a great deal of work on Brazilian cattleyas, laelias and allied genera. He suggested that it might be a *Laelio–cattleya* hybrid, possibly between *L. pumila** and *C. intermedia.** Neither of these species, however, flowers in winter, as this taxon does. The lip certainly has the dark apical lobe and more open appearance of *C. intermedia*, while the sepals resemble those of *L. dayana* or *L. pumila*.

We hope to raise seedlings from a selfing of one of these plants, and these may in due course offer more clues to the true identity of this taxon.

Actual flower size: 8–9 cm across.

Lanium avicula (Ldl.) Bentham & Hooker

Belonging to a small genus from northern South America, this creeping epiphyte with its dainty flowers is closely related to the epidendrums. Indeed, it was first described by Lindley in 1841 as *Epidendrum avicula*. Bentham and Hooker, who created the genus *Lanium*, transferred this species to it in 1881. A relatively little-known species, *L. avicula* is native to Brazil and Amazonian Peru, growing in tall forests from the lowlands up to 1,800 m. Its branching rhizomes form extensive patches.

Mid-green pseudobulbs are set at 2 cm intervals and are 1–3 cm tall, narrow, with two spreading leaves at the apex. Typically 1.5–3.2 cm long, these leaves may be acute or rounded at the apex. Flowering in autumn or winter, this species produces terminal spikes 6–12 cm long carrying several well-spaced flowers about 1.2 cm in diameter. Both the spike and the outside of the sepals are covered with microscopic white hairs. The translucent yellow-brown to yellow-green flowers sometimes carry red spotting. The narrow petals are shorter than the broad 0.7 cm-long sepals, and are slightly reflexed. The shovel-shaped lip with its upturned edges is about 0.5 cm long by 0.4 cm broad.

This species, because of its rambling habit, is best mounted on treefern or similar material. It may also be grown in very shallow pans of coarse material such as chopped treefern chunks. Give medium to bright indirect light with water all year round. Although preferring intermediate to warm temperatures, this species will grow in cool conditions once well established.

Actual flower size: approximately 1.2 cm across.

Leptotes bicolor Lindley

This species, the seed capsules of which were once used to flavour ice-cream, was discovered by Harrison near Rio de Janeiro and described by Lindley in 1833. It belongs to a small genus related to cattleyas and laelias. Synonyms include *Bletia bicolor*, *Leptotes glaucophylla*, *L. serrulata* and *Tetramicra bicolor*. It is a native of southern Brazil and Paraguay, from coastal mountains to subtropical rainforests at 500–900 m.

The clustered cylindrical pseudobulbs are only 1–2 cm tall with a single succulent leaf which is usually 4–8 cm long, occasionally reaching 12 cm. Almost terete, the leaf is green, more or less spotted with purple, acutely pointed, and grooved on the upper surface. The 2 cm spike rises from the apex of the pseudobulb in winter and spring, with one to three fragrant flowers which open successively and last from four to six weeks. The fleshy flowers are 3–5 cm across, with narrow sepals which are sharply curved inward at the acute apex and whose margins are somewhat deflexed. The 1.5–2.0 cm lip has white or greenish lateral lobes which are erect on each side of the column, and a convex magenta-rose mid-lobe with a white upturned apex ending in a sharp point.

This delightful little species is an easy subject in cultivation, doing well when mounted on treefern or grown in a shallow pan of fibrous material. Intermediate temperatures suit it well. It should be given moderate shade with fairly high humidity and should never be allowed to dry out completely for any length of time.

Actual flower size: 3–5 cm across.

Leptotes tenuis Reichenbach (f.)

Originally described by Reichenbach, this attractive species originates from the cool humid mountains in the southern states of Espírito Santo, São Paulo and Santa Catarina. Its synonyms include *Leptotes minuta* and *L. pauloensis*.

The very slender 2 cm pseudobulbs are densely clustered on a creeping rhizome. Covered with papery bracts, they each bear a very narrow leaf 2–6 cm long which is minutely dimpled, almost terete, and sharply pointed. It is dark green, sometimes tinged with purple, and has a narrow groove on the upper surface. Flowers, 1.5 cm across, are borne on a 3–5 cm spike which rises from the apex of the pseudobulb in winter or spring. The colour is variable. The sepals and petals may be translucent creamy-white or yellowish-green, while the lip may be cream to pinkish with or without a maroon blotch in the centre. The lateral sepals are narrowly triangular, while the dorsal sepal and the petals are oblong with an acute apex. The sepals have a pale midvein. The white to pale-pink lateral lobes of the lip are erect and rounded, while the broad mid-lobe is rather convex with fringed edges.

L. tenuis does well when mounted on a good-sized treefern slab. It needs intermediate to cool conditions with light shade and fairly high humidity. It may also be grown in small pots of chopped treefern fibre or similar material. Year-round moisture suits it best, with some reduction in winter.

Actual flower size: approximately 1.5 cm across.

Leptotes unicolor Barbosa Rodrígues

This species was discovered in Minas Gerais by Barbosa Rodrígues, who described it in 1877. *L. paranaensis* is a later synonym by the same author. Confined in Brazil to the states of Minas Gerais and Paraná, where it inhabits the cooler mountains, *L. unicolor* is also found in Argentina.

The terete 0.4–1.0 cm tall pseudobulbs are only 0.2 cm in diameter. Each bears a single fleshy leaf, which is flat above and rounded beneath. Typically 2–5 cm long and 0.3–0.5 cm wide, the leaf has a central groove above, an acute apex and minute dimpling. It may be slightly curved and is often tinged or spotted with purple. In winter, a short more or less pendent spike from the apex of the pseudobulb carries up to three flowers about 2.0–2.5 cm across. These range in colour from white to pale rosy-pink to bright violet. The lanceolate sepals and linear petals all curve inward and are 2.0–2.5 cm long with acute apices. The sepals are about 0.3 cm wide. The three-lobed lip, from 2.0–2.5 cm long, is fleshy and may be vaguely recurved. The small lateral lobes are almost triangular, while the lanceolate to triangular mid-lobe has a short tapering point.

L. unicolor is easily managed in cultivation. It does best for us when mounted on either treefern, paperbark or cork. It prefers an intermediate to cool environment with moderate shade and relatively high humidity. Copious water should be given when the plant is in active growth, with a significant reduction in winter. However, plants should never be allowed to dry out completely, and regular misting are beneficial.

Actual flower size: 2–2.5 cm across.

Lockhartia lunifera (Ldl.) Reichenbach (f.)

This species was discovered by Descourtilz and described in 1839 by Lindley as *Fernandezia lunifera*. Reichenbach transferred it to *Lockhartia* in 1852. *L. lunifera* occurs in the hot humid lowlands of Amapá and Pará, and in the cooler mountains and warmer lowlands of Bahia, Espírito Santo, Rio de Janeiro, São Paulo, Santa Catarina and Rio Grande do Sul.

It is an epiphyte with a cluster of flat leafy stems 10–35 cm long and about 1.5 cm wide, with overlapping tongue-shaped to almost triangular leaves clasping the stem. From 1.6–2.0 cm long and 0.5–0.7 cm wide near the base, these mid-green leaves are somewhat fleshy. In summer or autumn wiry spikes about 4 cm long are produced from between the leaves, mostly near the apices of the stems. They carry from one to three golden yellow flowers about 1.8 cm long with red-brown markings on the lip. These open in succession and have tepals which are 0.5–1.0 cm long and up to 0.6 cm wide. The sepals are more or less ovoid with a short sharp point at the apex. The petals, whose undulating lateral margins are somewhat deflexed, are oblong to rounded. The 0.8–1.2 cm-long lip has long arm-like lateral lobes which curve forward and upward. The mid-lobe is somewhat fiddle-shaped, deflexed in the basal half, and bilobed at the apex. The disc has a large warty callus. The ear-like column wings have toothed margins.

L. lunifera prefers a humid warm to intermediate environment with semi-shade and year-round moisture. It may be mounted on treefern slabs or grown in small pots of fairly tightly packed treefern fibre or similar material.

Actual flower size: 1.3–2 cm long.

Loefgrenianthus blanche-amesii (Loef.) Hoehne

Still quite rare in collections, this epiphyte was originally described by Loefgren, a Swede who became head of the Botanical section of the Botanical Gardens in Rio de Janeiro. He named it *Leptotes blanche-amesii* in honour of Blanche Ames, noted botanical artist and wife of well-known Harvard botanist, Oakes Ames. Hoehne, Director of the Botanical Institute of São Paulo, later separated it from *Leptotes*, creating the genus *Loefgrenianthius*, which remains monotypic. A native of the states of Rio de Janeiro, São Paulo and Paraná, *L. blanche-amesii* grows on mossy trees in the cool damp mountain ranges. It shares at least part of its range in the Serra da Mantiqueira at 1,000–2,000 m above sea level with orchid species which include *Isochilus linearis,** *Oncidium crispum** and *Sophronitella violacea.**

The more or less zigzag pendulous stems of this species may reach 30 cm or more. The fleshy leaves are approximately 3–6 cm long and are slightly recurved at the acute apex. The relatively large flowers are borne on short stems. The petals and sepals are usually white, while the lip is orange and/or yellow. The lanceolate to oblong sepals are about 1.2 cm long, with the dorsal narrower than the lateral sepals. The more or less linear petals are narrow, about 1 cm long, and slightly recurved. The 0.9 cm-long lip is pointed at the apex. The purple anther cap lends a nice contrast to the rest of the flower.

L. blanche-amesii does best when grown on a moisture-retentive mount such as treefern, with year-round moisture and moderate shade in a humid cool environment.

Actual flower size: approximately 2 cm across.

Lycaste macrophylla (Poepp. & Endl.) Lindley

Described in 1836 by Poeppig and Endlicher as *Maxillaria macrophylla*, this species was transferred to *Lycaste* by Lindley in 1843. Synonyms include *L. plana* and *L. dowiana*. *L. macrophylla* occurs from Costa Rica to Peru, Bolivia and Brazil, where it is found in Mato Grosso and Amazonas. It grows epiphytically or as a terrestrial in hot humid forests at relatively low altitudes, although in Peru it is found up to 2,400 m above sea level.

The ovoid to oblong-cylindrical pseudobulbs are 4–10 cm tall and 3–6 cm wide. At the base are several papery bracts and a pair of leaf-bearing bracts. At the apex are two or three deciduous plicate leaves 40–80 cm long and 10–22 cm wide. Single fragrant flowers are produced at various times, mostly in spring to summer, on 8–20 cm spikes (occasionally longer) from the base of the pseudobulbs. The lanceolate to elliptic sepals, which are olive-green to coppery brown or brownish-purple, are 4.5–7.0 cm long. The dorsal is 1.5–2.5 cm wide. The slightly wider laterals are joined to the foot of the column to form a short chin. The shorter and narrower petals are white to cream, often streaked or spotted with pink-red. They lie parallel to the column before recurving. The white 3–5 cm-long lip is often spotted with pink-red. The lateral lobes are erect, while the deflexed mid-lobe is ovate to elliptic with hairy undulating margins.

L. macrophylla is relatively temperature tolerant, and requires a humid environment with diffuse bright light. A medium to coarse potting mix is required, which should be kept a little drier in winter.

Actual flower size: 8–12 cm across.

Masdevallia curtipes (?) Barbosa Rodrígues

Using the key and drawings from Pabst & Dungs' *Orchidaceae Brasilienses*, we have tentatively identified this species as *M. curtipes*, described by Barbosa Rodrígues, but there remains some uncertainty in our minds. It clearly belongs, however, to the subgenus *Masdevallia*, section *polyanthae*, subsection *alaticaules*. The plant arrived from Brazil some years ago in a batch of *M. infracta*,* which it resembles vegetatively. *M. curtipes* is reported to grow on mossy trees in the mountains of Rio de Janeiro.

The clustered fleshy leaves are sub-erect to arching, with papery sheaths on the short petioles. About 2 cm wide and 8–15 cm long, they are minutely toothed at the obtuse apex. The three-angled flower spike rises from the base of the leaf. It carries only one flower, but should not be removed until quite dead, as it will produce up to five flowers over a period of time. The sepals are joined to form a short tube, with a very small chin at the base. The concave dorsal sepal is yellow with reddish markings and an erect 2.0–3.5 cm-long yellow tail. It is about 1.3 cm long, excluding the tail, as are the maroon lateral sepals which spread more widely than in *M. infracta*, and also have yellow tails. The more or less oblong petals are yellow, with or without red streaks, 0.6 cm long and only 0.15 cm wide, and point forward. The narrow maroon lip is about 0.6 cm long and somewhat fiddle-shaped, with a sharp point in the middle of the apex.

This species grows best in a cool to intermediate shady environment with year round moisture. As with all species which favour cool damp conditions, good ventilation or air movement is especially important.

Actual flower size: approximately 2 cm across.

Masdevallia infracta Lindley (1)

L indley described *Masdevallia infracta* early in the 1830s. *M. longicaudata* and probably *M. forgetiana* are conspecific. This epiphytic species occurs in Peru and in the Brazilian states of Espírito Santo, Minas Gerais, Rio de Janeiro and São Paulo.

The plants have no pseudobulbs. The clustered glossy green leaves are sub-erect to spreading. From 8–15 cm long, including the short grooved petiole, and 2.0–2.5 cm wide, they are oblong to elliptic with a minutely three-toothed apex. They are fleshy, with a few sheaths covering the petiole. Flower spikes from 10–20 cm long are produced from the base of the leaf in spring or early summer. Although spikes carry only one flower at a time, they should not be removed until obviously dead as they will produce up to five flowers over a period of time. Flower colour is extremely variable (see *M. infracta* Lindley (2)). The sepals are joined at the base to form a tube about 1.3 cm long. The free part of the dorsal sepal is triangular, concave, and ends in a more or less erect tail of 4 cm or more. The lateral sepals are joined for almost their entire length, except for their tails. Near the base is a sharp bend, producing a prominent chin and a swollen 'stomach' — as is seen clearly in the clone pictured here. The narrow 0.8 cm-long petals are linear to oblong with a sharp point at the apex, and lie parallel to the column. The oblong to fiddle-shaped lip is 0.6–0.8 cm long, with a reflexed apex. *Masdevallia* species were immensely popular a century ago, and in recent years have regained much of that popularity.

Actual flower size: 6.5–8 cm long.

Masdevallia infracta Lindley (2)

D iscovered by Descourtilz in the mountains near Rio de Janeiro in 1809, *M. infracta* was one of the first *Masdevallia* species to be cultivated in Europe.

It usually has a three-angled flower spike, which places it in the subgenus *Masdevallia*, section *polyanthae*, subsection *alaticaules*. *M. infracta* is one of the more easily obtainable masdevallias, and its ease of culture has ensured its continuing popularity. The colour variation in the flowers is so great from one clone to another, that it is well worth growing several clones of the species. The sepals may be almost white, pale yellow, orange, pale lilac, reddish-purple, wine-red or amethyst, usually with darker longitudinal veins. Regardless of general flower colour, the lateral sepals normally have some violet or reddish-purple on the inside. Of the three sepals, the dorsal is usually paler than the laterals. The tails of the sepals are usually yellow, while the largely hidden petals are white. The deflexed lip tends to be red or purple, especially near the apex. Despite the enormous colour variation in the flowers, there is only one named variety. *M. infracta* var. *purpurea* was described by Reichenbach in 1883 as having larger flowers which are almost completely a rich violet-purple.

M. infracta needs a shady position in a cool to intermediate environment. It may be mounted on treefern slabs with a little moss about the roots or potted in a freely draining mixture. It should never be allowed to dry out completely. This species is a little more tolerant of higher summer temperatures than many high-altitude *Masdevallia* species.

Actual flower size: 6.5–8 cm long.

Maxillaria desvauxiana Reichenbach (f.)

Reichenbach described this species in 1855, naming it in honour of Desvaux, of Paris, in whose collection it had flowered. *M. coriacea* is conspecific, along with *M. petiolaris* (A. Richard ex Reichenbach, *not* Schlechter). *M. desvauxiana* occurs in Colombia, Venezuela, Guyana, Suriname and French Guiana, from sea level to 1,500 m. In Brazil it grows epiphytically in the humid lowlands along the east coast from Bahia to Santa Catarina.

The ovoid, slightly compressed pseudobulbs are dark green with purple-black markings. They are 2–6 cm tall and 2.5–3.5 cm wide. At the base are a few brownish bracts. Each pseudobulb carries a single lanceolate leaf 15–40 cm long including the short petiole. Single fleshy flowers are borne on spikes up to 6 cm long from the base of the pseudobulb. They are pleasantly redolent of watermelon. The lanceolate to more or less elliptic sepals are yellowish-pink suffused with maroon. From 2.6–3.0 cm long and up to 1.3 cm wide, they have reflexed margins. The shorter, wider petals are rounded with slightly recurved apices. They are held forward and are darker than the sepals. The 2.4 cm-long lip is maroon with paler edges. The long narrow lateral lobes are erect with rounded front edges, while the rounded mid-lobe is recurved. The disc has an oblong fleshy callus, and there is a dark, very warty callus on the apical lobe.

M. desvauxiana requires a humid, intermediate to warm environment with semi-shade. A freely draining substrate is essential. Water copiously when in growth, and never allow to dry out completely.
Actual flower size: 5–6 cm across.

Maxillaria discolor (Lodd. ex Ldl.) Reichenbach (f.)

Closely related to *M. crassifolia*, this epiphyte was described as *Dicrypta discolor* by Lindley in 1839, using material from Loddiges. Reichenbach transferred it to *Maxillaria* in 1863. *M. longifolia* is a later synonym. In Brazil, *M. discolor* inhabits the hot humid lowlands of Amazonas, Amapá, Pará and Bahia. It also occurs in Venezuela, Colombia, Peru and the West Indies.

The mid-green, ovoid to oblong pseudobulbs are strongly compressed, 6–10 cm long and 2–3 cm wide. They are almost completely obscured by four to six basal leaves, which — along with the single apical leaf — form a loose fan. The leathery leaves, which are 16–35 cm long and up to 5 cm wide, are folded at the base and have a sub-acute asymmetrical apex. Flowering is mostly in summer, but may occur at other times. Single very fleshy flowers are borne on very short spikes from the leaf axils. The tepals are yellow to greenish-yellow. The oblong to lanceolate sepals are 1.6–2.0 cm long and about 0.6 cm wide. The petals are slightly smaller and project forward. These oblong petals have an acute triangular apex. The hinged lip is orange, often spotted with purple. From 1.4–1.6 cm long, it has curved, erect lateral lobes and a more or less triangular, slightly deflexed, apical lobe. An oblong callus runs the length of the lip, except for a break in the middle.

Although originating from hot lowland areas, this species adapts well to cooler conditions. Our plants do well with an 8°C minimum night temperature. Plants need moderately bright light and a well-drained medium with year-round moisture.
Actual flower size: 3–3.5 cm across.

Maxillaria juergensii Schlechter

Discovered in 1922 by Juergens, after whom Schlechter named it in 1925, this species grows on mossy trees in the mountains of São Paulo, Paraná, Santa Catarina and Rio Grande do Sul at elevations of 350 m and above.

Each plant comprises a cluster of branching rhizomes covered with papery bracts which also partly cover the 1–2 cm pseudobulbs. Roots are produced only towards the base of the rhizome, so that plants tend to become pendulous. Set from 0.25–1.0 cm apart, the ridged pseudobulbs are more or less spindle-shaped and bear one or two sub-erect leaves 3–4 cm long. These are dark green, sharply acute, and have a prominent keel. Single flowers are borne in spring on erect spikes 1–2 cm long arising from the base of the pseudobulbs. The fleshy 2.5–3.0 cm flowers are globular with maroon tepals which are paler towards the base. The dorsal sepal, which is slightly shorter than the 1.2–1.5 cm laterals, is concave and hoods the column. The 1 cm-long petals are parallel to the column and turned up at the apex. The base of the broad lip is pale yellow-green heavily spotted with maroon. The rest of the lip is maroon. There is an elongated glossy callus on the basal section, and a rounded apical half which is bent at a 90 degree angle. The whole flower is extremely glossy.

This species does well on a treefern mount, but may also be grown in a suspended pot, allowing the plant to trail over the edges. We use a mixture of treefern, pine-bark, and a small amount of fresh sphagnum moss. It should be kept moist all year round. Intermediate to cool conditions in semi-shade suit this species.

Actual flower size: 2.5–3.5 cm across.

Maxillaria leucaimata Barbosa Rodrígues

Described by Barbosa Rodrígues in the late nineteenth century, *M. leucaimata* grows epiphytically in the hot humid lowlands of Amazonas, Pará and Ceará, and also in the cooler mountains of Espírito Santo and Minas Gerais, and south as far as Santa Catarina.

The clustered pseudobulbs are more or less ovoid and strongly compressed. From 2.5–4.0 cm long and 1.5–2.0 cm wide, each has one or two leaf-bearing bracts at the base and a single arching leaf at the apex. This elliptic to lanceolate leaf, from 16–23 cm long and up to 3.5 cm wide, is folded at the base to form a petiole about 4 cm long. In late winter or spring a single flower is borne on an erect spike about 8 cm long from the base of the pseudobulb. The fleshy tepals are somewhat translucent, and pale yellow more or less suffused with maroon-purple. The sepals resemble an elongated triangle. The dorsal sepal, which curves forward, is about 3 cm long and nearly 1 cm wide at the concave thickened base. The slightly longer lateral sepals are partly twisted, and then curve downward. The narrower, more or less lanceolate petals point forward, and are 2.5 cm long. The 2 cm-long hinged lip is covered with very fine powder. The erect lateral lobes are suffused and edged with maroon-purple, while the obtuse to rounded apical lobe is very fleshy and has irregularly notched margins. There is a raised callus near the centre of the lip.

M. leucaimata needs a semi-shaded position in an intermediate to warm environment with year-round moisture. It grows well for us in suspended pots of chopped treefern fibre.

Actual flower size: approximately 3.5 cm across.

Maxillaria lindleyana Schlechter

Lindley was the first to describe this species, naming it *Maxillaria crocea*. However, this name had already been used by Poeppig and Endlicher in 1836 for a Peruvian maxillaria, thus rendering Lindley's name invalid. Schlechter later renamed the species in Lindley's honour. Like so many maxillarias, it comes from mountain areas from Espírito Santo to Santa Catarina.

The somewhat compressed pseudobulbs are oval, 1.5–2.5 cm tall and up to 1.5 cm across at the widest point. They are yellowish-green and have several sheaths at the base. A single matt-green leaf, 11–20 cm long, is borne at the apex of the pseudobulb. It is folded at the base, otherwise more or less flat, with an uneven apex and a prominent mid-vein beneath. The erect spike is 5 cm or more long and carries a single yellow flower. The tepals all taper sharply to acute tips, with the 2 cm dorsal sepal hooding the column. The spreading lateral sepals are 2.5 cm long. The petals, about 1.7 cm long, project forward and curve inward at the tip, sometimes even meeting and crossing. The 1 cm oval lip is marked with reddish brown and has a long raised callus which is covered with minute hairs at its apex. The apex of the lip is irregular.

This species does well in intermediate to cool conditions and semi-shade. We grow our plants in suspended pots of treefern fibre, pine-bark and sphagnum moss. Pots are well crocked with broken polyurethane pieces to reduce weight. Plants may also be mounted. They should be kept moist all year round.

Actual flower size: approximately 4 cm across.

Maxillaria notylioglossa Reichenbach (f.)

More commonly known as *Maxillaria meirax*, this species, which closely resembles *M. cerifera*, was described by Reichenbach in 1854. It occurs throughout most of Venezuela as well as in southern Brazil, where it inhabits the cool mountains of São Paulo and Rio de Janeiro as well as the savannah country of Minas Gerais.

The 2–3 cm-tall pseudobulbs are set 2 cm apart on a creeping rhizome covered with several sheaths. The flattened pseudobulbs, 2–4 cm long, curve upward, and become wrinkled with age. The two narrow leaves are 5–12 cm long, flat, and bilobed at the ends. The erect 3.5–5.0 cm spike carries a single pale green flower which does not open widely. The 1.0–1.2 cm sepals have sharp protruding points at the somewhat rounded apices. The lateral sepals, which form a shallow chin at the base, are projected forward. The narrow 0.7 cm petals are acute, and lie alongside the column. The obscurely three-lobed lip has a short claw with a raised ridge. The erect lateral lobes are rounded, whereas the mid-lobe is triangular. It has a rounded callus near the base, in front of which is a dark brown spot. A frosty white v-shaped ridge extends from midway along the sides to near the apex. The anther cap is dark purple.

This interesting little species grows well in a suspended pot or basket, which allows the plant to trail over the edges. Our plants are grown in a mixture of treefern chunks, pine-bark and leaf-mould or moss. *M. notylioglossa* prefers intermediate conditions with moderate shade and all-year-round moisture.

Actual flower size: 1.5–2 cm across.

Maxillaria ochroleuca Loddiges ex Lindley

Closely related to *M. bradei* and *M. rodriguesii*, this epiphyte was described by Lindley in 1832, using material from Loddiges. *M. ochroleuca* occurs in Venezuela, as well as in the Brazilian states of Espírito Santo, Minas Gerais, Rio de Janeiro, São Paulo, Paraná and Santa Catarina, where it inhabits the cooler mountain areas.

The ovoid pseudobulbs are compressed, 4.0–7.5 cm long and 2.0–3.5 cm wide. They are yellow-green to mid-green with two to four leaves at the base and a single strap-like leaf, 20–30 cm long and up to 2.7 cm wide, at the apex. The leaves are bilobed at the asymmetrical apex. In late spring or summer several single flowers are produced on short spikes from the base of the pseudobulbs. (The var. *longipes* from Venezuela has much longer spikes.) The spidery flowers are usually cream to pale yellow with a dark orange lip, although Pabst and Dungs also show a yellow form in *Orchidaceae Brasilienses*. Flowers do not open fully. The narrow tepals taper to sharp apices, with the sepals about 4 cm long and 0.4 cm wide at the base. The shorter, narrower petals are usually held forward and sometimes cross over. The hinged 1 cm-long lip has erect lateral lobes and a rounded to sub-acute apical lobe which is sparsely haired. In the throat is an oblong fleshy callus with minute hairs and a rounded apex.

M. ochroleuca may be mounted, but does well when grown in a suspended pot of well-drained medium. It needs partial shade in cool to intermediate conditions. Give plenty of water while in growth, with some reduction in winter.

Actual flower size: approximately 3 cm across.

Maxillaria parahybunensis Cogniaux

This is a little-known species, described about the end of the nineteenth century by Cogniaux. It is found in the cool shady mountain forests of São Paulo and Minas Gerais, where it grows on mossy trees at moderate elevations.

The dark green to purplish-green pseudobulbs are closely set on a very short rhizome which produces roots only near the base, so that plants tend to the suberect or pendulous. The 1 cm-long pseudobulbs are cylindrical with prominent ribbing and basal sheaths. The single fleshy leaf is keeled beneath and more or less flat above with a central groove. From 3–5 cm long, it tapers to a sharp point. The flowers are very similar to those of *M. juergensii*,* and are borne on a very short spike in late spring or early summer. The 1.2 cm sepals and 0.9 cm petals are pale yellow-green and very heavily suffused with pinkish-brown. All have rounded or obtuse apices. The concave dorsal sepal is hooded over the column and forward pointing petals, while the partially spreading lateral sepals are broadly triangular. The oblong 1 cm lip is bent halfway along its length, with small erect lateral lobes and a broad rounded mid-lobe. The longitudinal callus at the base is a very glossy dark brown.

This species does well when mounted on small blocks of treefern or placed in small pots of treefern fibre, etc. It prefers an intermediate to cool environment with semi-shade and year-round moisture. Large mounts or pots should be avoided, as these may retain too much water.

Actual flower size: approximately 1 cm across.

Maxillaria phoenicanthera Barbosa Rodrígues

Barbosa Rodrígues described this species, which belongs to the *M. picta** alliance, in the latter half of the nineteenth century. Schlechter's *M. punctata*, is synonymous, but not that of Loddiges. *M. phoenicanthera* inhabits the cooler mountains of Minas Gerais, Espírito Santo, Rio de Janeiro, São Paulo and Paraná.

The clustered ovoid to oblong pseudobulbs become strongly ridged with age. Laterally compressed, they are 4–5 cm tall and about 2 cm wide. Several brown papery bracts clasp the pseudobulb, which has two oblong to lanceolate leaves at the apex. From 17–26 cm long and up to 2.6 cm wide, these are folded at the base to form a short petiole. Several spikes about 3 cm long are produced in winter from the base of the pseudobulb. Each carries a single fleshy flower with a 3 cm-long ovary. The lanceolate sepals and narrow 1.5–2.0 cm petals are pale yellow with a few purple spots on the outside. The sepals are 1.8–2.7 cm long and up to 0.8 cm wide, with the dorsal projected over the column and the laterals spreading. The petals are held forward. The creamish, 1.3 cm-long lip is finely edged with purple. The long narrow lateral lobes have purple streaks, while the recurved mid-lobe has a few spots on the reverse. An oblong fleshy crest runs down the centre of the lip to the base of the apical lobe. The pale yellow column is streaked with purple and topped with a maroon-purple anther cap.

M. phoenicanthera does well when mounted on a treefern slab, but may also be potted. It needs a shady intermediate environment with good ventilation or air movement.

Actual flower size: approximately 2.5 cm across.

Maxillaria picta Hooker

Harrison introduced this species to England by sending plants, which he had collected near Rio de Janeiro, to a relative. Hooker described it in 1832. Synonyms include *M. leucocheile* and *M. fuscata*. Occasionally lithophytic, *M. picta* usually grows epiphytically in the cooler mountain regions of Minas Gerais, Rio de Janeiro and the southern states.

The slightly flattened ovoid pseudobulbs are 3.0–5.5 cm tall and up to 3.5 cm broad, and become furrowed with age. Each has two strap-like leaves 20–47 cm long at the apex. From 1.5–2.0 cm wide, they are folded at the base to form a short petiole. In winter several single flowers are produced on spikes up to 10 cm long which rise from the base of the pseudobulb. These fleshy flowers last well and are usually strongly fragrant. The oblong tepals are pale yellow with purple blotches on the outside, and darker golden yellow on the inside. The 2.5–3.0 cm-long dorsal sepal is 0.8 cm wide and curves forward above the purple column, while the shorter narrower petals, which have red-purple blotches inside at the base, point forward. The somewhat spreading lateral sepals are 3.0–3.5 cm long. The 1.8–2.5 cm-long lip is pale yellow with purple on the narrow erect lateral lobes, which are about 1 cm long with rounded margins. The tongue-like mid-lobe is reflexed and has irregular slightly wavy edges. An oblong callus runs from the base down the centre of the lip for half its length.

M. picta is a very hardy species, doing well either mounted or potted in a semi-shaded position in intermediate, cool, or even cold conditions.

Actual flower size: 4–5 cm across.

Maxillaria plebeja Reichenbach (f.)

Closely related to *M. pumila*, *M. parahybunensis** and *M. spannagelii*, this little-known maxillaria was described by Reichenbach in the nineteenth century. It is not Hoehne's *M. plebeja*, which is synonymous with *M. ferdinandiana*. *M. plebeja* grows on mossy trees and rocks in the cool coastal mountains of Rio de Janeiro, São Paulo, Paraná and Santa Catarina.

The pendent plants have roots only on the basal pseudobulbs. The dark green pseudobulbs are closely set on a rambling rhizome and are almost covered by brown papery sheaths. About 1 cm long, they are more or less oval with several grooves. Each bears a single very fleshy leaf about 3–6 cm long and 0.5 cm wide. It is linear to lanceolate with a very sharp acute apex, triangular in cross-section, and has one or more shallow grooves on the upper surface. Single greenish-yellow flowers appear in mid-winter on extremely short spikes from the base of the pseudobulb. They do not open widely. The oblong to lanceolate dorsal sepal, which is about 1 cm long and 0.5 cm wide, is projected over the column. The wider lateral sepals are somewhat recurved. The shorter, narrower petals are linear and point forward before recurving at the apex. The vaguely three-lobed lip is 0.8 cm long. It is suffused with red-brown and gently deflexed. The rounded lateral lobes are erect, and the more or less oblong mid-lobe is indistinctly bilobed at the 0.4 cm-wide apex.

M. plebeja does well mounted on a treefern slab and grown in a cool environment with semi-shade and year-round moisture.

Actual flower size: approximately 0.8 cm across.

Maxillaria porphyrostele Reichenbach (f.)

This species is related to *M. picta*,* *M. phoenicanthera** and *M. rupestris*, and was introduced into England from Rio Grande do Sul by Bull of Chelsea. It first flowered in England in 1873. Reichenbach described it shortly afterwards, naming it for its purple column. *M. porphyrostele* inhabits the cooler areas of São Paulo, Paraná, Santa Catarina, Rio Grande do Sul and Minas Gerais.

The slightly compressed, ovoid to almost globose pseudobulbs are 2.5–3.5 cm tall and become wrinkled and furrowed with age. Each has several papery bracts at the base and two strap-like spreading leaves at the apex. From 12–30 cm long, these are 1.5 cm wide and folded at the base. From mid-winter to early spring spikes up to 12 cm long carry single long-lasting flowers about 4 cm across. The more or less oblong dorsal sepal and petals and the lanceolate to narrowly triangular laterals are bright yellow, sometimes sparsely spotted with purple on the reverse. The 2.3 cm-long dorsal sepal and the shorter narrower petals, which have a few red-purple streaks at the base, point forward. The spreading laterals are 2.5 cm long and 0.7 cm wide near the base. The three-lobed 1.8 cm-long lip is pale yellow with reddish streaks on the erect almost oblong lateral lobes. The almost square mid-lobe is recurved, with a rounded apex and irregular undulating edges. There is a raised warty callus in the throat.

M. porphyrostele is a very hardy species, tolerating even cold winter conditions as long as it is kept fairly dry. It prefers, however, intermediate to cool temperatures with semi-shade and good air movement.

Actual flower size: approximately 4 cm across.

Maxillaria rodriguesii Cogniaux

This robust epiphyte from the mountains of Rio de Janeiro was described about the end of nineteenth century by Cogniaux, who named it in honour of Barbosa Rodrígues. Barbosa Rodrígues' *M. longipetala* is conspecific, but not that of Ruíz and Pavón.

The closely set pseudobulbs are yellow-green, 5–8 cm tall and 2.5–3.0 cm wide. They are more or less elliptic and somewhat flattened. At the apex is a single sub-erect leaf 18–26 cm long and up to 2.5 cm wide. There are two leaf-bearing bracts on either side of the base of the pseudobulb. Single flowers are borne predominantly in summer, but occasionally also in winter, on 3–5 cm-long spikes, several often appearing from the base of a single pseudobulb. The tepals are pale, almost translucent, yellow with darker fleshier apices, which are long and tapering. The 2.5 cm-long dorsal sepal is 0.5 cm wide at the concave base and, together with the slightly shorter narrower petals, point forward. The lateral sepals form a short chin at the base. The inside of the hinged lip is covered with minute white hairs, less so on the more or less oblong erect lateral lobes. The throat and the lateral lobes are a translucent pale yellow with purple-red spots and margins. The oblong apical lobe is very fleshy, rounded at the apex, and a solid yellow colour. An oblong callus runs down the centre to the base of the apical lobe.

M. rodriguesii is an easy plant in cultivation and a vigorous grower. It does well in a semi-shaded position with intermediate to cool conditions. It needs year-round moisture, with some reduction in watering during winter.

Actual flower size: approximately 3 cm across.

Maxillaria rufescens Lindley

Introduced into cultivation from Trinidad, this epiphyte was described by Lindley in 1836. Synonyms include *M. abelei* and *M. vanillodora*, the latter name indicating its vanilla-like fragrance. *M. rufescens* is widespread from Mexico to Peru and Brazil. In Brazil it grows in the hot humid lowlands of Acre, Amazonas, Bahia, Minas Gerais, Espírito Santo and the southern states. In other countries it is found at altitudes up to 1,700 m above sea level.

The compressed dull-green pseudobulbs are 1.5–6.5 cm long and up to 2 cm wide. They are ovate to oblong, with several brownish bracts at the base. The fleshy apical leaf is 4–35 cm long, 2–5 cm wide, and strap-like with an acute apex. Single flowers are produced on 1.5–7.0 cm-long spikes from the base of the pseudobulb, mostly in early winter. The oblong to lanceolate tepals may be yellow, orange, reddish, pinkish-brown or even white. The petals are often yellow, regardless of the colour of the sepals. The concave dorsal sepal is 0.9–2.4 cm long and 0.3–0.9 cm wide, while the lateral sepals, which are joined to the column to form a short chin, are slightly wider. The petals are narrower and shorter. The lip is typically yellow with some red-purple spotting. The erect lateral lobes are somewhat falcate, while the reflexed mid-lobe is oblong. The yellow to orange disc has a linear to oblong ridge extending to the middle of the lip.

M. rufescens does best in intermediate to warm conditions, with high humidity and moderate light. It may be mounted or potted.

Actual flower size: 3–4 cm across.

Maxillaria seidelii Pabst

A relatively recent discovery, this species was named by Pabst in honour of Alvim Seidel, proprietor of one of the oldest orchid nurseries in Brazil, who has collected a number of new species. Confined to the state of Rio de Janeiro, this species inhabits the cool mountain ranges at moderate elevations. The area of its habitat, where it favours mossy tree trunks as hosts, is cool, moist and subject to nightly mists.

The mid-green pseudobulbs of *M. seidelii* are densely clustered on a short creeping rhizome which may be erect or pendent, as roots are formed only on the basal portion. These oblong pseudobulbs, which are partially hidden by brown sheaths, are up to 1 cm tall and 0.4 cm in diameter. They have several very shallow grooves and bear two sharp-pointed needle-like leaves 3–4 cm long. Single flowers are borne on very short spikes from the base of the pseudobulb in spring or summer. These yellow bell-shaped flowers are about 1 cm long. The oblong sepals are 1 cm in length and curved at the acute apex, while the petals are slightly shorter. The 0.75 cm lip is oblong with a blunt apex. The area near the base of the callus is suffused with reddish-brown.

M. seidelii grows well mounted on small treefern slabs, but may also be grown in small pots of fairly fine material such as treefern fibre and sphagnum moss. It prefers intermediate to cool conditions with year-round moisture, good air movement and semi-shade.

Actual flower size: approximately 1 cm long.

Maxillaria species — *subulata* alliance

This epiphyte belongs to the *M. subulata* alliance, which includes *M. acicularis*, *M. juergensii** and *M. seidelii.** These species all inhabit the mountains of Minas Gerais, Espírito Santo, Rio de Janeiro and the southern states, and we suspect that the species illustrated here does, too.

The plants are mostly pendent, with roots only on those pseudobulbs closest to the host. The closely-set dark green pseudobulbs, which are 1.2–1.8 cm long and 0.5 cm wide, are almost totally covered with brown papery bracts. They are furrowed, and taper at both ends. The two apical leaves are linear, tapering to an acute apex. From 2.0–4.5 cm long and up to 0.3 cm wide, they are semi-circular in cross-section, with a single channel on the upper surface when young. Several shallow grooves become apparent as leaves age. Single flowers, similar to those of *M. juergensii*, are borne on 1 cm-long spikes from the base of the pseudobulb. They are buff to pale green, very heavily suffused with pink-brown. The lanceolate concave dorsal sepal is hooded over the column. The wide lateral sepals are slightly spreading, while the petals lie parallel to the column before reflexing at the apex. The lip has a large, almost black, glossy callus on the disc. The narrow lateral lobes are erect, while the mid-lobe is oblong with an almost triangular recurved apical section. The apical section of the lip in *M. juergensii* is wider and more rounded.

This species may be mounted, or potted and allowed to trail over the pot rim. It needs intermediate to cool conditions, and a shady position.

Actual flower size: approximately 1 cm across.

Maxillaria ubatubana Hoehne

Described by Hoehne sometime prior to 1959, this species is closely related to *M. picta,** *M. porphyrostele,** *M. rupestris,* etc. *M. ubatubana* grows epiphytically — and occasionally on mossy rocks — in the cool moist mountain ranges of Espírito Santo, Rio de Janeiro and São Paulo.

The mid- to dark green pseudobulbs are clustered, with brown papery bracts at their bases. From 4–5 cm tall and about 2 cm wide, they are vaguely four-angled. At the apex are two strap-like leaves 30–40 cm long and about 2 cm wide. Single flowers are borne in late spring or early summer on erect spikes up to 10 cm long which rise from the base of the pseudobulbs. The oblong tepals, which have tapering apices, are yellow, often suffused with maroon on the edges. The sepals are about 4 cm long and 1 cm wide, with the dorsal sepal curving over the column and the laterals more or less spreading. The slightly incurved petals lie parallel to the column. The 2.8 cm-long lip is pale yellow with maroon blotches. The erect to sub-erect lateral lobes are more or less oblong with rounded apices. The mid-lobe has irregular margins, a thickened callus in the throat and a deflexed, somewhat triangular apical lobe.

M. ubatubana grows well in cool to intermediate conditions with semi-shade. It requires plenty of water when in active growth, with some reduction winter. It may be mounted, but grows very well for us when placed in suspended pots of chopped treefern fibre. Good drainage is essential, but plants should not be allowed to dry out completely for any extended period.

Actual flower size: approximately 4 cm across.

Miltonia candida Lindley

Lindley based his 1838 description of this species on material which was originally imported by the Earl of Arran and sent to the Botanic Garden at Glasnevin in Scotland. Found in the states of Espírito Santo, Rio de Janeiro, São Paulo and Minas Gerais, *M. candida* grows as an epiphyte in both cooler mountain regions and the warmer lowlands.

The tapering pseudobulbs are strongly compressed and closely set on a branching rhizome. From 6–9 cm tall, they are 2–3 cm wide at the base. There are two or more leaf-bearing bracts at the base and two strap-like leaves at the apex. From 20–30 cm long and 2.0–2.5 cm wide, these taper to an acute apex. From three to eight long-lasting flowers are borne in autumn on a sub-erect spike 12–30 cm long which rises from the base of the pseudobulb. The fleshy tepals are chestnut-brown, more or less barred and blotched with yellow, and sometimes have recurved margins. The sepals are about 4 cm long and 1.5 cm wide, while the petals are about 3 cm long. The scoop-shaped lip is almost round to oval, and curves up at the base to touch the column. From 3.0–3.5 cm long, the lip is white with or without two violet spots in the centre. It has wavy edges, and typically bears five raised keels on the basal half. The column has a roundish wing on each side of the stigma, and two prominent spurs beneath the wings.

M. candida appreciates intermediate to warm conditions, moderately bright light, and plenty of water when in growth followed by a slightly drier rest after flowering. It may be potted, but grows well for us when mounted on treefern slabs.

Actual flower size: 6–7 cm across.

Miltonia clowesii Lindley

Discovered by Gardner, and described by Lindley in 1839, this species was named in honour of the Rev. Clowes, whose plants were the first to flower in England. *Odontoglossum clowesii*, *Oncidium clowesii* and *Brassia clowesii* are synonyms. *M. clowesii* grows in the cooler mountains of Rio de Janeiro, Espírito Santo and Minas Gerais.

The olive-green pseudobulbs are 7.5–10 cm tall, and set 2.5–4.0 cm apart on the stout rhizome. They are compressed, 2 cm wide near the base, and taper to 1 cm at the apex. There are two to four leaf-bearing bracts at the base. The two apical leaves, 22–65 cm long and 1.8–2.5 cm wide, are folded at the base and have an acute apex. Spikes from 35–65 cm long are produced in autumn from the base of the pseudobulbs. They carry five to ten flowers 7–8 cm long and 5–6 cm wide. The acutely pointed tepals are yellow-brown, barred and blotched with chestnut-brown. The oblong to lanceolate sepals are keeled. The dorsal sepal is 3.5 cm long and 1 cm wide, the laterals slightly longer but narrower. The petals are similar, or slightly falcate, 3.0–3.4 cm long, with undulating margins. The somewhat fiddle-shaped lip is 3.0–3.2 cm long and 2 cm wide. The edges of the basal half, which is dark mauve, are strongly reflexed. The white apical half has a sharp point at the apex. There are five to seven raised keels in the throat.

M. clowesii appreciates intermediate conditions with moderate to bright indirect light. Give plenty of water when in growth, followed by a drier winter rest. It may be potted, but because of its rather rambling habit is easier to manage on a mount.
Actual flower size: 7–8 cm long.

Miltonia x *cogniauxiae* Peeters

Described by Peeters, this natural hybrid between *M. spectabilis** and *M. regnellii** grows as an epiphyte in the cooler mountain areas of Rio de Janeiro.

Its habit resembles that of *M. regnellii*, with yellow-green oblong to conical pseudobulbs set at intervals of 2–5 cm on a stout rhizome. Somewhat compressed, they are 7–11 cm long and 1.5–2.0 cm wide near the base. There are three or four leaf-bearing bracts at the base of the pseudobulb. At the apex are two oblong to lanceolate leaves 25–30 cm long, which have an unevenly formed apex. In autumn, a spike about 35 cm long from the base of the pseudobulb bears one to three flowers about 6 cm across. The 3.5–4.0 cm-long tepals, which are recurved at the acute apices, are creamy-white suffused with very pale mauve. The slightly falcate lateral sepals are about 1 cm wide and strongly keeled, while the slightly wider dorsal sepal and 1.0–1.5 cm-wide petals are only keeled near the apex. The ovoid petals have irregular margins, as does the lip. The lip is pale mauve with dark amethyst veins and suffusions, and is edged with cream. From 2.5–4.0 cm long and 2.5–3.0 cm wide, the lip is rounded, with a point in the centre of the apex. It has three ridges at the base. These are white or pale mauve, and the central one is shorter than the others. The anther cap is mauve.

Although *M.* x *cogniauxiae*'s habit lends itself better to mounting, it may be potted. It needs an intermediate environment with moderate shade. Plenty of water should be given when the plant is in growth, followed by a short dry rest after flowering.
Actual flower size: approximately 6 cm across.

Miltonia cuneata Lindley

This epiphyte was described by Lindley in 1844. *M. speciosa* and *Oncidium speciosum* are later synonyms. *M. cuneata* grows in the cooler mountains and also in the warm humid lowlands of Espírito Santo, Rio de Janeiro and São Paulo.

The matt-green pseudobulbs may be closely set or spaced well apart on the rhizome. From 4.0–7.5 cm tall (occasionally to 10 cm), these pseudobulbs are ovate to oblong, slightly compressed, and about 3 cm across near the base. There are two to four leaf-bearing bracts at the base and two or three oblong to lanceolate apical leaves from 20–45 cm long and 3–4 cm wide. From late winter to spring a 30–60 cm-long spike carries four to eight flowers which last for about a month. The more or less lanceolate tepals are chestnut-brown with pale yellow recurved apical sections, and often a few yellow bars or streaks near the base. They have wavy margins. The lateral sepals and the petals are 3.2–4.0 cm-long and up to about 1.4 cm wide, while the dorsal sepal is shorter. The 3.5–4.0 cm-long white lip has a long narrow claw, which is more or less suffused with mauve. The blade of the lip is sub-quadrate. On the claw are two long keels which are sometimes marked with pink-mauve. Near the base they are covered with tiny hairs. Between the keels the claw is yellow. The narrow column wings join above the anther, with these sections strongly toothed.

M. cuneata is a strong grower if given the right conditions. It prefers a moist intermediate environment with diffuse bright light. Keep a little dry in winter. It may be potted or mounted, and grows well in hanging baskets.

Actual flower size: 5–7.5 cm across.

Miltonia flavescens (Ldl.) Lindley

This species was discovered early in the nineteenth century in Minas Gerais by Descourtilz. It was introduced into England in 1832, when Harrison sent plants from Rio de Janeiro to his brother in Liverpool. Lindley described it in the following year as *Cyrtochilum flavescens*, and transferred it to *Miltonia* in 1839. *Oncidium flavescens* and *Cyrtochilum stellatum* are conspecific. *M. flavescens* is widespread in warm lowland areas from Pernambuco in the north to Rio Grande do Sul in the south. It also occurs in Paraguay and Argentina.

The strongly compressed pseudobulbs are about 3 cm apart on a stout rhizome. They are yellow-green to mid-green, more or less oblong, 5–14 cm tall and 2.0–2.5 cm wide. There are one or two leaf-bearing bracts at the base and two strap-like leaves 16–35 cm long at the apex. In late spring to summer a somewhat flattened spike up to 1 m long (sometimes longer) rises from the base of the pseudobulb. It carries seven to fifteen fragrant flowers about 7.5 cm across which last quite well. The pale yellow tepals are linear-oblong, with acute apices. The sepals are 3.5–5.0 cm long and 0.4–0.6 cm across, while the petals are slightly wider but shorter. The 2.5 cm-long lip is more or less oblong with ruffled margins which are sometimes turned upward. The lip is white with reddish-purple streaks, which may form four to six radiating lines on the minutely hairy basal half.

M. flavescens does well in intermediate to warm conditions with semi-shade and high humidity. It may be potted, but because of its extended rhizome is probably better mounted on a fairly large slab.

Actual flower size: approximately 7.5 cm across.

Miltonia regnellii Reichenbach (f.)

Although discovered in 1846 by Regnell, in whose honour Reichenbach named it in 1848, *M. regnellii* was not introduced into cultivation until 1855 in Hamburg. *M. cereola* and *Oncidium regnellii* are conspecific. Regnell reputedly discovered this species in Minas Gerais, but Pabst and Dungs list it as only occurring in the cooler mountain areas of São Paulo, Paraná, Santa Catarina and Rio Grande do Sul. It may also have occurred at some time in Rio de Janeiro.

The yellow- to mid-green pseudobulbs, compressed and tapering, are 5–12 cm long, 1.2–2.0 cm across near the base, and are set up to 4 cm apart on a stout rhizome. From two to five leaf-bearing bracts are set at the base, with two strap-like leaves at the apex. These are 19–35 cm long and 1.0–1.8 cm wide, folded at the base and irregularly notched at the apex. In autumn an arching spike 30–55 cm long from the base of the pseudobulb carries three to five flowers 5.0–7.5 cm across. The tepals are glistening white and may be tinged with pale rose near the base. The lanceolate sepals are 3.0–3.5 cm long and about 1 cm wide, with a keel on the back of the lateral sepals. The wider petals are 2.7–3.0 cm long. The pale mauve lip has several dark violet streaks and is edged with creamy-white from 3.0–3.5 cm long. It bears three main ridges and several shorter ones at the base.

M. regnellii may be potted or mounted on fairly large slabs of treefern or similar material. It needs intermediate semi-shaded conditions, with plenty of water when in growth followed by a drier resting period after flowering.

Actual flower size: 5–7.5 cm across.

Miltonia russelliana (Ldl.) Lindley

Introduced into England from Rio de Janeiro in 1835, this epiphyte was originally described by Lindley as *Oncidium russellianum* in 1836. He transferred it to *Miltonia* in 1840. *M. quadrijuga* is synonymous. Its habitat is the cool mountain regions of Rio de Janeiro, São Paulo, Paraná, Santa Catarina and Rio Grande do Sul.

The dull olive-green pseudobulbs are slightly compressed, ovate to oblong, and closely set on the rhizome. From 5–7 cm tall, they have one or two leaf-bearing bracts at the base, and two narrow strap-like leaves 15–25 cm long at the apex. In late autumn or winter an erect to arching spike 40–60 cm long is produced from the base of the pseudobulb. It carries five to nine flowers which do not open widely. The oblong-lanceolate tepals are reddish-brown with pale yellow on the apical section, which is more or less recurved. The sepals are approximately 3 cm long and 1 cm wide, while the petals, which are held parallel to the column before curving outward, are about 2.6 cm long and slightly wider than the sepals. The oblong lip is 3 cm long and up to 1 cm wide, rose-lilac on the basal two-thirds and white or pale yellow on the recurved apical third. There is a 'waist' just below the apical third, a sharply tapered point at the apex, and three keels on the disc.

M. russelliana may be mounted or potted in a well-drained medium such as treefern fibre. It should be grown in an intermediate, moderately shady environment with good air movement. Plenty of water should be given when the plant is in growth. After flowering water should be reduced and the plant allowed a short dry resting period.

Actual flower size: 3–5 cm across.

Miltonia spectabilis Lindley

This species, which is the type for the genus, was first sent to England from Brazil by Fry in 1835. It flowered in Loddiges' nursery in 1837, and was described by Lindley shortly afterward. Knowles and Westcott's *Macrochilus fryanus*, published one month later, is synonymous, as is *Oncidium spectabile*. M. *spectabilis* occurs in both cool mountain and warm lowland areas, growing epiphytically in the eastern states of Brazil from Pernambuco to São Paulo, and also occurs in Venezuela.

The yellow-green to mid-green pseudobulbs are set 1–2 cm apart. They are compressed, ovate to oblong, 4–10 cm long and about 2 cm wide. There are one or two leaf-bearing bracts at the base, and a pair of narrow strap-like leaves 10–30 cm long at the apex. One or two flowers are borne, usually in late spring or early summer, on a flattened spike 7–15 cm long (occasionally longer). The oblong to lanceolate sepals are white, more or less suffused with pink. The keeled sepals are 3.5–4.0 cm long and about 1.6 cm wide. The slightly broader petals are often recurved. The single-lobed lip is 4.5–5.0 cm long and up to 4.6 cm wide. It is usually rose-pink with deeper red-purple at the base and darker veins throughout. The undulating margins are sometimes white or pale mauve. The oblong to triangular column wings are usually rose-purple.

M. *spectabilis* requires a humid, intermediate to warm environment with semi-shade and good ventilation or air movement. It may be mounted or grown in pots or shallow pans of well-drained material such as treefern fibre.

Actual flower size: approximately 7.5 cm across.

Miltonia spectabilis var. *alba* & other varieties

The elegant flowers of M. *spectabilis*,* with their flat shape and sparkling texture, show a great deal of variation in colour. Indeed, we have a number of clones in our collection, and no two plants are identical. Consequently, there are quite a number of named and accepted horticultural varieties. White varieties of all orchid species are always popular, and M. *spectabilis* var. *alba* is no exception. This variety is pure white, with a little yellow restricted to the callus on the lip. The clone pictured here was photographed at the Petropolis section of the Florália nursery in early December 1989. Another white variety of this species is the var. *virginalis*, which is very similar. The following varieties were in cultivation in England in the late nineteenth century, and are listed in Veitch's *Manual of Orchidaceous Plants* (1887–94): M. *spectabilis* var. *bicolor* has glistening white flowers except for a large purple blotch at the base of the lip; while in M. *spectabilis* var. *lineata* the lip has a purple blotch at the base from which seven to nine purple lines radiate to the lip margins. M. *spectabilis* var. *radians* Reichenbach (f.) has white flowers with six radiating purple lines on the disc of the lip; whereas the flowers of M. *spectabilis* var. *rosea* range in colour from pale pink to rose, with a number of purple lines on the lip.

All varieties require the same treatment in cultivation as the type.

Actual flower size: approximately 7.5 cm long.

Miltonia spectabilis var. *moreliana* Henfrey

A favourite of orchid growers everywhere, this splendid variety of *M. spectabilis** was first sent from Brazil to the French grower Morel at St Mandé, near Paris, in 1846 by his correspondent Porte. Henfrey recognised it as a variety of *M. spectabilis*, while Warner regarded it as a separate species, based on its colour alone. His *M. moreliana* and *M. spectabilis* var. *purpureoviolacea* are synonyms for Henfrey's var. *moreliana*.

M. spectabilis var. *moreliana* has the same flattened pseudobulbs as the type species. They lie 1–2 cm apart on the creeping rhizome and are covered with papery bracts. The one or two flowers last for about six weeks and, at up to 10 cm long, are slightly larger than the flowers of the type species. Colour is rather variable, but the petals and the sepals are commonly plum-purple with a white or pale pink base. The large skirt-like lip, which is about 5 cm long, is a pale rose-purple with a network of darker veins. *M. spectabilis* var. *moreliana* 'Atrorubens', which is pictured here, is one of the most desirable clones of the variety. It has dark satiny flowers. Only the petals have a pale patch at the base, while the white anther cap provides a nice contrast to the deep colour of the flower, as do the yellow keels near the base of the lip. The column wings on this clone are dark purple.

Cultural requirements are as for the type — intermediate to warm conditions, semi-shade and good ventilation. All the Brazilian miltonias are much easier to manage in warmer climates than the cool-growing *Miltoniopsis* species of the high mountain areas of northern South America.

Actual flower size: approximately 10 cm long.

Mormodes buccinator Lindley

Lindley described this species in 1840. Synonyms include *M. brachystachyum* and *M. wagenerianum*. *M. buccinator* occurs from Mexico to Ecuador, Venezuela and Brazil, often growing on dead trees at altitudes of up to 1,500 m above sea level. In Brazil it appears to be restricted to the state of Amazonas.

It is an extremely variable species. The clustered cylindrical to spindle-shaped pseudobulbs, which are covered by the bases of the leaves, are 5–25 cm tall and about 3.5 cm in diameter. The five to nine deciduous leaves are oblong to lanceolate, up to 30 cm long and 8 cm wide. They are pleated, with several prominent veins. An erect to arching spike 15–40 cm long is produced from near the base of the leafless pseudobulb, usually from winter to spring. It bears from three to many fleshy flowers, which may be white — like the var. *alba* pictured here — to greenish-yellow, yellow, pale pink or brownish-purple. Flowers may be spotted or striped. The oblong to lanceolate tepals are 2–3 cm long and up to 1.5 cm wide, with recurved margins and acute apices. The sepals are more or less strongly reflexed, while the slightly wider petals curve forward over the column. The 2–3 cm-long lip is more or less rounded, with a short sharp point at the apex. It curves upward, with the sides very strongly reflexed. The 1.8 cm-long column is twisted to one side of the lip.

M. buccinator does best in humid, warm to intermediate conditions with bright light. It needs plenty of water while in growth, followed by a fairly dry winter rest.

Actual flower size: 4.5–5 cm long.

Nanodes discolor Lindley

This is an extremely widespread species, occurring from the Pacific coast of Mexico, where it grows at altitudes of up to 1,100 m, south to Peru and the state of Amazonas in Brazil. It also occurs in Trinidad and Jamaica. It was first described in 1832 by Lindley, based on a plant from Amazonian Brazil. Bentham later renamed it *Epidendrum discolor*, while Ames in 1924 called it *E. schlechterianum*. Fifty years later Garay and Dunsterville resurrected the genus *Nanodes*, thus reinstating Lindley's original name. This species grows epiphytically or lithophytically in a wide range of habitats, from dry highlands to humid oak forests and rainforest.

The branched stems are 2.5–8.0 cm long and form dense mats. They are covered by the bases of the broad succulent leaves which are 1–3 cm long with a bilobed apex. Succulent and often suffused with red, they have a dark red mid-vein, are channelled above and keeled below. The flowers, which appear from spring to autumn near the apex of the stems, may be yellow-green, red-green, bronze-green or pale pink to purple. The one to three stemless flowers, 2.5 cm long, nestle in foliage. The translucent tepals are acute. The broad lip is joined to the column for half its length with the remainder having upturned edges.

N. discolor can be difficult to establish in small pieces, and rather resents disturbance. Once established, though, it is not a difficult subject. It grows well when mounted on cork and hung in an intermediate environment with fairly bright light.

Actual flower size: approximately 2.5 cm long.

Notylia barkeri Lindley

Described by Lindley in 1838, this species has numerous synonyms, including *N. trisepala*, *N. bipartita* and *N. guatemalensis*. In the 1970s it was proposed to divide this variable taxon into two species — *N. trisepala* and *N. tridachne* — depending on whether the lateral sepals are free or joined respectively, but this proposal has not been widely accepted. *N. barkeri* grows epiphytically from Mexico to northern South America in dense humid deciduous or mixed forest, ravines and swamps, from sea level to 1,600 m. In Brazil it appears restricted to the warm lowlands of Amazonas, Pará and Pernambuco.

The clustered pseudobulbs are compressed, wrinkled, from 1.0–3.5 cm tall and are partly obscured by several bracts and one or two leaves at the base. The single apical leaf is 3.5–20.0 cm long and folded at the base. It is leathery, strap-like, and more or less three-toothed at the broadly rounded apex. Flowers are produced from late winter to summer on pendent spikes from the base of the pseudobulbs. From 5–32 cm long, they carry many 0.5–0.7 cm flowers. These are faintly fragrant, greenish-yellow to white with a few orange spots on the curving petals. The 0.7 cm lateral sepals are joined for about half their length, or free with recurving apices. The slightly concave dorsal sepal is also recurved. The clawed lip is white, and shaped like a spearhead, with an acute apex.

This species prefers a humid, intermediate to warm environment, semi-shade, and plenty of water when in growth.

Actual flower size: approximately 0.8 cm long.

Notylia cordiglossa Reichenbach (f.)

Closely related to *Notylia barkeri* and *N. hemitricha* and endemic to Brazil, this species was described by Reichenbach in the latter half of the nineteenth century. It is a native of the northern states of Amazonas and Pará at elevations of less than 500 m above sea level. It grows on trees along forest edges, near streams, on open slopes or in clearings — places where fresh moving air is available in these hot humid regions far from the cooling influence of the sea. It has also been reported from the warm lowland areas of Rio Grande do Sul in the far south.

The small clustered pseudobulbs are wrinkled and partially hidden by bracts and leaves at the base. The broadly oval leaf at the apex of the pseudobulb is about 15 cm long. The pendent spike rises from the base of the pseudobulb with twenty-four or more pale green to yellowish-green flowers. The oblong concave dorsal sepal is 0.6 cm long and bent forward over the horizontal column. The 0.6 cm lateral sepals are joined for almost their entire length and are slightly recurved. The 0.5 cm petals curve down and forward, tapering to an acute apex. The lip is whitish with a keel on the claw at its base and a spear-shaped blade.

This species grows well when mounted on a piece of natural cork, or placed in a small pot of well-drained fibrous material. It prefers a warm to intermediate environment with high humidity and good air movement. Moderate shade seems best, with plenty of water when in growth. Reduce watering in winter, but give regular mistings.

Actual flower size: approximately 0.8 cm long.

Octomeria chamaeleptotes Reichenbach (f.)

A member of a genus related to *Pleurothallis* and whose generic name signifies its eight pollinia, *O. chamaeleptotes* was described by Reichenbach and is closely related to *O. caldensis*, *O. hatschbachii* and *O. riograndensis*. It occurs in the cooler mountain regions of Rio de Janeiro, Paraná, Santa Catarina and Rio Grande do Sul, where humidity is high all year round.

The clustered stems are 2.5–9.0 cm tall, and bear single very fleshy leaves 4–8 cm long, but only 0.3–0.5 cm across. The dull matt-green leaf is curved, more or less triangular in cross-section with a shallow furrow above, and tapers to an acute apex. In summer, almost stemless flowers are produced in clusters of two to twelve from the apex of the petiole. Approximately 1 cm across, these may be nodding or may have spreading recurved sepals and petals. The narrow glistening tepals are a pretty translucent pale yellow with darker apices, more or less lanceolate, and taper to blunt points. The sepals are 0.6–1.0 cm long, while the petals are slightly shorter. The obscurely three-lobed lip is 0.3–0.5 cm long and 0.2 cm wide. The lateral lobes are erect, while the irregularly edged mid-lobe curves slightly upward. There is one raised ridge near the front of each lateral lobe, and a slight ridge down the centre of the mid-lobe.

O. chamaeleptotes does well mounted on treefern slabs or potted in a fairly fine well-drained mixture such as chopped treefern fibre and sphagnum moss. It needs a shady position in a cool to intermediate environment with high humidity and constant moisture.

Actual flower size: approximately 1 cm across.

137

Octomeria concolor Barbosa Rodrígues

Closely related to *O. stellaris* and *O. pusilla*, this species was described by Barbosa Rodrígues about the end of the nineteenth century. *O. concolor* grows in the mountain regions of Espírito Santo, Rio de Janeiro, São Paulo, Paraná and Santa Catarina. It is also reported from the hot lowlands of Amapá in the north-east, where it favours positions on trees along watercourses and bordering clearings, where cooler moving air is present.

The very thin terete stems are 3.0–8.5 cm long, and are covered with brown papery bracts. Each bears a single very succulent leaf 4–6 cm long and up to 1 cm across. This stiff lanceolate leaf is almost triangular in cross-section with a flat upper surface. From one to four flowers appear in autumn and winter on very short stalks from the apex of the stem. They are about 0.9 cm across and do not open widely. The tepals are pale yellow with darker apices. The lanceolate sepals are 0.5–0.7 cm long and 0.2–0.25 cm wide near the base. The petals have more tapered acute apices. The hinged lip is 0.3–0.4 cm long. The tiny ear-like lateral lobes are erect, while the mid-lobe is oblong to fiddle-shaped, with a tiny point in the middle of the apex. A single line runs down the centre of the lip, and a ridge on either side extends diagonally from the base of the lateral lobe on to the mid-lobe.

O. concolor grows well in cool to intermediate conditions but is one of the relatively few pleurothallids which will tolerate higher temperatures. It may be mounted or potted, and needs a shady position, high humidity and year-round moisture.

Actual flower size: approximately 0.9 cm across.

Octomeria crassifolia Lindley

Described by Lindley in the first half of the nineteenth century, this is one of the lesser-known octomerias, and entered our collection more or less by accident, arriving mislabelled in a shipment of plants from Brazil. It is a native of the cool — even cold — southern mountain regions of Rio de Janeiro, São Paulo, Paraná, Santa Catarina and Rio Grande do Sul. It is also found in Uruguay and Paraguay.

The terete stems are closely set on a creeping rhizome. Covered with pale brown papery bracts for most of their length, they have two or three internodes and are 8.5–14.0 cm long and 0.3–0.4 cm wide near the apex. Each bears a single stiff leaf which is very fleshy, lanceolate and erect to curving. The 8–10 cm-long leaves are mid-green and 1.5–2.0 cm wide. Three or more almost sessile flowers, which do not open widely, appear at the apex of the stem in autumn. The sepals and petals are a translucent pale yellow with darker acute apices. They are approximately 1 cm long and 0.4 cm wide. The petals are slightly narrower than the sepals. The petals and dorsal sepal are lanceolate, while the lateral sepals are more or less triangular. The tepals all point forward. The hinged mobile lip is pale yellow with a dark maroon blotch in the throat. The rounded lateral lobes are erect, while the mid-lobe is rounded on the sides, and has a bluntly pointed apex. The lip is 0.6 cm long and 0.2–0.3 cm wide across the base of the mid-lobe.

O. crassifolia may be mounted or potted in a fairly fine well-drained mixture. It needs a cool semi-shaded position with year-round moisture.

Actual flower size: approximately 1 cm across.

Octomeria decumbens Cogniaux

Endemic to Brazil, this species was described by Cogniaux, curator of the Brussels Herbarium. It occurs in the states of Rio de Janeiro, São Paulo, Paraná and Minas Gerais. It is usually found growing on mossy trees in the cool damp mountain regions, which are subject to nightly fogs and mists.

The very narrow leaves are borne on creeping rhizomes. Together with their rather long slender stalks, which are covered with papery bracts, the pale to mid-green leaves reach 10–18 cm long, and have an acutely pointed apex. They are fleshy, and may be slightly curved. The upper surface is flat with three shallow longitudinal furrows, while the underside is rounded. The leaves are thus semi-circular in cross-section. Flowers are produced in clusters from the top of the leaf stalk. They are translucent pale creamy-yellow with darker tips and have a sparkling crystalline texture. The sepals and petals, which are held quite free of each other, are approximately 0.75 cm long. The dark 0.4 cm lip is hinged, three-lobed, and has two keels on the disc.

Like most of the octomerias, this species is floriferous and of easy culture. It may be potted or mounted — treefern is ideal — and grown in a cool to intermediate environment. It prefers semi-shade and year-round moisture, with a slightly drier spell in cold weather. It is an ideal companion plant for masdevallias, though not quite so heat-sensitive.

Actual flower size: approximately 1 cm across.

Octomeria grandiflora Lindley

Lindley described this species in 1842, using material imported from Brazil by Loddiges. *O. arcuata*, *O. surinamensis*, *O. robusta*, *O. ruthiana* and *O. truncata* are conspecific. It inhabits both the cooler mountain regions of Rio de Janeiro, São Paulo, Paraná, Santa Catarina and Minas Gerais, and the hotter lowland areas of Amazonas and Amapá, where it is found growing on the edges of forests and along stream banks, wherever cooler air currents are present. It is also found in Trinidad, Suriname, Bolivia and Paraguay.

The fleshy leaves are 15–28 cm tall, including the 5–12 cm-long laterally compressed basal stalks. The latter are covered with whitish papery bracts. Approximately 2 cm wide at the centre, the leaf blades are lanceolate, with a prominent mid-vein. The undersides are sometimes suffused with red. Several almost sessile flowers are produced at the base of the leaf in spring or summer. The bluntly pointed elliptic tepals are pale translucent yellow with darker apices and several faint veins. The sepals are 1.0–1.5 cm long and 0.5 cm wide. The dorsal sepal and the 1.0–1.5 cm long petals are slightly spreading. The three-lobed lip, 0.6–0.8 cm long and 0.4–0.6 cm wide, is hinged at the base of the reddish column. The somewhat falcate lateral lobes are erect and almost completely maroon, while the mid-lobe is maroon at the base and yellow at the bilobed apex.

O. grandiflora is more temperature tolerant than many other octomerias, and does well in shady, cool to intermediate, or even warm, conditions. It needs high humidity, year-round moisture, and good air movement.

Actual flower size: 1.5–2.2 cm across.

Octomeria juncifolia Barbosa Rodrígues

One of the prettiest of the octomerias, this species was described by Barbosa Rodrígues about the end of the nineteenth century. It is related to *O. decumbens,** O. geraensis, O. palmyrabellae, O. rodeiensis* and *O. unguiculata*. This robust epiphyte grows in the cool humid mountain regions of Espírito Santo, Rio de Janeiro, São Paulo, Paraná and Santa Catarina.

The clustered arching stems are 8–20 cm long and up to 0.3 cm in diameter. When young they are covered with one or two thick sheaths, which are often marked with maroon. The heavy fleshy leaves are terete with a single furrow on the upper surface. From 14–35 cm long and up to 0.4 cm wide, they are marked with maroon and taper to a sharp point. From two to seven bright yellow flowers are produced in clusters from the apex of the stem in spring. The 1.0–1.5 cm-wide flowers open only about halfway. The more or less elliptic sepals are 1.0–1.2 cm long and 0.4 cm wide, while the oblong to elliptic petals are slightly shorter and narrower. The hinged, 0.5 cm-long lip is more or less fiddle-shaped with erect ear-like lateral lobes. The apex of the mid-lobe is blunt, with a point on either side. The lip is yellow, with red spots at the base. At the base of each lateral lobe is a keel, which extends on to the apical lobe. A single almost imperceptible line runs down the centre of the lip.

This attractive species needs a cool moist environment with semi-shade and year-round moisture. It may be mounted or potted. As plants have a semi-pendent habit, they make good subjects for small baskets or suspended pots.

Actual flower size: 1–1.5 cm across.

Octomeria oxycheila Barbosa Rodrígues

This is another little-known octomeria, and was discovered in the state of Rio de Janeiro by Barbosa Rodrígues, who described it in 1882. It also occurs in Espírito Santo, São Paulo, Paraná, Santa Catarina and Rio Grande do Sul.

The terete stems, which are clustered on a creeping rhizome, have two or three internodes and a few brown bracts. They are 2–11 cm long, but only 0.1–0.2 cm in diameter. Each bears a single very stiff fleshy leaf, which tapers to a very sharp apex. From 5–12 cm long and 0.5–1.5 cm in width, the lanceolate leaf is more or less rounded beneath with a single central groove above. In autumn, almost stemless flowers appear from the joint between stem and leaf. Over time, this joint will produce several flowers, which are starry in shape with a glistening texture. They are a translucent to almost transparent pale yellow. The 0.5–0.6 cm-long sepals and slightly smaller petals are more or less triangular with three barely perceptible veins on each. The three-lobed fiddle-shaped lip is about 0.4 cm long, with erect ear-shaped lateral lobes. The mid-lobe has a minute point in the middle of the apex. There is a single unbroken keel down the centre and a curved darker ridge on either side near the base of the lateral lobes.

This species may be mounted or grown in pots of fine well-drained medium such as chopped treefern fibre with the addition of a little sphagnum moss. It needs a cool humid environment and semi-shade, year-round moisture and good ventilation or air movement. Like most octomerias, this is a trouble-free plant in cultivation and deserves to be better known.

Actual flower size: approximately 0.8 cm across.

Octomeria species

Brazil has about one hundred described (and probably many still undescribed) octomerias, few of which are well known or well documented, making it difficult in many cases to arrive at a definite identification. As far as we can tell, this robust species belongs to the *grandiflora* alliance, and within that most closely resembles the drawings of O. *edmundoi* in Pabst and Dungs' *Orchidaceae Brasilienses*.

The closely set stems are approximately 5–8 cm long, with a few papery sheaths, and are compressed near the apex. Each bears a single leathery leaf up to approximately 12 cm long and 2.5 cm wide. The oblong to lanceolate leaf is folded at the base and has an acute apex and a keel below. Three or more flowers are all produced at the same time on very short stalks from the apex of the stems. The translucent white sepals and petals are lanceolate to ovate with long tapering apices. They are approximately 1 cm long, with the more or less erect dorsal sepal slightly concave at the base. The lateral sepals are joined for a quarter to one-third of their length. The hinged lip is obscurely three-lobed, with a dark red marking on the basal half, which is held parallel to the slender column. The deflexed apical half is white and fan-shaped to rounded, with irregular margins and two or three small points at the apex.

Like most of the octomerias, this pretty species does well when potted in a freely draining fibrous material. It needs intermediate to cool conditions, year-round moisture, and should never be allowed to dry out for long periods.

Actual flower size: 1.5–2 cm across.

Oncidium barbatum Lindley

This species was discovered by Swainson, who sent plants to the Glasgow Botanical Gardens where it flowered in 1819. Lindley described it soon afterwards. It is closely related to O. *ciliatum*,* with which it is sometimes held to be conspecific, and to O. *micropogon*.* It can be distinguished from both by the minute beak-like mid-lobe of the lip. It is endemic to Brazil, occurring at moderate elevations in Ceará, Pernambuco, Bahia and Minas Gerais.

The waxy compressed pseudobulbs are somewhat quadrangular, from 3–6.5 cm tall and 2.0–3.5 cm in diameter. Each has one or two leaf-bearing sheaths at the base and a single leaf 6–10 cm long at the apex. This is erect to spreading, dark green and usually paler beneath. Several flowers, each 2.0–2.5 cm wide, are borne on a spike 30–60 cm long. The acute sepals and rounded petals are yellow, blotched and barred with red-brown, while the lip is bright yellow with some markings on the callus. The more or less oblong tepals are very wavy, and the lateral sepals are joined for about one-third of their length. The flat lip is about 2 cm wide with large rounded lateral lobes and a tiny mid-lobe. The callus has several rounded protuberances and the disc is toothed.

Not a difficult species in cultivation, O. *barbatum* prefers intermediate temperatures with moderate to bright filtered light and good air movement. Water copiously in summer and allow a drier, cooler rest in winter.

Actual flower size: 2–2.5 cm across.

Oncidium bifolium Sims

Sims described this species in 1812, using a specimen from Uruguay which flowered in Loddiges' nursery in England. *Oncidium vexillarium* and *O. celsium* are conspecific. As well as growing epiphytically in the Brazilian states of Paraná, Santa Catarina and Rio Grande do Sul, *O. bifolium* also occurs in Uruguay, Argentina and Bolivia in a variety of habitats — from the hot lowlands, where it favours shady streamside positions, to cold mountain areas up to 1,000 m or more above sea level.

The clustered pseudobulbs are 3–4 cm long (occasionally to 7 cm), and become furrowed with age. At the apex are two rather fleshy strap-like leaves 6–15 cm long with an acute apex. The 20–35 cm flower spike, which may be branched, appears in summer with five to twenty flowers from 2.0–2.5 cm across. The tepals are yellow, barred and spotted with red-brown, while the broad three-lobed lip is yellow with red-brown markings on the callus. The concave dorsal sepal and fiddle-shaped petals have undulating edges, with the petals curved inward at the rounded or notched apices. The 1 cm lateral sepals are joined at the basal halves, have pointed tips, and are obscured by the lip, which is about 2 cm long and 2.0–2.5 cm wide. The small lateral lobes are rounded, while the skirt-like mid-lobe dominates the flower. At its base is a fleshy callus with several finger-like protuberances.

This is a very adaptable species, tolerant of a range of conditions. We grow our plants in intermediate temperatures with moderate shade and generally high humidity. Allow plants to dry out a little in winter. *Actual flower size: 2–2.5 cm across.*

Oncidium blanchetii Reichenbach (f.)

Described by Reichenbach in the second half of the nineteenth century, *O. blanchetii* occupies a variety of habitats from the cooler mountains to the hot humid lowlands and inland savannahs. It tends to grow as a semi-terrestrial in sandy areas between rocks or in rock crevices filled with decaying vegetable matter. It occurs in Minas Gerais, Pernambuco, Bahia, Rio de Janeiro, São Paulo, Paraná, and Santa Catarina, as well as in Bolivia.

The clustered pseudobulbs are ovoid to elongated, 4.5–10.0 cm tall and 3–4 cm wide, with one or two leaf-bearing bracts at the base. At the apex are two or three strap-like leaves 24–46 cm long and up to 2.5 cm wide. In late winter or spring an erect spike from 80 cm–1 m or more bears twenty-five or more flowers on the apical quarter. The greenish-yellow tepals are striped or spotted with maroon to chestnut-brown. They are clawed, somewhat reflexed, and have undulating margins. The lanceolate dorsal sepal and curving laterals are about 0.6 cm long and 0.3 cm wide. The 1–2 cm-long petals are sub-quadrate, and 0.5–0.6 cm wide. The yellow 2 cm-long lip has small ear-like lateral lobes and a skirt-like apical lobe. This is 1.5–2.0 cm wide, bilobed with undulating edges, and may have red spots on the reverse. The callus is marked with red, and comprises about seven to nine finger-like projections.

O. blanchetii is fairly temperature tolerant, and will grow in conditions ranging from warm to cool. It needs moderately bright light and a reduction of water in winter. It does well potted or hung in baskets of a coarse well-drained mixture. *Actual flower size: 2.5–3 cm long.*

Oncidium cebolleta (Jacq.) Swartz

Probably the most widespread of all oncidiums, this epiphyte was discovered in Colombia by Jacquin, who described it as *Dendrobium cebolleta* in 1760. In 1800 it was transferred by Swartz to his new genus *Oncidium*. It is very closely related to *O. ascendens*. Synonyms include *O. juncifolium* and *O. brachyphyllum*. *O. cebolleta* is found from Mexico to Brazil, Paraguay and Argentina from sea level to the 1,800 m mark. It inhabits both semi-arid areas, where it experiences long dry spells, and humid forests. It is found almost throughout tropical Brazil, including the western states of Acre, Amazonas and Roraima.

The 1.5–2.0 cm-long conical pseudobulbs are covered by white sheaths which also cover the base of the leaf and inflorescence. Each pseudobulb has a single erect to sub-erect leaf 7–50 cm long and 1.0–2.5 cm wide. The grooved terete leaves taper to a sharp point. From late winter to spring a 1.0–1.5 m spike bears many yellow to yellow-green flowers with red-brown markings. The 0.7–1.7 cm-long sepals are spoon-shaped, with the concave dorsal more or less hooding the column. The oblong to elliptic petals have wavy margins. The yellow lip occasionally has red spots on the reverse. The spreading oblong lateral lobes are separated from the bilobed skirt-like apical lobe by a narrow isthmus. The callus, which is spotted with red, comprises a long nose-like protuberance in front with one large tooth, and several smaller warts on each side.

O. cebolleta grows best for us when mounted on cork, hung in a humid warm environment with fairly bright light and watered all year round.

Actual flower size: 1.6–3.5 cm across.

Oncidium ciliatum Lindley (1)

Described by Lindley, this species is closely related to *O. barbatum*,* with which it is often confused, and *O. micropogon*.* Synonyms include *O. bahiense* and *O. barbatum* var. *labiosum*. *O. ciliatum* is more widespread than *O. barbatum*, occurring in Ceará in the north-east, and in the eastern part of the country from Bahia to Rio Grande do Sul. It is found in both the cooler mountains and in the hot humid lowlands.

The four-angled waxy pseudobulbs are compressed, about 3–7 cm long and up to 4 cm wide. Each has one or two leaf-bearing bracts at the base and a single erect to spreading leaf at the apex. This apical leaf is 6–12 cm long and 2–3 cm wide. Several to many flowers are borne on a 30–60 cm spike in autumn or winter. Pabst and Dungs, in their *Orchidaceae Brasilienses*, show two forms of this species. Form 1, shown here, has yellow to greenish-yellow tepals more or less heavily barred or blotched with chestnut-brown. The broadly to narrowly lanceolate dorsal sepal and the slightly rhomboidal petals are about 1.2 cm long and 0.8 cm wide. The lateral sepals, more or less oval with a pointed apex, are joined at the base, and are usually shorter than the 1.5–2.0 cm-long lip. The lip is yellow except around the crest, with five or more protuberances and is marked with red. The large rounded lateral lobes are joined to the large kidney-shaped apical lobe by a rounded toothed isthmus. The variability of this species has caused some confusion in identification over the years, and no doubt will continue to do so.

Cultural requirements are the same as for *O. ciliatum* Lindley (2), following.

Actual flower size: 2.5–3 cm across.

Oncidium ciliatum Lindley (2)

Although the habit of *O. ciliatum* varies little, the flowers of different clones often show marked variances, which may be attributable to the wide distribution of this species (see previous entry). Form 2, pictured here, as in *Orchidaceae Brasilienses*, is the one most often confused with *O. barbatum.** The sepals and petals are almost completely olive-green to brown with reddish bars and or spots at the base. As in Form 1, they have undulating margins. The petals and the dorsal sepal are similar in both forms, but in Form 2 the lateral sepals are more or less oblong with pointed apices, up to about 2 cm long and 0.5 cm wide. The lip is much less well developed in this form, being about 1 cm long, so that the lateral sepals are clearly visible instead of being obscured as in Form 1. The lateral lobes are narrow at the base and otherwise rounded, but are much smaller than those of Form 1. The oblong to kidney-shaped apical lobe is also smaller, but it is not the tiny triangular apical lobe of *O. barbatum*. The five-lobed callus is also slightly different from that of Form 1, with a more prominent nose-like central protuberance. This form has quite inconspicuous column wings, while those of Form 1 (and of *O. barbatum*) are larger and more or less rounded. It seems to us that this may possibly warrant treatment as a separate species; alternatively, it may be a natural hybrid between *O. ciliatum* (Form 1) and *O. barbatum*.

O. ciliatum grows best when mounted and placed in a humid, intermediate to warm environment with indirect light.
Actual flower size: 3–3.5 cm long.

Oncidium concolor Hooker

Although not commonly cultivated until the late nineteenth century, this beautiful species was described about 1839 by Hooker, based on plants sent to England by Gardner in 1837. Among its synonyms are *O. ottonis* and *Cyrtochilum citrinum*. It grows in the mountains of southern Brazil from Minas Gerais, Rio de Janeiro and Paraná to Rio Grande do Sul, and in Argentina, sometimes in areas which experience frequent winter frosts.

The clustered dull-green pseudobulbs are rather egg-shaped, and become wrinkled with age. They are usually from 2–5 cm tall and 1.0–2.5 cm in diameter. Two acute strap-like leaves are borne at the apex of the pseudobulb and reach 9–15 cm in length. They have a prominent mid-vein beneath. An arching to pendulous spike carries up to twelve well-spaced flowers about 5 cm long in spring or summer. The pointed, more or less concave sepals are yellow to yellow-green, with lateral sepals joined for about half their length. The more rounded oblong petals, which are held upright in front of the dorsal sepal, are yellow with some green on the back. The tepals are 1.4–2.0 cm long. The dominant feature of the flower is the broad, more or less ruffled lip, which is about 3.5 cm long. The 1 cm claw has two parallel keels tipped with orange, and a short protuberance on either side of the mid-point. The column has two very broad wings at the apex.

This species may be mounted or potted. We use treefern for both purposes. It prefers a cool to intermediate environment with moderately bright light, good ventilation and a dry rest in winter.
Actual flower size: approximately 5 cm long.

Oncidium cornigerum Lindley

First cultivated in England in 1830, this species was described by Lindley in 1832. It belongs to the same alliance as *O. cruciatum,** which it closely resembles, *O. lietzii** and *O. pubes.** *O. pubes* var. *flavescens* is a synonym. *O. cornigerum* ranges from Minas Gerais and Espírito Santo to Rio Grande do Sul and is also found in Paraguay.

The dark green pseudobulbs are almost terete. From 4.5–10.0 cm tall, they bear a single 7.5–15.0 cm-long leaf, which has an acute apex and is 1.5–2.5 cm wide. A 10–60 cm-long spike carries several flowers in autumn. The tepals vary in colour from yellow barred with red-brown to chestnut-brown with yellow only at the base and apex. The sepals are 0.7–1.0 cm long, with the slightly concave dorsal bilobed at the apex. The lateral sepals are joined for almost their entire length, each ending in a tiny point. The oblong petals are slightly longer but narrower, with the outer half curving forward. The 0.9–1.2 cm-long lip is joined to the column by a short claw, and is yellow with red calli and spots. The oblong lateral lobes are arm-like, while the mid-lobe is rounded. The claw has two finger-like protrusions. There is a large raised plateau between the lateral lobes, and several gland-like calli just extend on to the apical half of the mid-lobe. The column has two very narrow arms above the stigma, which has a rectangular projection on either side.

O. cornigerum does best on a mount of treefern or similar material, and needs a semi-shaded position in intermediate conditions with a drier winter rest after flowering.

Actual flower size: approximately 2 cm across.

Oncidium crispum Loddiges

This immensely popular species is related to *O. enderianum,** *O. forbesii,** etc., and was described in 1832 by Loddiges, who named it for the much-crisped margins of all its floral segments. *O. crispum*'s natural habitat is the cooler mountains of Espírito Santo, Rio de Janeiro, São Paulo, Paraná, and Minas Gerais.

The compressed ovoid pseudobulbs are closely set and become ridged with age. They are dull olive- to brownish-green, 5–10 cm long, and up to 5 cm wide. At the apex are usually two leathery lanceolate leaves 15–23 cm long and 2.5–5.0 cm wide. Many flowers up to 7.5 cm across are produced in late spring or summer on a branched spike 70 cm–1.1 m long. The clawed tepals are chestnut-brown to olive-brown, very narrowly edged with pale yellow. The sepals may have yellow blotches. The 2.2 cm-long laterals are joined for a third of their length. The erect dorsal is about 2 cm long and 0.7 cm wide, while the slightly longer, rounded petals are about 1.8 cm wide. The 2–3 cm-long lip is yellow at the base with red-brown on the callosities, which comprise a long 'hook' with a ridge on either side at the base and several 'blob'-like calli along each side. There is a 1.0–1.2 cm-wide chestnut band on the mid-lobe, often with fine yellow edging. The tiny lateral lobes are rounded. The toothed, almost oblong column wings are red-brown with or without yellow markings.

O. crispum does best in intermediate to cool conditions with semi-shade (although we have seen plants in the Organ Mountains growing in full sun) and moderate humidity. Reduce watering in winter.

Actual flower size: 4.5–7.5 cm across.

Oncidium cruciatum Reichenbach (f.)

Described by Reichenbach in 1878, this epiphyte is closely related to *O. cornigerum*,* *O. lietzei** and *O. pubes*.* *O. phantasmaticum* is a synonym. It comes from the cool mountain areas of Rio de Janeiro, São Paulo, Paraná, Santa Catarina and Rio Grande do Sul.

The clustered, almost terete pseudobulbs are dark olive-green, covered by dry papery bracts when young, and becoming wrinkled with age. They are 9–15 cm tall, 1 cm in diameter, and bear one or sometimes two apical leaves 12–15 cm long and about 2.5 cm wide. These are lanceolate and folded at the base. From twenty to forty flowers 1.5–2.5 cm across are produced in autumn or winter on branched spikes 17–30 cm long. Their colour varies from chestnut-brown with pale yellow only at the base of the segments, to chestnut-brown with yellow bars and blotches. The slightly concave dorsal sepal and the petals are more or less paddle-shaped and 0.8–1.0 cm long by 0.5 cm wide. The wavy petals are spreading or curved inward near the apex. The 0.6–0.8 cm-long lateral sepals are joined for almost their entire length. The 1 cm-long lip is joined to the microscopically-hairy column by a long claw. It is three-lobed, with narrow spreading lateral lobes and a roundish mid-lobe which is usually recurved at the apex. There are many callosities from the claw to the centre of the mid-lobe. The column has a curved projection on either side of the stigma.

An easy and rewarding species in cultivation, *O. cruciatum* does well when grown on mounts of treefern or similar material in a cool to intermediate environment with indirect bright light.

Actual flower size: 1.5–2.5 cm across.

Oncidium dasystyle Reichenbach (f.)

Introduced into cultivation by B. S. Williams in 1872, this species was described by Reichenbach the following year. Belonging to the same section as *O. concolor*,* it is limited to the state of Rio de Janeiro, where it grows in the cool coastal ranges. The latitude here is roughly on the Tropic of Capricorn, and the mountains experience bright days and cool nights with heavy dews.

The clustered pseudobulbs of *O. dasystyle* are compressed and become furrowed with age. About 3 cm tall, they bear two rather thin leaves 12–15 cm long. Flowers are borne in winter on a slender arching to pendulous spike 30–45 cm long. There are usually three to six flowers on a spike, each nearly 4 cm across. The 2 cm pointed tepals are pale yellow blotched with red-brown. The concave dorsal sepal is hooded over the column. The petals are sometimes twisted at the base. The lateral sepals are joined for half their length and are obscured by the large skirt-like lip, which is pale yellow to almost white except for the large glossy callus which is almost black. There are no distinct lateral lobes, but two tiny ears near the base of the 3 cm lip. The conspicuous column wings are almost square.

This beautiful species is fairly easy to cultivate although not as strong a grower as many other Brazilian oncidiums. Intermediate temperatures suit it best, with moderate to fairly heavy shade and high humidity. Avoid extremes of temperature. It may be mounted or potted in a medium that is a little on the fine side.

Actual flower size: 3–4 cm across.

Oncidium divaricatum Lindley

Discovered by Descourtilz in the early nineteenth century, this species was sent to London in 1826 by Heatherly, the British vice-consul in Brazil. Lindley described it in 1827. It is very closely related to *O. pulvinatum,* * *O. sphegiferum* * and *O. robustissimum. O. divaricatum* grows epiphytically in the mountains of Espírito Santo, Minas Gerais and Rio de Janeiro, often on the trunks of large trees.

The strongly flattened, clustered pseudobulbs are roundish, yellow-green, and 2–4 cm in diameter. There are a few papery bracts at the base and a single fleshy leaf at the apex. The oblong to elliptic leaf, which is 12–30 cm long and 4–11 cm wide, is folded at the base, has a prominent keel below, and undulating margins. In spring a slender, arching, branched spike up to 2 m long bears many flowers about 2.5 cm across. The tepals are yellow-orange at the apex and chestnut at the base. The spathulate sepals are 1.1–1.2 cm long and about 0.6 cm wide, while the more or less oblong petals are slightly longer and wider. The petals have a short claw at the base and slightly undulating margins. The yellow lip is spotted with red-brown and is up to 2 cm long. The large rounded lateral lobes are minutely and irregularly serrated, while the oblong to kidney-shaped mid-lobe is somewhat crisped. The large callus comprises four cushion-like lobes covered with tiny hair-like glands.

Because of its long arching spike, this species is best grown in baskets or on mounts. It does well mounted on treefern or cork in a humid intermediate environment with bright indirect light.

Actual flower size: approximately 2.5 cm across.

Oncidium enderianum (hort.)

This species was known and in cultivation as early as the beginning of the twentieth century, at which time it was thought to be a natural hybrid between *O. crispum* * and *O. curtum.* Since recognised as a separate species, it resembles *O. crispum* very closely. *O. enderianum* is found in the cooler mountains of São Paulo and Rio de Janeiro.

The oblong to elliptic pseudobulbs are dull olive-green and slightly compressed with a few vertical ridges. From 4.0–7.5 cm tall, they are 2–4 cm wide with two (occasionally one) lanceolate to oblong leaves at the apex. These are 14–23 cm long and 2.5–5.0 cm wide, and are often tinged with reddish-purple below. Several showy flowers are borne usually in autumn to early winter, with the occasional plant flowering in spring. The spike is up to 1 m or more long. The tepals are about 3 cm long and have undulating margins. The light brown sepals are sometimes barred with yellow, while the somewhat rounded petals are light brown with yellow edges and yellow bars at the base. The 4 cm-long lip is light brown with a narrow yellow edge and a large golden patch at the base of the skirt-like apical lobe and on the callus, which is marked with red. The lateral lobes are rounded, and the callus has two diverging projections in front. (*O. crispum* has a single nose-like protuberance). There are also several warts behind and beside these projections.

O. enderianum may be potted, but does best for us when mounted on a treefern slab and hung in partial shade in an intermediate environment. Watering should be reduced in winter.

Actual flower size: 5.5–6 cm across.

Oncidium fimbriatum Lindley

Although this species was described in 1832 by Lindley from a botanical drawing by Francis Bauer, it did not find its way into cultivation in England until the 1880s. *O. godseffianum*, *O. chrysorapis* and *O. hecatanthum* are all conspecific. This species is closely related to *O. lietzei** and *O. pubes.**

O. fimbriatum inhabits the cool mountains and also the warmer lowlands of Rio de Janeiro, São Paulo, Paraná, Santa Catarina and Rio Grande do Sul. It also occurs in Paraguay.

The 8–15 cm-long pseudobulbs are almost terete, and about 1 cm wide. They are dark green and bear two strap-like leaves 18–21 cm long and up to 3 cm wide with acute apices. An arching to pendulous spike 60–90 cm long carries several to many flowers in autumn. The bright yellow tepals, which have a very short point in the middle of the apex, have reddish bars and streaks. The sepals are about 1 cm long. The ovate dorsal sepal, which is about 0.7 cm wide, hoods the column. The narrower lateral sepals are joined only at the base. The clawed, more or less oblong petals are slightly longer, but only 0.5 cm wide. They are irregularly edged at the apex and have undulating margins. The 1 cm-long lip is predominantly yellow, with long arm-like lateral lobes, which curve forward and/or upward. The apical lobe is usually bilobed. Between the lateral lobes and the isthmus is a warty callus, which is bilobed in front and marked with red.

O. fimbriatum is not a difficult subject, and grows well mounted and given intermediate to warm conditions with moderately bright light and good ventilation.

Actual flower size: 2–2.5 cm across.

Oncidium flexuosum Sims

This easily grown species was described by Sims in 1821. *O. haematochrysum*, *O. haematoxanthum* and *Epidendrum lineatum* are all synonyms. *O. flexuosum* is widespread in the eastern part of Brazil, from Pernambuco and Bahia in the north to Santa Catarina in the south, and occurs also in Pará. It grows epiphytically — often in swampy situations — in the hot humid lowlands. It has also been reported from Argentina and Paraguay.

The strongly compressed pale green to yellow-green pseudobulbs may be closely set or up to 12 cm apart on the rhizome. From 4–8 cm tall and 2–4 cm wide, they are ovoid to oblong with one to three bracts at the base and usually two strap-like leaves at the apex. These are 10–23 cm long and up to 3 cm wide. Branched spikes from 60 cm–1 m long are produced from summer to early winter with many flowers. The tepals are yellow, barred with red to chestnut-brown. The concave dorsal sepal is oblong to oval, 0.35–0.40 cm long and up to 0.3 cm wide. The lateral sepals are joined for approximately half their length while the wavy, often reflexed petals are oblong. The 1.2–1.5 cm-long lip is yellow with red-brown markings around the callus. The lateral lobes are ear-like, while the wide apical lobe is skirt-like with wavy edges and a bilobed apex. The fleshy callus is two-lobed — the basal one is downy while the front lobe has three to five protuberances.

O. flexuosum is reasonably tolerant of a wide range of temperatures, doing well in warm to cool conditions. It prefers high humidity and bright indirect light. Reduce watering if plants are grown in cool conditions in winter.

Actual flower size: approximately 2 cm long.

Oncidium forbesii Hooker

Closely related to *O. gardneri** and *O. crispum*,* this superb species was discovered by Gardner in 1837 in the Serra dos Orgãos near Rio de Janeiro. He sent plants to England, and Hooker described the species in 1839. *O. crispum* var. *forbesii* and *O. crispum* var. *marginatum* are later synonyms. *O. forbesii* grows on trees in the mountains of Minas Gerais, Espírito Santo, Rio de Janeiro and São Paulo.

The oblong, elliptic or ovoid pseudobulbs are somewhat flattened, and from 5–8 cm tall and 2–4 cm wide. They are a dull olive-green, often marked with brown. At the base are one or two leaf-bearing bracts, with one or sometimes two leathery apical leaves. These are lanceolate to oblong, 15–30 cm long, and up to 4 cm wide with an acute apex. In autumn an erect to arching spike 40–90 cm long bears several showy flowers. All segments are chestnut-brown with narrow yellow edges, with or without red-brown spotting. The clawed, oval to elliptic dorsal sepal is 2–2.3 cm long and up to 1.5 cm wide, while the longer narrower lateral sepals are joined for less than one-third of their length. The clawed petals are 2.6–2.8 cm long and 2–3 cm wide. They are strongly crisped and have a bilobed rounded apex. The 3.0–3.4 cm-long lip has tiny yellow ear-like lateral lobes. The broad isthmus has deflexed margins, while the large skirt-like apical lobe, which is bilobed, has very wavy edges. The red and yellow callus is five-lobed, with two spreading calli in front.

O. forbesii requires an intermediate environment with moderately bright indirect light. It does well mounted, and needs a moderately dry winter rest after flowering. *Actual flower size: 5–6 cm across.*

Oncidium fuscopetalum (Hoehne) Garay

Described by Hoehne as *Oncidium macropetalum* var. *fuscopetalum*, this species was elevated to specific rank by Garay. It differs from *O. macropetalum** in the colour of its petals and the configuration of the callus. It is endemic to Brazil, growing in the hot lowlands of Mato Grosso on the edges of the forests and along stream banks.

The clustered pseudobulbs are 2.5–5.0 cm tall and become wrinkled with age. They are slightly flattened and ridged, with one or two leaf-bearing bracts at the base and one or two dark green strap-like leaves at the apex. These leaves are 6–15 cm long, strongly arching and acute at the tip. Several flowers are produced in winter on an arching spike up to 30 cm long. The wavy tepals are dark brown, occasionally mottled with yellow. The erect 0.75 cm dorsal sepal and the 1 cm lateral sepals, which are joined for half their length, are elongated with blunt slightly recurved apices. The irregularly edged petals are 0.75 cm long and about 0.5 cm wide, with a narrow claw at the base. The 1.3 cm lip is yellow with red-brown blotches on and around the callus, which comprises several raised glands. The lateral lobes are acute with rounded upper edges. The broad midlobe is skirt-like and the isthmus is irregularly serrated.

This attractive species grows well mounted on treefern or similar material and given intermediate to warm conditions with moderate light and good air movement. *Actual flower size: approximately 1.5 cm across.*

Oncidium gardneri Lindley

Lindley described this species in 1843, naming it to honour Gardner, who had discovered it in the Serra dos Orgãos near Rio de Janeiro in about 1840. Synonyms include O. *flabelliferum* and O. *praetextum*. O. *gardneri* inhabits the mountain regions of Espírito Santo, Rio de Janeiro, São Paulo, Paraná and Minas Gerais.

The ovoid compressed pseudobulbs, which are 5–7 cm long and 2.5–4.0 cm wide, become furrowed with age. Each bears one or two leathery leaves 15–30 cm long and up to 5 cm wide. The oblong to lanceolate leaves are dark green, sometimes suffused with purple below. A branched spike 45–90 cm long carries several to many flowers in summer or autumn. The clawed sepals are yellow with red to brown bars. The concave rounded dorsal sepal is 1.2–1.6 cm long and 0.7–0.9 cm wide, while the lateral sepals, which are joined for about half their length, are slightly longer and narrower. The paddle-shaped to oval petals are predominantly red to chestnut-brown with yellow markings, especially along the irregular undulating margins. They are about 1.6–1.8 cm long and up to 1.4 cm wide. The 2.0–2.5 cm-long lip is bright yellow with a wide band of red to brown blotches which usually merge. The spreading ear-like lateral lobes are joined to the wide skirt-like apical lobe by a reasonably wide isthmus. The apical lobe is bilobed with wavy edges. The fleshy callus, which is marked with red, is warty at the base, with two finger-like protuberances at the front.

Cultural information for this species may be found under the entry for O. *gardneri* var. *flavum.**

Actual flower size: approximately 5 cm across.

Oncidium gardneri var. *flavum* (hort.)

Ever since its introduction into cultivation in England by Rollison in 1856, O. *gardneri* (along with O. *forbesii,** O. *crispum,** O. *marshallianum*, and O. *sarcodes,** all of which are closely related to it) has remained a very popular species. This is hardly surprising, considering its large showy flowers, which are well displayed and which tend to dance in any breeze. Together with the group mentioned above, O. *gardneri* has provided the basis for many of the excellent modern hybrid oncidiums. Not unnaturally, any unusually coloured forms of this species are eagerly sought. One such is the variety pictured here, O. *gardneri* var. *flavum*.

The discovery of this beautiful variety is credited to Arturo Mello, an orchidist from Rio de Janeiro, who collected it in the area east of Teresopolis in the Serra dos Orgãos in relatively recent times. Except for its lip, which lacks the band of red or brown blotches, the flowers of this variety are identical to those of the type. A pure yellow form has also been reported. Since it shares much of its habitat with O. *forbesii,** and since their flowering times coincide to a large extent, it is not surprising that cross-pollination should have occasionally occurred. The resulting natural hybrid has been given the name O. x *punctatum*.

O. *gardneri* and its varieties may be grown in pots, using a fibrous well-drained material. But it does best for us when mounted on medium-sized slabs of treefern. It prefers diffuse bright light and humid intermediate environment with good ventilation. Watering should be reduced in winter.

Actual flower size: approximately 5 cm across.

Oncidium gracile Lindley

Belonging to the same section as *O. concolor** and *O. dasystyle*,* this species was described by Lindley in the nineteenth century. Originating from the hot dry savannah country of Minas Gerais, it grows as a semi-terrestrial among grasses in sandy soil or in rock crevices amid stunted vegetation. It is found usually between 500–1,000 m.

The tightly-clustered pseudobulbs are pale yellow-green to mid-green, and sometimes produce adventitious plantlets at their apices. From 2–5 cm tall, these plump pseudobulbs have papery bracts at the base and two stiff more or less erect leaves at the apex. Folded at the base, these leaves are 6–10 cm long with a prominent mid-vein and edges which are slightly curled back. The spikes, which range from 30 cm to 1 m or more in height (thus elevating the flowers above the long grass in their habitat) bear six to twelve long-lasting well-spaced flowers. The tepals are about 0.8 cm long, and curve slightly at the apices. They are chestnut brown, edged with olive-green. The 1.6 cm lip is yellow, long and narrow at the base, with a single orange-yellow callus ending in two prominent points. The kidney-shaped apical portion of the lip is about 1.6 cm wide.

This is one of the 'terrestrial' oncidiums which deserve to be more widely grown than they are. Easy to manage, they flower regularly and prolifically. We grow our plants in suspended pots of coarse treefern chunks with a little broken sandstone. They do very well in intermediate conditions with moderate light and plenty of water when in growth.

Actual flower size: approximately 1.5 cm across.

Oncidium harrisonianum Lindley

Named after its discoverer, Harrison, who sent plants to England, this species was described by Lindley in 1832. Synonyms include *O. pallidum*, *O. pantherinum* and *O. pentaspilum*. It is endemic to Brazil, and grows in the cooler mountain ranges of Rio de Janeiro, São Paulo, Espírito Santo, and also on the inland tablelands of Minas Gerais up to 1,000 m.

The almost round pseudobulbs are compressed, with a prominent ridge on either side. They are 2.0–2.5 cm in diameter and bear a single very fleshy leaf 6.5–15 cm long. This sub-erect to curved leaf is dull green, and covered with minute grey spots. It has a prominent keel below and is more or less acute. The erect to arching spike is 12–30 cm long with branches on the lower half. Flowers are borne in summer or autumn on the branches and on the terminal half of the spike. They are about 1.6 cm across, with yellow or orange-yellow tepals blotched with red-brown. The yellow lip has red-brown spots or stripes on the small lateral lobes and about the callus. The concave dorsal sepal and spreading laterals are more or less oblong with sub-acute apices, while the oar-shaped petals have slightly reflexed margins. The wide mid-lobe of the lip is often curved upward at the apex. At the base is a cushion of hairs and five finger-like calli.

This species grows well for us on treefern mounts when hung in a semi-shaded position and given intermediate to cool conditions. It appreciates good ventilation or air movement. Plenty of water is needed when the plant is in growth, with a drier winter rest.

Actual flower size: approximately 1.6 cm across.

151

Oncidium heteranthum Poeppig & Endlicher

Described by Poeppig and Endlicher in 1836, this species was discovered by the former in the Bolivian Andes. Synonyms include *O. bryolophotum*, *O. megalous* and *O. zonatus*. *O. heteranthum* is a widespread species, occurring not only in Brazil but in Costa Rica, Panama, Venezuela, Ecuador, Bolivia and Peru. In Peru it is found mostly at elevations of 1,500–2,300 m above sea level. In Brazil, on the other hand, it inhabits the hot humid lowlands of Pará, close to the equator.

The clustered pseudobulbs are 5.0–8.5 cm tall and about 3 cm wide. They are slightly grooved, with two leaf-bearing bracts at the base and usually two straplike leaves 4–34 cm long at the apex. The erect to drooping flower spike up to 1.2 m long has several branches each about 7–12 cm long. Only the one to three terminal flowers on each branch are perfect, while the others are more or less abortive. In these abortive flowers, the segments, which are narrow and only 0.3–0.4 cm long, are whitish in colour and reflexed. The tepals of the perfect flowers are creamy-white or pale yellow to green, with two or three broad brown bars. The 0.6–1.0 cm-long sepals are 0.2–0.3 cm wide. The broader petals are spoon-shaped, while the three-lobed lip is fiddle-shaped and 1.0–1.5 cm long. The base of the lip is red-brown, whereas the apical part is yellow. The lateral lobes are triangular with recurved edges. The crest, which is white marked with brown, usually comprises nine finger-like projections in three transverse rows, with those in front recurved.

This is a temperature-tolerant species which prefers shady positions.
Actual flower size: 1–2 cm across.

Oncidium hians Lindley

Introduced into England in 1838, this species was described in the same year by Lindley. It is synonymous with *O. leucostomum*, *O. quadricorne* and *O. maxilligerum*. It is restricted to the cool mountains of Pará and the inland tablelands of Minas Gerais where it grows in areas of stunted vegetation at elevations up to 1,000 m.

The almost round pseudobulbs are 1–2 cm tall and somewhat flattened. A single leathery leaf arises from the apex. It is 5–10 cm long and about 2.5 cm wide, spreading or strongly curved, folded at the base and with a keel beneath. In late spring or summer a more or less erect branched spike 12–30 cm long rises, carrying numerous well-spaced flowers from 1.0–1.5 cm across. The oblong tepals are typically reddish-brown with yellow edges, but may be completely yellow-brown, or yellow with red-brown longitudinal stripes. They curve slightly forward at their rounded apices. The obscurely three-lobed lip is pale yellow with or without red-brown spots. It is 0.6–0.8 cm long with tiny rounded lateral lobes and a spreading mid-lobe which is narrow at the base and about 0.45 cm at the apex. The large crest is whitish, with four upward-curving finger-like calli.

This is an easily grown species if given even moderate care, and takes up little space. It appreciates intermediate to cool conditions with moderate shade, and does best for us when mounted. A relatively small treefern slab will accommodate plant for many years.
Actual flower size: 1–1.5 cm across.

Oncidium hookeri Rolfe

Very closely related to *O. loefgrenii** and *O. raniferum,** this species was first collected by Gardner near Rio de Janeiro in 1837. Originally mistaken for *O. raniferum*, it remained undescribed until 1887. The differences between the two species are fairly minor and, indeed, *O. raniferum* var. *majus* is a synonym for *O. hookeri*. It is confined to the cool mountain ranges of Minas Gerais, Rio de Janeiro, Paraná and Rio Grande do Sul, where it grows as an epiphyte.

The 1.5–3.0 cm pseudobulbs are narrowly conical and distinctly ridged, with one or two leaf-bearing bracts at the base. There are one or two erect or arching leaves at the apex of the pseudobulbs. They are 8–20 cm long, narrow, and more or less rounded at the apex. In autumn or winter an erect to sub-erect spike 15–20 cm long carries up to about sixty flowers, each 0.7–1.0 cm long. The oblong tepals are creamy-yellow with some brownish tinges, while the three-lobed lip is yellow with reddish-brown markings on and about the callus. The dorsal sepal and the petals curve inward at the tips, while the lateral sepals extend behind the relatively large lateral lobes of the lip. The 0.6 cm mid-lobe is fan-shaped and has a very fleshy concave callus at the base. This callus comprises about five rather flattened lobes.

An undemanding species, *O. hookeri* appreciates a position in moderate shade with intermediate to cool conditions. It grows well for us when mounted on treefern. Plenty of water when in growth, but allow to dry out a little in winter. *Actual flower size: 0.7–1 cm long.*

Oncidium hydrophyllum Barbosa Rodrígues

This species, endemic to Brazil, was described in the late nineteenth century by Barbosa Rodrígues. It grows in the cooler mountains from Rio de Janeiro to Rio Grande do Sul, and in the drier savannah country of Minas Gerais and Goiás, where it experiences a continental climate. It is found growing in humus-filled rock crevices or in sandy soil among tall grasses, as well as in the cool misty forests.

The tightly clustered pseudobulbs are dull yellow-green, slightly compressed with acute edges, and sometimes produce new plantlets at their apices. They are ovoid, typically 3–6 cm tall and up to 3 cm wide, with papery bracts at the base and two strap-like leathery leaves 6–20 cm long at the apex. The erect spike is from 30 cm to 1 m or more to reach above the grasses. It bears several 2–3 cm flowers about 1 cm apart near its apex. The tepals are greenish-yellow, heavily blotched with reddish-brown or purple-brown with a few paler spots. The concave 0.6–0.8 cm dorsal sepal lies almost along the column, while the 1 cm ovoid lateral sepals are spreading. The very crisped, broad petals have a narrow base. The 1.6 cm lip is bright yellow with brown markings on the callus, which has several finger-like protrusions. The very small lateral lobes are ear-shaped, while the 2 cm-wide mid-lobe is skirt-like. The rhomboidal column wings are held well forward.

This is an easily grown and attractive species. It may be mounted, but we grow it in suspended pots of treefern fibre and a little broken sandstone, in moderate light and intermediate conditions. *Actual flower size: 2–3 cm long.*

Oncidium jonesianum Reichenbach (f.)

Saint Léger discovered this attractive species in northern Paraguay in 1878. Reichenbach described it in 1883, dedicating it to the Rev. Jones, an avid orchid enthusiast of the day. In Brazil, *O. jonesianum* inhabits the savannah country of Mato Grosso, Minas Gerais and São Paulo, where it grows usually on trees near watercourses.

The erect or pendulous plants have ovoid pseudobulbs up to about 1 cm long, which are covered by a white sheath. The single, almost terete leaf has a single furrow when young, and may be tinged with purple. Leaves are 15–40 cm long and 0.4–1.5 cm in diameter, with sharply pointed apices. In autumn, arching to pendulous spikes from 30–60 cm long carry five to sixteen showy flowers. The tepals are cream to pale creamy-green with large red-brown spots. They are about 2.0–2.7 cm long and 0.7–1.0 cm wide, with undulating margins and recurved apices. The sepals are oblong to spathulate, with the dorsal curving forward, while the petals are oblong to elliptic. The 2.0–2.5 cm-long lip has a large white apical lobe, which usually has a few red spots at the base, or may even be covered with spots. The ear-like lateral lobes are yellow with reflexed margins, while the yellow or whitish crest is spotted with red. There is a large warty callus on the disc.

O. jonesianum has the reputation of being a difficult plant in cultivation. It resents 'wet feet' and does best for us when mounted on pieces of cork or paperbark. It needs fairly bright light and high humidity in an intermediate environment, plenty of water when in growth, then a drier rest. *Actual flower size: 4–5.5 cm across.*

Oncidium lanceanum Lindley

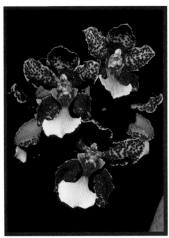

Lindley described this species in 1836, naming it in honour of John Lance, who had introduced it into England from Suriname in 1834. *Lophiaris fragrans* is conspecific. Occurring also in Colombia, Venezuela, Guyana, Suriname, French Guiana and Trinidad, this species is confined in Brazil to the hot humid lowlands of Amazonas.

The strongly flattened pseudobulbs of this 'mule-ear' oncidium are usually insignificant, but may be up to 2 cm tall. Each one bears a single more or less erect leaf which is 30–50 cm long and 7.5–12.5 cm wide and is said to resemble the ear of a mule. It is dark green, leathery, very stiff, folded at the base and spotted with reddish purple. Flowering is predominantly in summer on erect often branched spikes rising from the base of the newest growth. From 25–55 cm long, each spike carries up to twenty or more very fragrant long-lasting flowers. The oval to oblong tepals, which are narrow at the base, have undulating edges and are 3.5 cm long and about 2 cm wide. They are yellow or yellow-green, densely spotted or blotched with red to chocolate-brown. The 3.8 cm-long lip is usually dark purple to rose-purple at the base with a white to pink apical lobe. The lateral lobes are ear-like to oblong, while the large kidney-shaped mid-lobe has slightly irregular margins. The crest comprises an erect fleshy ridge with a forward-pointing projection on either side at the base.

O. lanceanum may be mounted — cork bark is ideal — or grown in a pot or basket. It prefers a warm humid environment, moderate shade and year-round watering. *Actual flower size: 5–6.5 cm across.*

Oncidium lietzei Regel

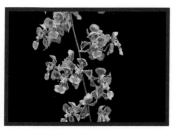

Very closely related to *O. pubes,** *O. fimbriatum** and *O. riograndense*, etc., this species was described in about 1880 by Regel, who named it after Lietze, the original collector. *O. hrubyanum* is a later synonym. Its distribution is confined to the cooler mountains and savannahs in Espírito Santo, Paraná and São Paulo. It is also found in Paraguay.

The cylindrical to conical pseudobulbs, which are slightly compressed, are 5–12 cm tall and up to 2 cm wide. They are partly covered by white papery sheaths, with one or two erect to spreading leaves at the apex. From 11–20 cm long and 3–5 cm wide, they are oblong to elliptic and have an acute recurved apex. In autumn a slender arching to pendulous spike 40–90 cm long carries several flowers on the apical half. The tepals are yellow or greenish-yellow, more or less heavily barred with reddish-brown. The spoon-like 1.0–1.5 cm-long dorsal sepal is bent forward over the column, while the shorter lateral sepals are joined for nearly half their length. The fiddle-shaped petals, which curve inward, are 1.1–1.6 cm long. The 1.2–1.5 cm-long lip is yellow with some red on the large warty callus which extends on to the base of the apical lobe. The narrow oblong lateral lobes curve inward and are separated from the rounded apical lobe by a narrow isthmus. The column has incurved wings with red at their bases.

O. lietzei does best for us when mounted on treefern slabs and given intermediate semi-shaded conditions. Plants need plenty of water when in growth, but should be allowed to dry out between waterings. *Actual flower size: 2.2–3 cm across.*

Oncidium limminghei Morren ex Lindley

This species was first collected in Venezuela by van Lansberg, who sent plants to Morren in Belgium in 1855. Morren sent this type material to Lindley, who described it in the same year. *O. echinophorum* is conspecific. The species is reported only from Venezuela and from the state of Rio de Janeiro in Brazil.

It is a curious little plant with flat heart-shaped pseudobulbs 1–2 cm long, which often overlap on the branching rhizome. Each pseudobulb bears a single leaf which is also heart-shaped and lies flat against the host. The leaf is about 3.5 cm long, and light grey-green with maroon-purple veins. The erect to horizontal spike rises from the base of the new pseudobulb in summer or autumn and bears one flower at a time, continuing to lengthen until up to five flowers, each 3–4 cm across, have been produced. The concave dorsal sepal and slightly incurved petals are dark reddish-brown, more or less barred with yellow-green, while the ovoid sepals are generally duller in colour. The three-lobed lip is yellow, spotted with orange-brown or red, with rounded lateral lobes that narrow at the base and curve inward at the tips. The mid-lobe has a long narrow isthmus and may be turned up or slightly incurved. The callus comprises three ridges. The column wings are deeply fringed.

One of the more difficult oncidiums in cultivation, this species should be mounted on material with excellent drainage such as cork or paperbark. It prefers moderate light, intermediate to warm conditions and high humidity. *Actual flower size: 3–4 cm across.*

Oncidium loefgrenii Cogniaux

Cogniaux named this species, which is very similar to *O. hookeri** and *O. raniferum*,* in honour of Loefgren, the Swedish botanist and explorer who became head of the Botanical section of the Botanical Gardens in Rio de Janeiro. *O. mellifluum* is synonymous. This species comes from the southern half of Brazil, growing in the cool mountain ranges and the warmer dry savannahs.

The slightly flattened pseudobulbs are closely set on the rhizome. From 1.5–2.5 cm tall, they are narrow, dark green with some purple spotting and are strongly ribbed. They bear two narrow strap-like leaves 7–13 cm long, which have a prominent mid-vein and are sub-erect to arching. The branched spike is up to 15 cm or more long and in autumn or winter carries many 1 cm-long flowers. The tiny tepals are yellow with a few reddish markings. The petals are swept upward with the dorsal sepal, which hoods the column. The pointed lateral sepals are joined for about half their length before spreading out. The three-lobed lip is yellow, with a bright red glossy callus made up of several very fleshy rounded lobes in three transverse rows. The tiny lateral lobes are rounded and often curved up at the ends. The 0.6 cm midlobe is narrow at the base, spreading to 0.45 cm at the more or less bilobed apex, which is often curved upward.

This unusual little species grows well when mounted and hung in moderate to fairly heavy shade. It prefers humid conditions with intermediate temperatures, plenty of water in the growing season, and a drier rest in winter.

Actual flower size: approximately 1 cm long.

Oncidium longipes Lindley

Introduced into England in 1850, this species has been widely cultivated since that time. Lindley described it in 1851. Synonyms include *O. janeirense* and *O. oxyacanthosmum*. It is native to Minas Gerais, Rio de Janeiro, São Paulo, Paraná, Santa Catarina and Rio Grande do Sul, where it grows in the cool moist mountain areas as well as in the warmer lowlands. In the latter areas it favours trees along watercourses as hosts.

The elongated pale green pseudobulbs are more or less clustered on a stout rhizome. From 2.0–2.5 cm tall, they are furrowed and have one or two glossy green leaves at the apex. These are 10–15 cm long, strap-like, and sharply pointed. *O. longipes* flowers freely on a zigzag spike up to 15 cm long from spring to autumn. The two to five long-lasting flowers are 2.0–3.5 cm across, with yellow tepals streaked with reddish brown. The bright yellow lip is spotted with dull red on and about the whitish callus. The oblong sepals have acute tips, while the broader petals are rounded. The lateral sepals are joined for about one-third their length. The ear-like lateral lobes of the lip have wavy edges, as does the broad mid-lobe. The callus at the base of the lip has many wart-like projections. The claw of the mid-lobe is more or less fringed.

This is a popular and easily grown species which quickly reaches specimen size in the right conditions. It does well for us when mounted on treefern and given bright indirect light in intermediate to cool conditions. Water copiously when in growth and give a drier rest in winter.

Actual flower size: 2–3.5 cm across.

Oncidium macronix Reichenbach (f.)

Described by Reichenbach in the second half of the nineteenth century, this attractive and unusual species belongs — along with *O. longicornu* — to the section *Rhinocerontes*, a name referring to the unusually elongated callus shaped like the horn of a rhinoceros. Also found in Argentina and Paraguay, *O. macronix* is confined in Brazil to Santa Catarina and Rio Grande do Sul where it grows epiphytically in both cooler mountain regions and warmer lowlands.

The dark green pseudobulbs are set about 1 cm apart on a stout rhizome. They are 4–5 cm tall and quite narrow, compressed, strongly ridged, and sometimes curved. They have papery bracts at the base, and usually bear two narrow tapering leaves 10–14 cm long. In autumn, branched 40 cm spikes bear many 1.0–1.5 cm flowers, each zigzag branch carrying five to ten blooms. The widely spreading tepals are predominantly pale to dark purplish-brown with some yellow-green mottling, especially near the apex. The more or less erect dorsal sepal is slightly recurved, and the relatively broad wavy petals curve inward at the apex. The three-lobed lip is yellow with a large orange-red blotch around the callus, which is usually orange-red, but may be yellow. The lateral lobes are rounded, as is the broad mid-lobe. The column is white.

A distinctive species which is easily cultivated, it does well for us when mounted on small treefern slabs and hung in moderate light in intermediate to cool conditions with good air movement. Give copious water when in growth, with a slightly drier rest after flowering.

Actual flower size: 1–1.5 cm long.

Oncidium macropetalum Lindley

This species, described by Lindley in the nineteenth century, comes from Paraguay, possibly from Bolivia, and from the states of Minas Gerais, Goiás, Mato Grosso and São Paulo in Brazil. Its habitat is the hot lowland savannah, up to 1,000 m.

The plump pseudobulbs, from 2.5–5.0 cm tall, are ridged and slightly compressed. They have one or two leaf-bearing bracts at the base and one or two arching leaves about 10–15 cm long at the apex. These leaves are acute, with a prominent midvein. In winter an arching spike bears a few to many well-spaced flowers about 3.2 cm long. The short wavy sepals are pale yellow with or without red-brown bars. The dorsal sepal is erect or slightly recurved and the lateral sepals are joined at the base. The 1.5 cm-long petals, together with the lip, dominate the flower. They are bright yellow with or without dark red markings at the narrow bases. Shaped like a rounded square, they have undulating edges and may be indented. Sometimes they have a sharp point in the centre of the outer edge. The three-lobed lip is yellow with red-brown blotches on and around the callus, which has several finger-like projections at the rear and three diverging rounded ones in front. The lateral lobes are rounded, as is the bilobed mid-lobe. The isthmus is serrated and the relatively large column wings are more or less rounded.

This species does best in an intermediate environment with moderate light, good air movement and plenty of water when in growth, followed by a drier resting period.

Actual flower size: approximately 3 cm long.

Oncidium micropogon Reichenbach (f.)

Although first grown in Europe as early as 1853, and described by Reichenbach a year later, this species did not come into general cultivation until re-introduced by Sander in 1886. Closely related to O. *barbatum** and O. *ciliatum,** it is synonymous with O. *dentatum*. It is reported from the hot lowlands of Bahia, where it favours riverside trees, and from the cooler mountain areas of Santa Catarina and Rio Grande do Sul.

The clustered ovoid pseudobulbs are compressed, with acute edges and several ribs. From 3.0–6.5 cm tall, they bear one or two strap-like leaves. These are sub-erect, 10–15 cm long, and more or less rounded at the tips. This species flowers from summer to autumn on 30–45 cm-long spikes which carry three to ten or more flowers about 4 cm long. The oblong sepals are yellow with red-brown bars, and the acute laterals are joined for about half their length. The dorsal sepal is more or less rounded. The bright yellow 2 cm petals are spotted at the narrow claw-like base. They are almost round with wavy irregular edges and a sharply pointed apex. The almost equally three-lobed lip is yellow with spots on and around the fleshy callus which has several conical projections. The lateral lobes are roundish, while the mid-lobe is fan-shaped with undulating edges and a sharp point. The edge of the isthmus is toothed.

This species does well if given intermediate conditions with moderate light and fairly high humidity. We grow our plants on treefern mounts.

Actual flower size: approximately 4 cm long.

Oncidium phymatochilum Lindley

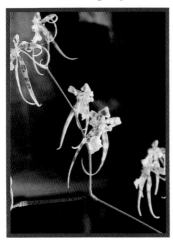

This unusual species was not described by Lindley until 1848, despite being first cultivated in England by Loddiges and by the Rev. Clowes of Manchester in about 1840. O. *phymatochilum* is a widespread but not common plant, occurring in Mexico, Guatemala and Brazil and inhabiting forests up to 1,300 m above sea level. In Brazil it favours the mountains of Pernambuco, Espírito Santo, Minas Gerais, Rio de Janeiro and São Paulo.

The compressed oblong to ovoid pseudobulbs are 5.5–12.5 cm tall and up to 5 cm wide. They are often brownish-purple with a single leathery leaf at the apex. The elliptic to lanceolate leaf is 24–35 cm long, 4.0–7.5 cm wide, and dark green suffused with red below. In spring or summer wiry spikes 60 cm–1.5 m or more long bear many well-spaced flowers on the zigzag upper portion. The recurved and sometimes twisted tepals may be ivory-white with orange-red spots, or yellow to pale green with red-brown blotches near the base. The long tapering sepals are 1.8–3.5 cm long and about 0.3 cm wide at the base, while the petals are shorter and slightly wider. The 1.5–2.5 cm long lip is white with reddish blotches on the basal part. The ear-like lateral lobes have wavy margins, while the isthmus has deflexed edges. The ovate to heart-shaped apical lobe has a sharp tapering point on the recurved apex. The crest has several tooth-like projections, with the front three being the largest.

O. *phymatochilum* does best for us when mounted. It needs a humid, intermediate to warm environment with moderately bright light and year-round watering.

Actual flower size: approximately 5 cm long.

Oncidium pubes Lindley

Discovered in the early part of the nineteenth century by Descourtilz, this species was not described until 1826, after Douglas sent plants to London from Brazil. Its synonyms include *O. bicornutum* and *O. pubescens*. It ranges from the cooler mountain regions of Rio de Janeiro, São Paulo and Minas Gerais to Paraguay and possibly Argentina.

The clustered dark green pseudobulbs are almost terete, tapering slightly near the apex. From 5–7 cm long and 1.0–1.5 cm in diameter, they usually have a pair of very dark green strap-like leaves 7–12 cm long and up to 3 cm wide with an acute apex. This species usually flowers in autumn on an arching to pendulous spike carrying many flowers on short branches. The tepals are glossy yellow more or less barred and spotted with red-brown — sometimes to such a degree that little yellow is visible. The 1.2 cm petals and dorsal sepal are paddle-shaped with the petals curving inward at the apex and the concave dorsal hooded over the column. The lateral sepals are joined for most of their length. The three-lobed lip is yellow with red-brown markings around the ridged callus, which is minutely haired, and toothed in front. The small lateral lobes are oblong, and the clawed mid-lobe is kidney-shaped.

This species grows easily and flowers regularly in cultivation and, with its bright glossy flowers, makes a nice show. It needs intermediate conditions, moderate light and plenty of water when in growth. It does well for us when mounted on treefern slabs.

Actual flower size: approximately 2 cm across.

Oncidium pulvinatum Lindley

Harrison introduced this species into Britain in 1838 when he sent plants which he had collected in Brazil to his brother in Liverpool. Lindley described it in the same year. *O. sciurus* is conspecific, while *O. divaricatum*,* *O. sphegiferum** and *O. robustissimum* are all closely related. *O. pulvinatum* grows epiphytically in the mountains in the southern part of Brazil, from Minas Gerais and Espírito Santo to Rio Grande do Sul.

The rounded pale green to yellow-green pseudobulbs, which are strongly flattened and 3.5–5.0 cm in diameter, bear single fleshy leaves at the apex. The oblong to lanceolate leaves are 20–30 cm long and up to 8 cm wide with an acute apex and a prominent keel. The slender arching spike is 60 cm–3 m long, with several branches and many flowers. The 1.0–1.3 cm-long tepals are yellow-green to olive-green, with chestnut-brown at the base. The spoon-shaped sepals are 0.6 cm wide and have a small point at the apex, as do the oblong petals, which have a short claw at the base. The dorsal sepal is more or less concave, while the laterals are spreading. The pale yellow lip has red spots and is approximately 1.4 cm long. The large semi-circular lateral lobes have irregular undulating margins. The bilobed mid-lobe also has wavy edges. At the base of the lip is a single circular callus, which is white with red spots and covered with tiny glands.

O. pulvinatum is quite a robust species. It does well when mounted on a treefern slab and placed in a humid, intermediate to cool environment with moderately bright light. Reduce watering in winter.

Actual flower size: 2–2.5 cm across.

Oncidium pumilum Lindley

This species, which is similar to *O. nanum* and synonymous with *Epidendrum ligulatum*, was described by Lindley in 1825. It occurs in Uruguay, Argentina, and in Brazil from Pará, Goiás and Bahia in the north to Rio Grande do Sul in the south. It grows in a wide range of habitats from hot humid lowlands to cooler mountain areas.

O. *pumilum* is a miniature 'mule-ear' oncidium, with clustered insignificant pseudobulbs only 0.3–0.5 cm tall. These are flattened and bear a single fleshy leaf 5–12 cm long and 1.6–3.5 cm wide. Often suffused with pinkish-brown and spotted with purple, the stiff leaf is more or less erect, pointed, and folded at the base. The erect spike is 8–15 cm long and carries many densely packed flowers on short branches in winter and spring. The tepals are yellow with red-brown markings, while the 0.5 cm lip is pale yellow with a brown line on either side of the callus. The dorsal sepal is concave and the petals curve forward. All tepals have blunt apices. The large lateral lobes of the lip are rounded on the upper edges and curve downward. The concave mid-lobe is more or less oval. The fleshy callus comprises two pairs of diverging ridges. The column has large curved wings.

This delightful and compact species does well for us when mounted on sections of paperbark trunk or cork and hung in a moderately bright position. It is tolerant of a wide range of temperatures. Water all year round, with a dry winter rest when grown in cool conditions.

Actual flower size: approximately 0.8 cm long.

Oncidium raniferum Lindley

Very closely related to *O. hookeri,** *O. loefgrenii** and *O. paranaense*, this species was first collected by Gardner in the Serra dos Orgãos and introduced into England by Knight. Lindley described it in about 1837. *O. raniferum* is endemic to Brazil, occurring in the mountains of the widely separated states of Pernambuco and Rio de Janeiro.

The clustered ovoid to elongated pseudobulbs are compressed, and have several ridges on either side. From 2.5–6.5 cm long and 0.7–2.0 cm wide, they have two or three leaf-bearing bracts at the base and two linear to oblong leaves at the apex. These are 6–20 cm long and up to 1.5 cm wide, with a sub-acute apex. The sparsely branched, erect spikes are 20–35 cm long and bear many dainty flowers, the sepals and petals of which are yellow to greenish-yellow with pale red bars and spots. The tepals are up to about 0.4 cm long and 0.2 cm wide. The lateral sepals are spreading, while the concave dorsal sepal is erect. The oblong to elliptic petals are sometimes reflexed. The 0.4–0.8 cm-long lip is the dominant feature of the flower. It is yellow with red-brown on the disc. The small, more or less oblong lateral lobes have rounded apices, while the somewhat wedge-shaped apical lobe is minutely notched at the apex. The large glossy callus comprises six lobes in two horizontal rows.

O. *raniferum* is an easily grown and attractive miniature. It does well mounted on small treefern slabs and hung in a moderately shady intermediate to cool environment with relatively high humidity. Reduce water in winter, but do not allow to dry out completely for long periods.

Actual flower size: 1–1.2 cm long.

Oncidium sarcodes Lindley

Lindley described this deservedly popular species in 1849, the year in which it was first cultivated in England by the Horticultural Society of London. O. *rigbyanum* is synonymous, while O. *forbesii,* O. *gardneri* and O. *curtum* are closely related. O. *sarcodes* grows on trees in the mountains and in the warm humid lowland areas of Minas Gerais, Rio de Janeiro, Paraná and São Paulo.

The closely set dark green pseudobulbs are 9–15 cm tall and 1.5–3.0 cm wide. Almost terete, they are slightly compressed. At the apex are two or, occasionally, three leathery oblong to lanceolate leaves, which are 15–30 cm long and 2.5–6.0 cm wide. In spring an arching spike 90 cm–1.8 m long bears many flowers on short well-spaced branches. The tepals are yellow with a large chestnut blotch or several smaller blotches. The spathulate to oval dorsal sepal, which is concave and curves forward over the column, is 1.3–1.6 cm long and about 1.2 cm wide. The narrower lateral sepals are oblong to lanceolate with a keel on the reverse. The somewhat paddle-shaped petals are about 2 cm long and have undulating margins. The 1.7–2.0 cm-long yellow lip may be spotted all over with red, but usually only has spots around and on the oblong callus, which has two spreading lobes at the front and a tooth on either side near the middle. The small more or less oblong lateral lobes have reflexed edges, while the edges of the skirt-like bilobed apical lobe are undulating.

O. *sarcodes* prefers a humid, intermediate to warm environment, semi-shade, plenty of water when in growth and a drier winter rest.

Actual flower size: 3.5–5 cm across.

Oncidium schwambachii (?)

We imported plants of this pretty species from Brazil several years ago, but have been unable to find any reference to it in the standard reference works. One of the 'mule-ear' oncidiums, it belongs to the O. *lanceanum* alliance within the section *plurituberculata*, and is thus related to O. *lanceanum,* O. *stramineum*, O. *nanum*, O. *pumilum* and O. *morenoi*, most closely resembling the last two.

The clustered pseudobulbs are up to 1 cm tall and are covered by papery sheaths, as is the base of both the single leathery leaf and the flower spike. The 8–12 cm-long leaf is dark green to yellow-red, with red to purple spots. The leaves are 2.3 cm wide and folded at the base and have an acute apex. A simple or, more typically, a branched spike up to about 13 cm long bears many very fragrant flowers about 0.8 cm long. The oblong to lanceolate tepals are white to pale straw-yellow and about 0.4 cm long. The dorsal sepal and the petals curve forward near the apex, while the lateral sepals are more or less spreading. The relatively large white lip has a fleshy yellow callus, which has three rounded lobes in front between the large more or less oblong lateral lobes. The smaller apical lobe is rounded.

We have no information about the origin or habitat of O. *schwambachii*, but have found that it grows well in intermediate conditions, that it prefers to grow on mounts of cork or paperbark, and that it should be allowed to dry out between waterings. It likes plenty of water when in growth, a drier winter rest, moderately bright light and good ventilation.

Actual flower size: approximately 0.8 cm long.

Oncidium species — section *barbata*

Although we imported this species several years ago as *O. croesus*, it does not fit the description of that species. It does however belong to the same section, i.e. the section *barbata*. This section is characterised by an uneven number of callosities on the lip, which is shorter than the lateral sepals and has a serrated or ciliate isthmus or area just above the isthmus.

This species has compressed ridged pseudobulbs set 1–2 cm apart on the rhizome. They are 3.0–5.5 cm tall and up to 1 cm wide, and are more or less oblong with papery bracts at the base and usually a single oblong leaf at the apex. The 9–20 cm-long leaf is 1.5–2.5 cm wide, with an unevenly bilobed apex and a prominent mid-vein. Up to twelve well-spaced flowers are borne in summer on a somewhat zigzag spike 12–32 cm long. The undulating tepals are yellow with red to chestnut-brown bars or blotches. The erect dorsal sepal and slightly curved petals are about 2–3 cm long and 0.5 cm wide. The spreading lateral sepals, which are oblong with an obtuse apex, are 3–4 cm long. The 2.5 cm-long lip is yellow with red-brown on and around the crest, which comprises many finger-like calli. Both the oblong to rounded lateral lobes and the kidney-shaped apical lobe have undulating margins. The area between the lateral lobes and the narrow waist has serrated deflexed edges.

This species does well when placed on treefern mounts and grown in intermediate to cool conditions. It prefers relatively high humidity and partial shade. It seems to need no distinct resting period in winter. *Actual flower size: 5–7 cm long.*

Oncidium sphegiferum Lindley

This species was introduced into England by Loddiges in about 1842, and was described by Lindley in 1843. It is very closely related to *O. divaricatum*,* *O. robustissimum* and *O. pulvinatum*.* It is found in the cooler areas of Espírito Santo, Rio de Janeiro, Paraná and Rio Grande do Sul.

The pale green to yellow-green pseudobulbs are strongly compressed and almost round. From 2.0–3.5 cm tall, they each bear a single very stiff, fleshy leaf 16–22 cm long and 3.5–7.5 cm wide. The leaves are elliptic to oblong, and have a prominent mid-vein below. In summer, autumn or winter an erect to arching spike rises from the base of the pseudobulb. From 24 cm–1.2 m long, it is branched and carries several to many flowers. The 1.0–1.4 cm-long sepals and petals are greenish-yellow to bright yellow-orange with heavy chestnut blotching on the basal half. The dorsal sepal is spoon-shaped, with the apical half hooded over the column, which has large rectangular wings with purple-brown stripes. The spreading lateral sepals are club-shaped, while the more or less rectangular petals have slightly deflexed irregular margins. The 1.5–1.8 cm-long lip is paler than the tepals and has several chestnut blotches. The large rounded lateral lobes are irregularly serrated on the side and lower edges. The large raised callus, which is white and orange, is covered with minute hairs.

O. sphegiferum does well when mounted on a slab of treefern or similar material, in semi-shaded intermediate conditions. Give plenty of water when in growth, with a reduction of water in winter. *Actual flower size: approximately 2.7 cm long.*

Oncidium spilopterum Lindley

L indley described this species in 1844, using plants imported by Loddiges. *O. saint-legerianum* and *O. ghillanyi* are later synonyms. Also found in Paraguay, *O. spilopterum* occurs in the hot lowlands and also the savannah country of Minas Gerais and Mato Grosso. (For more information on habitat, see the entry for *O. spilopterum* var. *album*.*)

The clustered pale green pseudobulbs are slightly compressed, typically 3–7 cm tall, and up to about 2.5 cm wide. They are ovoid to conical and become grooved with age. There are a few papery bracts at the base and one or two apical leaves. These are linear to lanceolate, 15–20 cm long and 1.5–2.5 cm wide, with a prominent midvein below and an acute apex. From six to ten flowers are produced in autumn to early winter on an erect to arching spike 30–90 cm or more long. The ovate to oblong tepals are greenish-yellow, heavily marked with violet-brown or even completely violet-brown, and have undulating margins. The lateral sepals, which are joined at the base, are about 1.3 cm long and 0.3 cm wide, while the dorsal sepal and petals are approximately 1 cm long and 0.5 cm wide. The yellow 2.0–2.5 cm-long lip dominates the flower with its maroon-violet callus and occasional reddish marks on the paler reverse at the base. The spreading lateral lobes are oblong to rounded, while the apical lobe, which has irregular undulating margins, is more or less kidney-shaped. The callus is a single multi-digitate mass.

For cultural information refer to the entry for *O. spilopterum* var. *album*. *Actual flower size: 3–3.5 cm long.*

Oncidium spilopterum var. *album* (hort.)

W ith many orchid species it is not uncommon to find 'alba' varieties the flowers of which, while not necessarily white, lack any red pigmentation. The variety of *O. spilopterum* pictured is one of these. This clone has greenish-brown tepals and a large yellow lip with white on and around the callus. The large curved column wings are pure yellow, whereas in the type they have a band of red at the base.

Knowledge of the habitat of an orchid species often gives valuable clues as to its cultural requirements. *O. spilopterum*, although sometimes found in the less elevated areas of Mato Grosso, mostly inhabits the savannahs of Minas Gerais at more than 800 m above sea level. It grows in the crevices of rocks or in sandy areas between rocky outcrops, in many places sharing its habitat with rupicolous laelias, *Pleurothallis teres*,* and other oncidiums such as *O. blanchetii*,* *O. hydrophyllum** and *O. warmingii*. The vegetation of these areas is stunted, with low shrubs (including *Vellozia* bushes) and tall grasses which afford some protection from the harsh conditions. The climate is continental, with often very large differences between day and night temperatures. Strong winds help to ameliorate high daytime temperatures in summer. Winter conditions are cold and dry and last for three to five months with only nightly dews to sustain plants.

It is not surprising, then, that in cultivation *O. spilopterum* prefers bright indirect light, intermediate to cool conditions, good ventilation, only occasional misting in winter, and a coarse freely draining medium. *Actual flower size: 3–3.5 cm long.*

Oncidium trulliferum Lindley

Introduced into cultivation in England by Loddiges, in whose nursery it flowered in 1838, this species was described by Lindley in 1839. *O. dimorphum*, *O. galeatum*, *O. ornithocephaloides* and *O. venustum* are all conspecific. *O. trulliferum* inhabits both the cooler mountains and the warm lowlands of Espírito Santo, Rio de Janeiro, São Paulo and the southern states.

The compressed dull-green pseudobulbs are more or less oblong, 10–21 cm tall and up to about 2.5 cm wide. They have several papery bracts at the base and two or three sub-erect to spreading leaves at the apex. These leaves are oblong to almost lanceolate with a narrow folded base. They are 15–23 cm or more long and 2.5–5.0 cm wide. Branched spikes about 60 cm long bear many pretty flowers about 2.5 cm wide. The bright yellow to greenish-yellow tepals are barred with red-brown. The sepals are somewhat spathulate, with the 0.8 cm-long concave dorsal hooded over the column. The spreading 1.0–1.2 cm-long lateral sepals, which are about 0.4 cm wide, are joined only at the base, while the almost rectangular petals are 1 cm long and about 0.7 cm wide with reflexed margins and blunt apices. The petals have irregular margins, as does the 1.5 cm-long lip, which is yellow with red on and in front of the callus. The rounded lateral lobes are ear-like, while the rounded apical lobe is vaguely bilobed. The callus has three main very warty lobes, the front one of which is saddle-shaped, while the rear two are spreading.

For cultural information, refer to the entry for *O. trulliferum* var. *album*.*

Actual flower size: approximately 2 cm across.

Oncidium trulliferum var. *album* (hort.)

Still a relatively rare species in cultivation, *O. trulliferum** is the only Brazilian oncidium belonging to the section *rostrata*. This section includes twenty-seven species, among them the very well-known *O. ornithorhyncum* from Mexico and Central America and *O. cheirophorum* from Costa Rica, Panama and Colombia.

The distinctive features of this section are the curved, almost s-shaped column and the elongated anther and rostellum, which together produce a 'beak' near the apex of the column. *O. trulliferum*'s fairly long-lasting flowers make a delightful display, especially if the spike — with its fifty to one hundred or more flowers — is allowed to follow its natural inclination to arch gracefully. Occasional 'alba' clones of this species, such as the one pictured here, are probably not as rare as most growers believe. This one cropped up by accident in a batch of plants imported from Brazil some years ago. The sepals and petals are a pale glossy greenish-yellow without any of the red markings found in the type. The fleshy lip is very pale yellow to almost white, with yellow on the large callus. The column and its spreading, narrowly oblong wings are also nearly white.

O. trulliferum (and the var. *alba*) requires a relatively humid, intermediate to warm environment with good ventilation and bright indirect light to semi-shade. It needs plenty of water when in growth, but the amount should be reduced greatly in winter. It does well when mounted on fairly large slabs of treefern, but it may be potted in a coarse freely draining medium such as treefern chunks or bark.

Actual flower size: approximately 2 cm across.

Oncidium varicosum Lindley

This species, which was described by Lindley in 1837, has a number of later synonyms, including *O. geraense*, *O. euxanthinum* and *O. lunaeanum*. *O. varicosum* favours sunny positions in semi-tropical rainforests at 600–800 m above sea level in the states of Minas Gerais, São Paulo and Goiás. It also extends to riverside and marshy forests on the central plateau of Goiás.

The clustered oval to oblong pseudobulbs are furrowed and spotted with purple. They are compressed and typically 4–8 cm tall and 2.0–2.5 cm in diameter, but may be larger. The two strap-like leaves at the apex are 15–30 cm long with an acute apex. Many flowers are borne in autumn or winter on an arching to pendulous spike 90 cm–1 m or more long. The tepals are yellow with red-brown bars. The concave oval to lanceolate dorsal sepal is 0.7–1.0 cm long, about 0.5 cm wide, and is held forward above the column. The slightly concave lateral sepals, which are joined for about half their length, are 0.9–1.2 cm long, 0.4–0.5 cm wide, and more or less lanceolate. The narrowly oblong petals are about 1 cm long, and are often recurved, with reflexed crisped margins. The large skirt-like lip, which is typically 2–3 cm across, is bright buttercup yellow with red-brown on and around the callus. The more or less rounded lateral lobes have wavy margins, as does the apical lobe, which is bilobed at the apex. On the crest is a central nose-like projection with two others attached to either side, as well as several tiny independent glands.

For cultural information, refer to the entry for *O. varicosum* var. *rogersii*.*

Actual flower size: 2–3 cm across.

Oncidium varicosum var. *rogersii*

Since its introduction into cultivation in Europe by de Jonghe of Belgium shortly after its rediscovery by Libon in 1846, *O. varicosum*,* which is closely related to *O. bifolium** and *O. flexuosum*,* has remained one of the most popular of all oncidiums or 'dancing ladies', as they are commonly called. The common name is particularly apt for this species, as the slightest breeze makes the blossoms dance. Its common Brazilian name — 'chuva de ouro', or rain of gold — is even more descriptive, alluding as it does to the cascade of brilliant yellow flowers which meets the eye when the long slender spike with its well-spaced branches is allowed to arch or hang naturally. *O. varicosum* var. *rogersii*, pictured here, was originally described as a separate species, but there seems to be substantial disagreement about the actual author. Veitch, in *A Manual of Orchidaceous Plants* attributes the description to Reichenbach (f.) (1870), while *Curtis's Botanical Magazine* gives Bateman (1865) the credit. Either way its varietal epithet gives recognition to Rogers, in whose collection it first flowered. Seemingly much rarer than the type, the var. *rogersii* generally has an even more dominant lip. Often regarded in the past as a distinguishing feature, lip size alone cannot be relied on to separate variety and type. A more reliable feature is the shape of the apical lobe of the lip, which in the var. *rogersii* has four rounded lobes instead of the two present in the type.

Both need fairly bright light and an intermediate environment, plenty of water when in growth, and a drier winter rest.

Actual flower size: 3–5 cm across.

Ornithocephalus myrticola Lindley

Descourtilz collected this species in the early nineteenth century in Brazil, where he found it growing on trees of the *Myrtaceae* family, hence its specific name. Lindley described it in 1840. Among its synonyms are *O. pygmaeum* and *O. reitzii*. It occurs in a range of habitats, from cool moist mountain regions to dry savannah country and hot lowlands, from Minas Gerais and Rio de Janeiro to Rio Grande do Sul, and also in Bolivia.

The plant has no pseudobulbs but comprises a fan of very fleshy leaves which are jointed near the base. The leaves are typically 5–7 cm long and 0.5–0.7 cm wide, tapering to an acute point. The flowers are borne on zigzag spikes 4–8 cm long which rise from the leaf axils. The flowers, which are redolent of lemon, are covered on the exterior with relatively long hairs, as are the spikes. There are about fifteen densely packed flowers on a spike, each measuring about 1 cm across. The irregularly edged sepals and petals are white with a central green stripe on the sepals and several stripes on the petals. The 0.5 cm lip is often held uppermost. Its edges are reflexed and its fleshy disc has five prominent yellow or green calli, the outer ones being hairy. There is a transverse green stripe in front of the calli. The narrow apex is white.

This species does well when mounted on cork or paperbark and placed in a semi-shaded intermediate environment with good humidity and air movement. Give it some water all year round, and never let it dry out completely.

Actual flower size: approximately 1 cm across.

Ornithophora radicans Garay & Pabst

This delightful miniature was first described by Linden and Reichenbach in 1864 from material collected in the Porto Alegre area of Rio Grande do Sul. It is also found in the states of Paraná, Espírito Santo, Rio de Janeiro, São Paulo and Santa Catarina. Originally classified as a sigmatostalix, it was reclassified by Garay and Pabst in 1951, when they created the new genus *Ornithophora*, of which it remains the only species.

It is an extremely popular and easily grown species with delicate thin apple-green pseudobulbs, each bearing a pair of narrow grassy leaves, spaced at intervals of 1–3 cm on the creeping rhizome. In late summer arching flower spikes emerge from the base of the pseudobulbs. Each spike bears about ten bird-like flowers (the generic name means bird-bearing) which are pale lemon-green with a white and yellow or orange lip and a purple column. The tiny tepals are slightly recurved. The lip has a long narrow claw, which is covered by a large yellow to orange callus. The more or less oblong lip has a horn-like protrusion near the upper corners and two diverging keels in front of the callus.

The plant's rambling habit makes it ideally suited to slab cultivation, although flat pans may also be used. It needs a position in moderate shade and should be kept moist all year round except for a slightly drier rest after new pseudobulbs have matured. The pseudobulbs, however, should not be allowed to shrivel unduly. *O. radicans* thrives in intermediate to cool conditions.

Actual flower size: 0.6–1 cm long.

Pabstia jugosa (Ldl.) Garay

Introduced into England by Loddiges, this species was originally described by Lindley in 1840 as *Maxillaria jugosa*. He transferred it to the genus *Colax* in 1843. However, *Colax* later proved to be a homonym, which invalidated the name. In 1973 Garay created the genus *Pabstia*, naming it in honour of Guido Pabst, and transferred this species to it. *Lycaste jugosa* and *Zygopetalum jugosum* are conspecific. *Pabstia jugosa* grows as an epiphyte or lithophyte in the cooler mountains of Rio de Janeiro and São Paulo.

The clustered pseudobulbs are 5–7 cm tall and 2–3 cm wide. They are ovoid to oblong, compressed and slightly grooved. The two somewhat pleated leaves at the apex of the pseudobulbs are 15–25 cm long and 3–5 cm wide, tapering to a sharp point. A 12–20 cm spike rises from the base of the new growth in early summer and carries two to four showy flowers. The oblong to lanceolate sepals are white to greenish-white, approximately 3 cm long and 1.3–1.7 cm wide. The dorsal sepal is slightly concave. The ovate petals are greenish-white blotched with dark maroon. They are 2.6–2.8 cm long, about 1.5 cm wide, and have an obtuse apex. The clawed lip is about 2.5 cm long. It is white with reddish-purple stripes and blotches on the roundish mid-lobe, and spots on the disc and erect lateral lobes. The disc has four grooves and is slightly hairy near the base.

Humid, moderately shady conditions in an intermediate environment suit this species. It may be mounted or potted. It requires plenty of water when in growth, less once the pseudobulbs have matured.

Actual flower size: approximately 6 cm across.

Pabstia viridis (Ldl.) Garay

This epiphyte was first described as *Maxillaria viridis* by Lindley, who later named it (invalidly) *Colax viridis*. In 1973 Garay used it as the type species for his new genus *Pabstia*. Its distribution is limited to the mountains of Rio de Janeiro, São Paulo and Santa Catarina.

The clustered, faintly four-angled pseudobulbs are a waxy olive-green. From 3–9.5 cm tall and 1.2–2.5 cm wide, they are wrinkled and slightly compressed. At the base of each pseudobulb are two leaf-bearing bracts, while the apex bears two leaves 16–22 cm long. These are tapered at both ends, 3.5–4.5 cm in width, and have three prominent veins beneath. In summer a single very fleshy flower is borne on a 4 cm spike from the base of the developing pseudobulb. The apple-green sepals are keeled on the reverse, and may have a few brownish spots. The concave dorsal sepal is 2.5–3.7 cm long and 1.5–2.0 cm wide. The lateral sepals are slightly shorter. The shorter narrower petals are heavily marked with dark brown-maroon. The mobile lip is white, densely suffused with purple, and is joined to the column by a 3.6 cm claw. The erect to spreading lateral lobes are rounded at the rear and acutely pointed at the front. The reflexed mid-lobe, which is 1.0–1.4 cm wide, is almost rhomboidal.

P. viridis is a pretty and easily grown species which deserves to be better known in collections. It does best for us when grown in suspended pots of chopped treefern fibre, and prefers a humid intermediate environment with semi-shade. It needs plenty of water when in growth with some reduction after pseudobulbs mature.

Actual flower size: 2.5–5 cm across.

Pabstiella mirabilis (Schltr.) Brieger & Senghas

This genus was created in 1975 by Brieger and Senghas to honour Guido Pabst, the Brazilian botanist. They regarded Schlechter's *Pleurothallis mirabilis* as being sufficiently distinct from all other pleuro-thallids to warrant its own genus. It is distinguished by the extremely long column-foot (about 0.5 cm) to which the 0.5 cm claw of the lip is attached. Luer did not accept the change, and in 1986 returned the species to *Pleurothallis*, creating the subgenus *Mirabilia* of which it is the only member. We have chosen to retain Breiger and Senghas's name. This unusual epiphyte inhabits the cool moist mountain ranges in the states of São Paulo, Paraná, Santa Catarina and Rio Grande do Sul.

The very fleshy leaves are held on long wiry stalks up to 5 cm long. The blade of the leaf is 2–5 cm long and 1 cm wide. In spring wiry spikes rise from the point where the leaf joins its stalk. The arching spikes are up to 5 cm long and carry about six delicate white flowers which may be faintly tinged with pink. They are about 1 cm long, including the spur formed by the lateral sepals to accommodate the long claw of the lip. The dorsal sepal is slightly hooded, while the narrow rounded petals point forward. The free parts of the lateral sepals curve outward under the lip. The minutely warty blade of the lip is held almost at right angles to the claw.

This species needs cool damp conditions with good air movement, moderate shade and relatively high humidity all year round. We grow our plants on small treefern mounts.

Actual flower size: approximately 1 cm long.

Phloeophila pubescens (Barb. Rodr.) Garay

This intriguing pleuro-thallid was originally described as *Physosiphon pubescens* in 1877 by Barbosa Rodrígues. In 1974 Garay transferred it to Hoehne and Schlechter's *Phloeophila*, a genus established in 1926. After renaming it *Sarracenella pubescens* in 1981, Luer has since transferred it to the genus *Pleurothallis*, renaming it *P. sarracenia*. (Lindley had already used the name *P. pubescens* for another species.) Despite this latest change, about which we have some reservations, we have continued to use the most commonly accepted name. This species inhabits the cool misty mountains of Minas Gerais, Rio de Janeiro, Paraná and Santa Catarina.

The succulent leaves are closely set on a creeping branching rhizome, which often grows away from its host so that segments hang freely. Green to yellow-green with purple spots, the almost stalkless boat-shaped leaves are up to 2 cm long with an acute tip. The unusual slug-like flowers are produced in late winter and early spring directly from the rhizome. The curved 1.5 cm flowers are dark reddish-purple, with all sepals joined to form a tube which is minutely hairy inside. The sepals contract to triangular points at the small opening. The narrow petals and tiny lip are hidden deep inside the tube. The lip is covered with minute warts, and the upturned sides at the base are edged with fine hairs.

An easy grower in intermediate to cool conditions, this species does well when mounted on treefern, paperbark or cork. A semi-shaded position suits it, with year round moisture.

Actual flower size: approximately 1.5 cm long.

Phragmipedium caricinum (Ldl. & Paxt.) Rolfe

Lindley and Paxton described this species as *Cypripedium caricinum* in 1850, using a herbarium specimen sent to them by Bridges, who had discovered the species in Bolivia. Rolfe transferred it to *Phragmipedium* in 1896. Synonyms include *Selenipedium caricinum* and *Paphiopedilum caricinum*. A native also of Bolivia and Peru, *P. caricinum* occurs in the far north of Brazil in the state of Roraima. It grows as a terrestrial in the rainforest, on rocks covered with humus — even in the middle of rivers — and very occasionally on trees.

Each growth comprises three to six strap-like leaves 25–50 cm long, but only 0.6–1.3 cm wide. From three to seven flowers are borne in spring on a spike 30–60 cm long, which is covered with short hairs. The spike elongates as flowers open successively. The tepals are whitish to pale or lime-green with darker green veins, and have more or less undulating margins. The lanceolate to nearly oval dorsal sepal is 2.5–4.0 cm long and about 1.3 cm wide, while the shorter lateral sepals are joined for their entire length. The narrow ribbon-like petals are 5–13 cm long, twisted, and rose-coloured near the apex. The pouch-like lip is up to about 3.5 cm long. Its colour is green to yellow-green, while the lateral lobes, which are folded inward, are green and ivory-white with green and brown-purple spots. The staminode has two almost black hairy 'eyebrows'.

P. caricinum is a species which resents disturbance, and if possible should be left undivided. It prefers moist, warm to intermediate conditions with high humidity, year-round water and semi-shade.

Actual flower size: 7–15 cm long.

Phragmipedium sargentianum (Rolfe) Rolfe

Introduced into England by Sander in 1892, this species was described by Rolfe as *Selenipedium sargentianum* in the same year. In 1896 he transferred it to his new genus *Phragmipedium*. It is very closely related to *P. lindleyanum*. *P. sargentianum* is endemic to the coastal ranges of Pernambuco at 600–1,000 m above sea level. It is predominantly terrestrial, growing in moist decaying vegetable matter in shady positions in the forest. It also occasionally occurs in bright indirect light among tall grasses in crevices in granite outcrops.

Each growth has up to seven dark green oblong to lanceolate leaves. Usually from 20–50 cm long, they may reach 1.2 m in very shady positions. They are about 3.5 cm wide, with a prominent mid-vein and acute apices. The tepals are green or yellowish-green, with reddish veins and are edged with minute hairs. The somewhat concave dorsal sepal is ovate to elliptic, about 3 cm long and 1.6 cm wide. The lateral sepals are joined for their entire length, while the narrow 5.5 cm-long petals are spreading. The petals have purplish-red nerves and edges, especially near the twisted, undulating apices. The yellow-green 4 cm-long lip is veined and suffused with purplish-red. The lateral lobes, which are heavily spotted and suffused with purple-red, are folded inward, and each has a white gland in the centre of its edge. The side and upper edges of the staminode have tiny reddish hairs.

P. sargentianum requires a warm humid environment with year-round moisture. It should be potted in a well-drained fibrous mixture and will flower in both shade and bright indirect light.

Actual flower size: 7–10 cm across.

Pleurothallis alligatorifera Reichenbach (f.)

Reichenbach described this species, naming it for the fancied resemblance of the flowers to the gaping jaws of an alligator. *P. blumenavii* is a later synonym. *P. alligatorifera* comes from the cool moist mountain regions of Rio de Janeiro, Santa Catarina and Rio Grande do Sul. It grows as an epiphyte on mossy trees in areas where the forests are saturated with dew each night.

The clustered terete stems are 2.5–4.5 cm long and about 0.3 cm wide at the thickened apex. Each carries a single leathery leaf which is 5–10 cm long and 1.7–2.5 cm wide. This leaf is lanceolate to elliptic, keeled below, and minutely three-toothed at the apex. An erect slightly zigzag spike up to 30 cm long rises from the apex of the stem and bears about twelve well-spaced nodding flowers on the apical half. They are orange-yellow with red stripes. The 1.2 cm dorsal sepal is concave, and curves forward over the column. The lateral sepals, which are joined for almost their entire length, have more or less incurved outer edges. The 0.2 cm-long petals are held forward and have a sharp point in the centre of the obtuse apex. The tiny 0.35 cm-long lip is three-lobed with erect narrow lateral lobes, which are rounded at the apex, and an elliptic midlobe.

Like most *Pleurothallis* species, *P. alligatorifera* will do well either mounted on treefern or similar material or in small pots of well-drained fibrous material, such as treefern fibre, pine bark and a little moss. It requires a moderately shady spot in a cool to intermediate environment with year-round moisture.

Actual flower size: approximately 1.2 cm long.

Pleurothallis grobyi Bateman ex Lindley

This species was first imported into England from Guyana by Bateman, who named it in honour of Lord Grey of Groby, a dedicated orchid grower. However, it was Lindley who first described the species in 1835. Its many synonyms include *P. surinamensis* and *P. marginata*. It ranges from Mexico through Central America and the West Indies and into South America as far as Peru and Brazil and is found from near sea level to 1,500 m. In Brazil it occurs in Bahia and from Espírito Santo and Minas Gerais to Santa Catarina.

The plants comprise neat clumps of paddle-shaped fleshy leaves from 1.5–7.0 cm long. They are usually suffused or mottled with purple beneath. The erect to arching spikes are produced in spring or summer. From 5–15 cm long, they are thread-like and somewhat zigzag, carrying several well-spaced flowers which do not open widely. Normally all flowers on a spike open at the same time. They are a translucent creamy-yellow or greenish-white with longitudinal reddish-purple stripes. The concave dorsal sepal is recurved at the apex, and the lateral sepals are joined for most of their length, with upturned sides which form a scoop. The petals are tiny, as is the tongue-shaped lip.

This little species grows quite happily when mounted on a small treefern slab or potted in a medium of pine bark, treefern fibre and sphagnum moss. It prefers a cool shady environment with good air movement and fairly high humidity. The plant should never be allowed to dry out completely.

Actual flower size: 0.5–0.75 cm long.

Pleurothallis hypnicola Lindley

This species, for which Cogniaux's *P. cuneifolia* is a synonym, was described by Lindley in 1842. It inhabits the cool damp mountains from Minas Gerais and Espírito Santo to Rio Grande do Sul, growing in association with many other pleurothallids including *P. sonderana** and *P. grobyi.**

The mid-green leaves are 6–12 cm long including the slender 2–4 cm stalks, which are covered with dark brown bracts. The acute leaves are minutely three-toothed and slightly reflexed at the apex. Flowers are produced in spring and at other odd times during the year on a spike which rises from the top of the leaf-stalk. Over a period of time many spikes are produced from the same leaf-stalk. Each one continues to elongate over an extended period, producing flowers on old spikes even after the leaves have dropped. The wiry, somewhat zigzag spike may reach an eventual length of 12 cm. The flowers, which may open simultaneously or in succession, are approximately 0.6 cm long. Colour is usually yellow, very heavily blotched with dark claret so that flowers may appear to be totally red. The lateral sepals are yellow at the base, and are joined for about half their length, forming a scoop under the 0.3–0.4 cm lip. The small petals have a thickened glossy apex.

This species prefers a cool moist environment in fairly heavy shade. It may be mounted or potted, but should be kept moist all year yound. Lacking pseudobulbs, like all pleurothallids, it can succumb quickly if allowed to dry out for long periods.

Actual flower size: approximately 0.6 cm long.

Pleurothallis platystachya Regel

This distinctive pleurothallis was described in the nineteenth century by the German botanist Regel. *P. acutangula* is conspecific. *P. platystachya* grows on mossy trees in the damp coastal ranges of Espírito Santo, Rio de Janeiro, São Paulo and Paraná.

The clustered stems are strongly flattened and covered with brown papery sheaths. They are 4.5–12.0 cm long and up to 0.6 cm wide near the apex. Each bears a single fleshy leaf, from 6.5–15.0 cm long and 1.8–3.0 cm wide, which is lanceolate with an acute minutely notched apex. The 13–20 cm-long spike is produced in spring from the apex of the stem. The spike and the eight or more flowers which it bears are both strongly compressed and flattened. The flowers are yellowish-green with maroon spotting. The oblong to lanceolate dorsal sepal, which is about 1.5 cm long and 0.3 cm wide, lies parallel to the column and is folded almost in half and thickened along the centre. The slightly longer lateral sepals are joined for two-thirds of their length to present an H-like cross-section. They curve upward under the lip and, like the other tepals, have acute apices. The very narrow petals are 0.6–0.7 cm long, point forward, and have upward-curving apices. The oblong mobile lip is about 1.1 cm long and 0.2 cm wide, with tiny erect lateral lobes and slightly deflexed margins. On either side near the margins is a keel which runs for two-thirds of the length of the lip.

P. platystachya is an easy grower, either mounted or potted. It needs a cool to intermediate environment with year-round moisture and semi-shade.

Actual flower size: approximately 1.5 cm long.

Pleurothallis prolifera Herbert ex Lindley

Described by Lindley early in the nineteenth century, this species is very closely related to *P. pectinata* and *P. tridentata*. Barbosa Rodrígues' *P. litophila* is a later synonym. A native of the states of Rio de Janeiro, São Paulo and Minas Gerais, it grows mostly as a lithophyte in rock crevices — together with *Laelia longipes*, *L. flava*,* *L. crispilabia** and *Bifrenaria tyrianthina** — but also on trees. These mountain areas experience hot dry days and cool nights with frequent heavy dews.

The leaves of *P. prolifera* are borne at intervals on a stout rhizome. The leaf stalk is 3–15 cm long and the 3–7 cm leaf blade is bent downward. The leaf is somewhat heart-shaped with a prominent mid-vein and turned-up sides. It is rather leathery in texture and mid-green in colour, suffused with purple, particularly when grown in bright light. A spike is produced in spring or summer from the base of the leaf, with several 0.5–0.6 cm-long dark maroon flowers which do not open widely and lie along the top of the leaf. The narrow 0.25 cm-long petals and lip have serrated edges. The petals point forward, while the lip lies along the joined lateral sepals. Sometimes small plantlets are produced on top of the leaf, instead of flower spikes.

A cool to intermediate environment suits this species. It does well in rather brighter light than most *Pleurothallis* species, and is also a little more tolerant of dry conditions. We grow our plants on treefern mounts hung in moderate shade.
Actual flower size: 0.5–0.6 cm long.

Pleurothallis saurocephala Loddiges

Loddiges described this robust epiphyte in 1830. Kuntze's *Humboldtia saurocephala* is conspecific. A fairly common plant in the cooler mountain forests of southern Brazil, it ranges from Minas Gerais and Espírito Santo as far south as Rio Grande do Sul.

The closely set stems are more or less erect and covered with brown papery sheaths. From 4–19 cm long, the stems are terete at the base and slightly compressed at the 0.4–0.6 cm wide apex. Each bears a very fleshy leaf 8–15 cm long and 2.5–5.0 cm wide. It is elliptic to lanceolate with a notch at the rounded apex. Erect to arching spikes from 7–20 cm long rise from the apex of the stem in late spring to summer with about twenty fleshy flowers, which do not open fully. The sepals, which are about 1 cm long, are greenish-yellow to pink-brown on the outside. Inside, they are covered with tiny maroon to almost black warts. The more or less oblong dorsal sepal is 0.3 cm wide, while the laterals, which are joined at the base, are held close together to present an oblong to elliptic blade about 0.4 cm across. The 0.2 cm-long petals, which are held forward, are yellow-green or pinkish, with or without stripes. The purplish lip is about 0.3 cm long, sometimes with green at the base. It is more or less oblong, with tiny erect lateral lobes and two keels from near the middle almost to the apex.

This is an unusual and easily grown *Pleurothallis* species, which is not as sensitive to dry conditions as many of the genus. It prefers high humidity, however, and an intermediate to cool environment with diffuse bright light to semi-shade.
Actual flower size: approximately 1 cm long.

Pleurothallis sonderana Reichenbach (f.)

Described over a century ago by Reichenbach, this is one of the better-known and more popular *Pleurothallis* species. It is indigenous to Brazil, but found there over a wide area, occurring in the southern states of Minas Gerais, Espírito Santo, Rio de Janeiro, São Paulo, Paraná, Santa Catarina and Rio Grande do Sul. It grows usually on the branches and trunks of trees in the cooler areas of the mountain ranges.

The fleshy erect leaves are 2–6 cm long, including the short stalk. They are narrow, with a central channel above and a rounded underside. The 3 cm-long spike rises from the top of the stalk from summer to winter. It bears three to five golden yellow to burnt-orange flowers which last for several weeks. They do not open widely, and tend to nod on their spikes. Both the acute dorsal sepal and the lateral sepals, which are joined for almost their entire length, are 0.6–0.7 cm long. The more or less oval petals are only 0.25 cm long. The slightly longer lip is minutely serrated near the apex and has a spur on either side near the base.

Like most of the pleurothallis, this species is easy to maintain in cultivation once the right conditions have been provided. It may be potted in any fine freely draining mixture or mounted on a piece of treefern with a little moss about the roots. It prefers a fairly well-shaded position and cool temperatures with good air movement. It should never be allowed to dry out completely.

Actual flower size: approximately 0.7 cm long.

Pleurothallis species — striped flowers

Brazil is extremely rich in pleurothallis, with over 300 species occurring there. The vast majority of these species are found growing on mossy trees in the cool humid mountains of Espírito Santo, Rio de Janeiro, São Paulo, Paraná, Santa Catarina and Rio Grande do Sul. Only a few species such as *P. barbulata* and *P. semperflorens* prefer the hot humid lowlands, while fewer still inhabit the savannah country of the interior. In Brazil *Pleurothallis* species are not highly regarded as horticultural subjects, and this, together with their large numbers, has led to a paucity of information on the genus. This in turn often makes it difficult, sometimes impossible, to identify plants even tentatively without access to herbarium material. The pretty little species pictured here falls, unfortunately, into this category.

The slender closely set stems are 3–5 cm tall with two or three sheaths and single fleshy leaf from 4–8 cm long and 1 cm wide. It is lanceolate with an acute apex. A short spike rises from the apex of the stem and bears a number of flowers consecutively. Only one flower opens at a time, with a new bud developing simultaneously. The tepals are buff-coloured with longitudinal maroon streaks. The concave dorsal sepal is almost 1 cm long, has an upturned apex and hoods the column and the 0.2 cm-long petals. The 1 cm-long lateral sepals are joined for almost their entire length. The small tongue-like hinged lip is dark brown-black.

This species grows well on small mounts in a cool to intermediate environment with semi-shade and year-round moisture.

Actual flower size: approximately 1 cm long.

Pleurothallis species — *strupifolia* alliance (?)

We have used Pabst and Dungs' classification to place this species in the section *brachystachyae-longicaules*. Probably belonging to the *strupifolia* alliance, it resembles very closely *P. pubescens* (Lindley 1836), and may even be that species.

The stout stems are faintly grooved and slightly compressed near the 0.2–0.3 cm-wide apex, which is wider than the rounded base. Each stem bears a single leathery leaf up to 25 cm long. The leaves, which are bluish-green, are oblong to lanceolate with deflexed margins. They are arching to pendulous. Flowering is in late spring, with about twelve alternating flowers which open successively over a very short period of time, then all remain open together. The spike is up to 10 cm long, with several often being produced from the apex of each stem. The more or less lanceolate dorsal sepal is cream with maroon stripes on the reverse. It is approximately 1 cm long, 0.3 cm wide, and very strongly recurved. The lateral sepals are joined for their entire length to form a lanceolate platform about 1 cm long and 0.6 cm wide. It is greenish with pale maroon blotches. The sides are turned up at the base to form a very short chin. The petals point forward, are 0.3 cm long, coloured the same as the dorsal sepal, and have obtuse apices. The tiny hinged lip is purple, with a somewhat rounded apex. The short winged column has a purple anther cap.

This species should be grown in an intermediate environment with semi-shade and high humidity. It needs year-round moisture with a slighty drier winter.

Actual flower size: approximately 1 cm long.

Pleurothallis species — yellow flowers

This very pretty species belongs to the group of pleurothallis for which Barbosa Rodrígues created a separate genus, *Anathallis*, in 1877. In his new genus he placed those *Pleurothallis* species whose flowers have lateral sepals that are joined only to the base of the column and not to each other. However, this treatment was largely ignored, and *Anathallis* is now accepted only as a synonym. Within this grouping, the species shown here most likely belongs to the *P. depauperata* alliance, whose members come from the cool mountain regions ranging from Minas Gerais and Espírito Santo to Rio Grande do Sul.

The stems are 4.0–8.5 cm long and covered with brown sheaths at the base. The blade of the leathery leaf is oval to oblong-elliptic, 3.5–9.0 cm long and about 2.5 cm wide. Arching to pendulous spikes about 25 cm long are produced from the apex of the stem, with several appearing from the same stem over a period of time. Each bears many nodding flowers which open only about three-quarters of the way. The tepals are translucent yellow with a darker central vein. The slightly concave lanceolate dorsal sepal is about 1 cm long, while the vaguely falcate lateral sepals are slightly longer and have a short sharp point at the apex. The 0.5 cm-long petals are more or less oblong with a blunt asymmetrical apex. The somewhat fiddle-shaped lip is about 0.5 cm long and has a brown vein down the centre for most of its length.

This is an easily grown species in a semi-shaded cool to intermediate environment with year-round moisture. It may be potted or mounted.

Actual flower size: approximately 1 cm across.

Pleurothallis strupifolia Lindley

Described in the nineteenth century by Lindley, this species has several synonyms, including *P. bicolor* and *P. hookeri*. It inhabits the cool mountain ranges of Rio de Janeiro, São Paulo, Paraná and Santa Catarina, growing epiphytically among mosses and lichens.

The stalk, which is covered with papery bracts, is up to 7 cm long, topped with a very fleshy stiff leaf 5–10 cm long. The curved leaf points downward and is notched at the tip. This species flowers in spring or summer with the spike rising from the base of the leaf. Each 3–5 cm-long spike carries about five fleshy flowers and lies along the middle of the leaf. The flowers, approximately 1 cm long, do not open widely, and are cream or pale yellow heavily spotted with very dark maroon — almost black in some cases — and more or less suffused with pink. The hooded acute dorsal sepal is recurved at the apex and striped with pink on the outside. The joined lateral sepals form a broad rounded platform, and are minutely toothed along their edges, as is the dorsal sepal near its base. The pale 0.4 cm-long petals are spoon-shaped, with irregular indentations around the apex. The minutely spotted lip is 0.4 cm long and has several fleshy calli.

This very attractive species does best for us when mounted and allowed to sprawl over a fairly large treefern slab. It should be given cool to intermediate conditions and a damp semi-shaded position. Water copiously in summer, less often in winter.
Actual flower size: approximately 1 cm long.

Pleurothallis teres Lindley

This unusual, little-known species was described by Lindley in about 1842. Unlike most other pleurothallids, it does not inhabit the cool damp forests but, rather, grows on rocks in bright light in the dry inland areas of the states of Rio de Janeiro and Minas Gerais, at 500–1,000 m above sea level. Here it experiences large diurnal variations in temperature and cold, very dry winters with dew as the only source of moisture. The vegetation is limited to grasses, stunted scrub and a few scattered trees.

In bright light the almost terete leaves become a dark red-brown, while in shade they remain green, tinged or mottled with red-purple. These leaves grow close together on a thick branching rhizome, which is anchored to the rocks with wiry roots. The pencil-shaped leaves are 4–12 cm tall with a single channel on top. *P. teres* flowers mostly in winter (although flowers may appear at almost any time) and sometimes again in summer. The erect spike rises from the base of the leaf-channel. Up to 9 cm tall, it bears up to a dozen or more nodding flowers up to about 0.7 cm long. These may be orange with dark red stripes or, more commonly, brick-red. The 0.5–0.7 cm-long sepals are concave, with the laterals joined for their entire length. The tiny petals and lip point forwards.

This species is very adaptable. It does well in intermediate to cool conditions, in either bright light or semi-shade. It may be potted or mounted, but we grow our plants in shallow terracotta pans of coarse mixture suspended where ventilation is good. Watering should be reduced in winter.
Actual flower size: 0.5–0.7 cm long.

Promenaea paranaensis (?) Schlechter

This species, as will be seen from the illustration, is very similar to *P. xanthina*.* On closer examination, however, several differences become apparent. It belongs, quite clearly, to the *P. xanthina* alliance, and most closely resembles the drawings of Schlechter's *P. paranaensis* in Pabst and Dungs' *Orchidaceae Brasilienses*. Like all promenaeas it inhabits the cool damp mountains of south-east to southern Brazil.

The vaguely four-angled pseudobulbs are 1.5–2.0 cm tall and 1.0–1.5 cm wide. They are oval to oblong with two spreading apical leaves, which are a glistening pale to mid-green with darker veins. From 4–7 cm long, the leaves are narrowly lanceolate with a prominent mid-vein and a tiny sharp point at the recurved apex. The plants are smaller in all their vegetative parts than all clones of *P. xanthina* we have seen. Like *P. xanthina*, this taxon flowers in late spring to early summer. The bright yellow lanceolate tepals are slightly more spreading than in *P. xanthina*, and the more or less oblong lip is considerably more deflexed. The large lateral lobes of the lip, which are spotted with red, have a distinct spur on the lower edge at the base. The column — narrower than that of *P. xanthina* — is streaked with red. Unlike *P. xanthina*, this taxon does not present a view of column wings and anther cap as three distinct points when viewed from the front. Also, the callus on the lip has only one tooth between the elevated sides, while that of *P. xanthina* has three.

All *Promenaea* species enjoy much the same conditions in cultivation as in nature, and this one should be treated similarly to *P. xanthina*.

Actual flower size: 4–5 cm across.

Promenaea riograndensis Schlechter

Schlechter described this little-known *Promenaea* species, which grows as an epiphyte in the cool mountain regions of Rio Grande do Sul and Santa Catarina, sometimes in association with *P. stapelioides*.*

The dull olive-green pseudobulbs are set about 0.5 cm apart on a creeping rhizome. From 2.0–2.5 cm tall and 1.0–1.5 cm in diameter, they are slightly compressed, furrowed and wrinkled. There are two or three leaf-bearing bracts at the base of the pseudobulb and two sharply pointed lanceolate leaves at the apex. These soft mid-green leaves have darker veins and are 11–13 cm long and 1.0–1.5 cm wide. Single flowers are borne in summer on 3 cm spikes from the base of the pseudobulb. All segments, which are cream with maroon-purple spots and blotches on the inside, project forward, so that flowers measure only about 2 cm across. The sepals and petals are recurved at their sharply pointed apices. The 2 cm-long sepals are 0.8 cm wide near the base and have a prominent keel. The dorsal sepal is concave, while the laterals are almost triangular. The more or less ovoid petals are 1.5 cm long and 0.8 cm wide. The three-lobed 1.8 cm-long lip is hinged to the base of the column, with the 0.7 cm lateral lobes curving inward. The 0.9 cm wide mid-lobe is rounded, with a sharp point at the apex. A raised dark callus extends to the base of the side-lobes and forms a jutting shelf above the mid-lobe.

P. riograndensis, although rather fragile in appearance, is not a difficult subject in cultivation. It needs a cool to intermediate environment and semi-shade with year round moisture.

Actual flower size: approximately 2 cm across.

Promenaea stapelioides (Link & Otto) Lindley

Link and Otto described this species early in the nineteenth century as *Cymbidium stapelioides*. The specific epithet refers to the resemblance of the flowers to the South African stapelias. In 1832 Lindley described it as *Maxillaria stapelioides*, transferring it to his new genus *Promenaea* in 1843. Reichenbach's *Zygopetalum stapelioides* is another synonym. Native to the cooler mountains from Rio de Janeiro to Santa Catarina, it grows mostly on trees, but also on damp rocks in shady positions at moderate elevations.

The clustered pseudobulbs are compressed and more or less four-angled. From 2–3 cm tall, they are enclosed at the base by two to four leaf-bearing bracts. Two soft grey-green leaves, from 5–6 cm long,

rise from the apex of the pseuodobulb. They are spreading, with a prominent mid-rib beneath and an acute apex. In summer or autumn one or two long-lasting flowers almost 5 cm across are produced on short spikes from the base of the pseudobulb. The keeled, slightly overlapping sepals and petals are greenish-yellow, densely blotched and barred with dark purple-maroon. The velvety lip is mostly a dark purplish-black. The paler lateral lobes project forward. The concave mid-lobe is almost round with a raised keel on the rounded crest.

This unusual species may be mounted, but we grow our plants in well-drained suspended pots of treefern fibre, pine bark and sphagnum moss. Intermediate conditions are preferred, with moderate shade to bright indirect light. Plants should never be allowed to dry out completely.

Actual flower size: approximately 5 cm long.

Promenaea xanthina (Ldl.) Lindley

Still commonly known by its synonym, *P. citrina*, this species was probably first collected in Minas Gerais at the beginning of the nineteenth century by Descourtilz, who called it *Epidendrum jonquille*. However, this was not published, so Lindley's *Maxillaria xanthina* of 1839 is the earliest valid name. Lindley transferred it to *Promenaea* in 1843. It is a beautiful and popular miniature from the cooler mountains of southern Brazil where it grows as an epiphyte, and occasionally on rocks, in forests up to 1,700 m.

The obscurely four-angled pseudobulbs are clustered on a branching rhizome. From 1.5–3.0 cm long, they have one or two leaf-bearing bracts at the base, and two sub-erect to spreading leaves at the

apex. From 5–7 cm long, they are soft, pale to mid-green, have an acute apex and a prominent mid-vein below. When not in flower, the plants are almost impossible to distinguish from those of *P. stapelioides*.* The one or two fragrant flowers are borne on an arching 5–10 cm spike which rises from the base of the pseudobulb in spring or summer. Lasting a month or more, they are clear yellow with reddish blotches on the base and lateral lobes of the lip and on the column. The sepals are about 2 cm long, the petals slightly shorter. The oblong 1.5 cm lip is more or less rounded at the apex. The lateral lobes are erect, and the broad mid-lobe is deflexed. The fleshy three-lobed callus has a raised protuberance inside the three-toothed apex of its mid-lobe.

We grow this species as we do *P. stapelioides*, but continue watering until late autumn.

Actual flower size: 3–4 cm across.

Pseudolaelia corcovadensis Pôrto & Brade

A small genus of only six species, all of which are endemic to Brazil, *Pseudolaelia* was established in 1935 by Campos Pôrto — the grandson of Barbosa Rodrígues and Director of the Botanical Gardens in Rio de Janeiro — and Brade. They also described this species, naming it *P. corcovadensis* because it grows on the Morro de Corcovada, a steep rocky outcrop which rises to about 700 m in Tijuca National Park within the city of Rio de Janeiro. It is the only pseudolaelia found in the state of Rio de Janeiro, the other species occurring in Minas Gerais, with *P. dutrae* and *P. vellozicola* also growing in Espírito Santo.

The elongated to ovoid pseudobulbs are set well apart on a stout rhizome. They are about 4–6 cm long and 2 cm wide. At the apex are up to six more or less erect leaves, which are linear to oblong and 10–22 cm long. A long apical spike carries several pale to dark mauve-pink flowers on the apical section. The spreading tepals are lanceolate to elliptic and approximately 2 cm long. The dorsal sepal and the petals are about 0.7 cm wide, while the laterals are slightly broader. The 1.5 cm-long lip has spreading, more or less oblong, lateral lobes and a skirt-like apical lobe, which has undulating margins. Seven creamy-yellow keels radiate from the base of the lip.

Because of its rambling habit, *P. corcovadensis* is best grown on a mount, preferably of freely draining material such as cork, which it seems to prefer to treefern. It should be hung in fairly bright light in a warm to intermediate environment with good ventilation or air movement.

Actual flower size: approximately 4 cm across.

Psygmorchis pusilla (L.) Dodson & Dressler

Originally described as *Epidendrum pusillum* by Linnaeus in 1753, this species has had a number of name changes over the ensuing years. Reichenbach moved it to the genus *Oncidium* in 1863 under the name *O. pusillum*. It has also been known as *O. iridifolium*. It was finally removed from the genus *Oncidium* when Dodson and Dressler created the genus *Psygmorchis* (meaning 'fan orchid') in 1972. It is found, usually in large colonies, from Mexico to Panama, in the West Indies, Bolivia, and in most parts of Brazil except the north-east corner and those states south of Rio de Janeiro. It is quite commonly encountered growing on coffee and citrus trees in cultivated orchards. Its natural habitat is the hot humid forest up to elevations of 800 m, where it often grows on smaller branches and twigs overhanging streams.

As is indicated by its generic name, the plants are fan-shaped. There are no pseudobulbs, but instead a series of equitant fleshy leaves up to 8 cm long. Flower spikes appear from the leaf axils in spring or summer and bear a succession, usually two or three, of single flowers. At 2.5 cm in diameter, the flowers are the largest in the genus.

This delightful little species has proved difficult to maintain in cultivation for any length of time. It has been suggested that the plants may in fact be short-lived in nature. For best results grow it in warm to intermediate conditions with fairly bright light. Plants should be mounted on twigs or small cork mounts and placed where humidity is high and air movement good. Plants seem very sensitive to over-watering.

Actual flower size: approximately 2.5 cm across.

Rodriguezia bracteata (Vell.) Hoehne

Described as *Epidendrum bracteatum* by Velloso in the late seventeenth or early eighteenth century, this species was finally renamed *Rodriguezia bracteata* by Hoehne early in the twentieth century. Synonyms include *Burlingtonia fragrans*, *R. fragrans* and Cogniaux's *R. venusta*. This last appellation often causes this species to be confused with Reichenbach's valid *R. venusta*, the flowers of which have eight to ten keels on the lip, whereas *R. bracteata* has only two. *R. bracteata* inhabits both the warm humid lowlands and cooler mountain areas, and occurs in the states of Bahia, Rio de Janeiro, São Paulo, Paraná and Santa Catarina.

The compressed oblong pseudobulbs, which are 3–5 cm tall and 1.5 cm wide, are obscured by three or four leaf-bearing bracts at the base. A single strap-like leaf 10–25 cm long rises from the apex. In autumn or early winter, several to many sparkling white flowers about 3 cm long are borne on a 10–20 cm arching to pendent spike which is produced from the base of the pseudobulb. The more or less spoon-shaped dorsal sepal, which is about 1.6 cm long and 0.6 cm wide, hoods the column, while the slightly longer lateral sepals are joined to form a scoop beneath the 2.3 cm-long lip. The petals have undulating margins and are recurved at the apex. The clawed lip has a yellow blotch in the throat. There are two deflexed ear-like lobules near the base, while the blade is bilobed. The column has a 'horn' on either side of the stigma.

R. bracteata does well mounted, as its many wiry roots like to dangle freely in the air. It needs intermediate conditions with moderate light and humidity.

Actual flower size: approximately 3 cm long.

Rodriguezia decora (Lem.) Reichenbach (f.)

This species reached Europe when Libon sent plants to de Jonghe in Belgium, where it flowered in 1851. Lemaire described it as *Burlingtonia decora* in 1852, and Reichenbach transferred it to *Rodriguezia* later in the same year. *Burlingtonia amoena* is another synonym. *R. decora* occurs in the cooler mountains of São Paulo, Paraná, Santa Catarina and Rio Grande do Sul, and also in the savannah country of the Distrito Federal around Brasília.

The ovoid compressed pseudobulbs are 10–30 cm apart on a thin rhizome. These pseudobulbs are about 2.5 cm tall and bear a single strap-like leaf at the apex and usually a single leaf at the base. The apical leaf is up to about 15 cm long and 2.5 cm wide with an acute apex. From five to fifteen faintly fragrant flowers are borne on the apical section of a 30–60 cm-long spike which rises from the base of the pseudobulb in autumn or winter. The white, more or less oblong tepals have reddish-brown spots. The 1.2 cm-long dorsal sepal and longer, wider petals are held forward, while the lateral sepals, which are joined for more than half their length, form a spur at the base. This spur encloses the base of the 2.5–2.8 cm-long lip. There are five spotted keels on the long claw, while the apical half comprises two rounded lobes. The column has two long hairy projections near the base.

R. decora, because of its extended rambling habit, needs a fairly long narrow mount. It does best in intermediate conditions with indirect bright light and fairly high humidity. Reduce watering in winter if temperatures are low.

Actual flower size: 3–3.5 cm long.

Rodriguezia decora var. *picta* Hooker

Bateman, who received plants from southern Brazil, introduced this variety of *R. decora** into cultivation in 1863. Later that year Hooker described it as *Burlingtonia decora* var. *picta*, presumably unaware that *B. decora* had already been transferred to the genus *Rodriguezia*. Like the type, *R. decora* var. *picta* is a native of the southern Brazilian states, where it grows as an epiphyte, often on the thin branches of deciduous trees. Its preferred habitat is along river banks or in swamps.

The plants of this variety differ from those of the type in that the 2.5 cm-tall pseudobulbs, which are still well spaced on the slender rhizome, are less compressed and have shorter, more acutely pointed leaves. The plants, which may produce a tangled mass of aerial roots, are often only tenuously anchored to their host. The flowers, which are borne on a long wiry spike, are usually more brightly and heavily spotted than in the type. The white sepals and petals, which have a sharp point at the apex, are spotted with maroon-purple. The dorsal sepal and petals are held forward and obscure the terete column. This column has two long minutely hairy 'arms' extending from near the apex. The long narrow five-keeled claw of the lip may be rose or orange-brown, while the kidney-shaped apical lobe is white.

Along with the type, *R. decora* var. *picta* can be a problem in cultivation due to its rambling habit and masses of aerial roots. Very large mounts are not a good idea, as they tend to retain too much moisture. A satisfactory compromise is to use a stick or branch of tea-tree, paperbark or oak.

Actual flower size: approximately 3 cm long.

Rodriguezia secunda Humboldt, Bonpland & Kunth

Although not introduced into cultivation in England until 1818, when plants were imported from Trinidad, this species was discovered some years before by von Humboldt and Bonpland in northern Colombia. With Kunth, they described it in 1815. Some authors regard this species as being synonymous with Ruíz and Pavón's *R. lanceolata* (1798), but most consider the latter to be a separate (even, in Schweinfurth's case, a dubious) species. Loddiges' *R. lanceolata* of 1822, *Burlingtonia rosea*, *Pleurothallis coccinea* and *R. bungerothii* are synonyms. *R. secunda* occurs from Panama and the West Indies to Brazil, where it is found in Amazonas, Pará, Amapá and Mato Grosso.

The flattened 2–5 cm-long pseudobulbs are 1.0–1.6 cm wide, and almost obscured by leaf-bearing bracts at the base. The one or two apical leaves are 7–25 cm long and up to 3.5 cm wide. Flowering may occur any time, one to six spikes from 12–40 cm long rising from the axils of the leaf sheaths. The flowers, which usually face upward, are typically rose-pink to blood-red. The oval to oblong 0.9–1.4 cm-long dorsal sepal and shorter wider petals are somewhat concave and do not open widely. The 1.0–1.5 cm-long lateral sepals, which have upturned margins, are joined for their entire length. The more or less fiddle-shaped lip is 1.2–1.5 cm long and up to 0.9 cm across. It has two erect ear-like lobes near the base and a fleshy furrowed crest extending from the base for about half its length.

A warm humid environment with no distinct dry resting period suits *R. secunda*.

Actual flower size: approximately 1.5 cm across.

Schomburgkia crispa Lindley

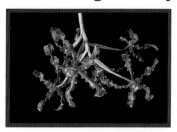

Lindley used this species in 1838 as the type for his new genus *Schomburgkia*, which he named in honour of Richard Schomburgk, who discovered plants of this species in Guyana. *S. fimbriata* and *Epidendrum fimbriatum* are conspecific. *S. gloriosa* is also regarded by most — though not all — authors as being synonymous. In Brazil *S. crispa* is found in a variety of habitats from the cooler mountains to the hot lowlands and the savannahs. It is found growing epiphytically in Amazonas, Pará, Pernambuco, Rio de Janeiro, São Paulo, Minas Gerais and the Distrito Federal. It is also native to Venezuela, Suriname and Guyana.

The spindle-shaped pseudobulbs are 10–30 cm tall and up to 5 cm wide. They are compressed, with several ridges on either side and may be marked with brown or purple. At the apex are two or three stiff fleshy leaves which are lanceolate, 16–30 cm long and 3.5–6.0 cm wide with a prominent mid-vein. An erect spike up to 1.2 m in length rises from the apex of the pseudobulb and carries several to many flowers near its apex. The almost equal petals and sepals are brown, linear to oblong, and have very crisped margins. They are approximately 2.5–4.0 cm long and 0.7–1.2 cm wide. The cream to pale pink to dark magenta lip is about 2 cm long with sub-erect narrow lateral lobes, a strongly recurved apical lobe, and three keels down the centre.

S. crispa is a tough and robust plant, and easily grown if given suitable conditions. It needs a warm to intermediate environment with high humidity, bright light and plenty of water when in growth followed by a drier rest.

Actual flower size: 5–7.5 cm across.

Scuticaria hadwenii (Ldl.) Hooker

Hadwen, for whom this species is named, introduced plants from Rio de Janeiro into England, where they flowered in 1851. Lindley described it as *Bifrenaria hadwenii*. William Hooker transferred it to *Scuticaria* in 1852. It has also been known as *S. strictifolia*. *S. hadwenii* grows epiphytically in the mountains of Bahia, Espírito Santo, Rio de Janeiro, São Paulo and Santa Catarina.

Plants have only rudimentary pseudobulbs and very thick fleshy roots. The dark green, more or less terete leaves are covered with papery brown bracts near the base and have a single groove on their upper surface. From 13–45 cm long and 0.5–0.7 cm in diameter, they are acutely pointed. Single (occasionally two) flowers are produced in summer on spikes from 4–5 cm long. The fleshy tepals are yellow-green with chestnut-brown blotches, or chestnut-brown with paler apices. The oblong to triangular sepals are 3.0–4.5 cm long and 1.2–1.5 cm wide with tapering acute apices. The slightly narrower petals may have recurved margins. The scoop-like lip is hinged to the base of the column, which is marked with maroon. The lip, from 2.5–3.5 cm long, is white to yellow, blotched and spotted with yellow-brown or pale to dark pinkish-purple. The lip is obscurely three-lobed, with the rounded midlobe divided into two near the apex. Three ridges at the base form an oblong 'ski-jump' callus.

S. hadwenii, because of its pendent or semi-pendent habit, is best mounted on slabs of treefern or cork. It prefers intermediate conditions with semi-shade and should be given a dry rest in winter.

Actual flower size: 6–7.5 cm long.

Scuticaria irwiniana Pabst

Pabst described this species in 1973, naming it in honour of Irwin, who had discovered it in 1971 on the Serra do Caraça in Minas Gerais at 1,750–1,900 m above sea level. Endemic to Minas Gerais, it is the only *Scuticaria* species to grow exclusively on rocks, with lichens and low vegetation providing some protection from the hot summer days and cold winter nights.

The erect terete leaves rise almost directly from the rhizome. From 5–12 cm long and about 0.8 cm in diameter, the leaves are grooved, with a white sheath at the base. In early summer a single flower is borne on an erect spike up to about 15 cm long. The more or less lanceolate tepals are brownish-red, with or without yellow-green tessellations. They are about 2.5 cm long and 1 cm wide with recurved margins. The petals are almost white on the reverse. The strongly three-lobed lip, which is about 2.5 cm long, is white to purplish on the reverse. The inner surface is white, striped and sometimes strongly suffused with purplish-red. The large lateral lobes are erect or curve inward towards the column. The more or less oblong mid-lobe has a blunt to rounded irregularly-edged apex. In the throat is an oblong callus which is vaguely four-lobed in front.

S. irwiniana is tolerant of fairly wide temperature variations. It may be potted in a freely draining material such as coarse treefern fibre with some broken sandstone added, or may be mounted on natural cork bark. It prefers fairly bright light. Give plenty of water when in growth followed by a dry winter rest when an occasional misting is all that is needed.

Actual flower size: 4.5–5 cm across.

Sophronitella violacea (Ldl.) Schlechter

Discovered by Gardner in 1837 and described by Lindley in 1840 as *Sophronitis violacea*, this species was separated from that genus in 1925 by Schlechter and placed in his new genus *Sophronitella*, of which it remains the only species. Distinguishing features include the short-winged column and the lip, which does not enfold the column. This species is common in the cooler mountains from Rio de Janeiro and São Paulo to Rio Grande do Sul, and also in the drier savannah country of Minas Gerais.

The spindle-shaped pseudobulbs are closely set on a branching rhizome. They are 1.5–3.0 cm long, shallowly ridged, sometimes suffused with purple and when young are covered with papery bracts. The single grassy leaf is erect to spreading with a prominent keel. The narrow leaf, 3.8–8.0 cm long, tapers to a sharp point. Spikes from 0.4–0.9 cm carry single starry flowers (occasionally two) in winter and early spring. The violet-purple flowers are paler at the centre and about 2 cm long. The acute petals and narrower sepals are 2 cm long, with the edges often curled up. The 1.7 cm lip, which is joined to the column, has a pouch at the base and a sharp point at the curled apex. The fleshy column wings are sickle-shaped.

This species likes a humid atmosphere, but resents 'wet feet'. It prefers a quick-draining mount such as paperbark or cork. Intermediate conditions are ideal, with moderate light and plenty of water when in active growth. Allow to dry out completely between waterings, and give plants a cool dry winter rest.

Actual flower size: approximately 2 cm long.

Sophronitis brevipedunculata (Cogn.) Fowlie

When Cogniaux described this species as *Sophronitis wittigiana* var. *brevipedunculata* at about the end of the nineteenth century, he suspected that it might in fact be a separate species, a suspicion which Fowlie confirmed in 1972. Restricted to the ridges and interior plateaux of Minas Gerais at 1,500–2,000 m, it grows on *Vellozia* bushes or on rocky outcrops where there is some humus. This area experiences very hot days and cold dewy nights.

The somewhat wrinkled pseudobulbs are globose to cylindrical and 1–2 cm long. They are arranged alternately in two rows on the rhizome and covered with fibrous bracts when young. Each bears a single thick leaf which is very stiff and may be ovate or elongated. From 2.0–4.5 cm long and up to 2.3 cm wide, the leaves are narrow at the base and rounded or sharply pointed at the apex. From autumn to winter very short spikes rise from the apex of the pseudobulbs carrying one to three flowers from 4.0–7.5 cm across. The tepals are light red to orange-red with darker veins. The 2.3–3.0 cm-long lip is yellow-orange, with veining in the tube formed by the lateral lobes. The oblong sepals taper to points, and the rounded petals may be notched on the upper edge. Blue, pale yellow and yellow varieties have been reported.

This beautiful and easily grown species does best for us when mounted on any rough-barked branch or slab. Give it moderate light, intermediate to cool conditions and a dry rest in winter. Drainage must be very good.

Actual flower size: 4–7.5 cm across.

Sophronitis cernua Lindley

Discovered by Harrison near Rio de Janeiro, this species was used by Lindley as the type for the genus *Sophronitis* in 1827. Synonyms include *S. modesta* and *S. hoffmannseggii*. It is quite common throughout eastern Brazil, in Bahia and from Minas Gerais and Espírito Santo to Rio Grande do Sul, growing on trees and rocks in the coastal lowlands and inland savannah country.

The flattened pseudobulbs are closely set on a branching rhizome. Arranged alternately in two rows (sometimes in a single row), they are 1–2 cm long and lie flat against the host. The single ovate leaves are 1.5–3.0 cm long, flat or arching, blunt or sharply pointed. Dark green above, they are usually suffused below with purple. The upper leaf edges and mid-vein may have a reddish tinge. Erect to arching spikes 2–5 cm carry two to seven flowers each from 2.2–2.7 cm across in autumn or winter. The flowers do not open flat. They are a sparkling cinnabar-red with white or yellow at the base of the lip and column. The ovate to oblong sepals are pointed at the apex. The petals are somewhat rhomboidal. The more or less scoop-shaped lip is 0.8–1.0 cm long with upturned sides at the base and an acute apex. A yellow form of this species exists.

S. cernua requires more warmth than other *Sophronitis* species and in our experience does better when mounted on cork or paperbark which dries out quickly after watering. It appreciates a warm to intermediate environment with fairly bright light. Give it year-round watering with a reduction in colder weather.

Actual flower size: 2.2–2.7 cm across.

Sophronitis coccinea (Ldl.) Reichenbach (f.)

This species was discovered by Descourtilz, who called it *Epidendrum ponceau* and made the careful painting upon which Lindley based his 1836 description. Lindley's *Cattleya coccinea* became this species' first valid name. Reichenbach transferred it to *Sophronitis* in 1864. *S. grandiflora* and *S. militaris* are synonyms. It inhabits a narrow band from 650–1,500 m on the coastal mountains in south-eastern Brazil, growing in the cool forests on slender moss-covered trees or rocky ledges in shaded or partly exposed positions.

The clustered, more or less erect pseudobulbs may be egg-shaped, cylindrical or spindle-shaped. From 1.5–4.0 cm tall and 0.2–0.6 cm in diameter, they bear a single fleshy leaf with a purple mid-vein and sometimes purple edges. This oblong to elliptic leaf is 3.0–7.5 cm long and up to 2.5 cm wide. An erect to arching spike 3.0–7.5 cm long carries a single flower 3–7 cm across, from autumn to early spring. There are many colour varieties, but the veined segments are usually scarlet with some yellow or orange at the base of the lip. The oblong sepals are 1.7–2.2 cm long. The rounded to diamond-shaped petals are longer and wider. The 1.3–2.0 cm lip has rounded to triangular lateral lobes which enclose the column, and a pointed oblong to triangular mid-lobe.

A very attractive and popular species, producing its brilliant red flowers in the dull days of winter, *S. coccinea* may be mounted or potted in coarse fibrous materials. It needs intermediate to cool conditions with moderate light and fairly high humidity, and reduced watering in winter. *Actual flower size: 3–7 cm across.*

Sophronitis coccinea 'Orange' & other varieties

The colour of *S. coccinea** is extremely variable. The unusual clone shown here has apricot- to peach-coloured petals and sepals, which have a clearly visible network of subdued orange to reddish veins. The yellow lip is lightly suffused with orange near the apex, while the lateral lobes are suffused with red on the outside near their edges. The inside of the lip has a few red streaks. There are several horticulturally accepted varieties of *S. coccinea*, which apparently flower just before or just after the typically red-flowered type. The pictured clone most closely resembles the colour drawings of the var. *rossiteriana* in Pabst and Dungs' *Orchidaceae Brasilienses*. This variety was originally described as a separate species by Barbosa Rodrígues in about 1899, and was later reduced to varietal status by Pabst and Dungs. Brazilians call it 'Cor de gemma', an allusion to its egg-yolk colouring of yellow with a little orange. Its lip is said to be paler, with just the slightest hint of red. It does not appear, however, to have the clear network of veins apparent in the pictured clone. A rarer, truly yellow variety is the var. *lobii*, which was described by Decker and is lemon-yellow in colour. One of the most unusual varieties is the var. *barboleta*, which has reddish-orange sepals and petals with darker veins. The petals have a yellow patch extending along the centre from the base for about half their length, giving the flower something of a 'butterfly' appearance, for which the variety is named. *Actual flower size: 3–7 cm across.*

Sophronitis coccinea subspecies *pygmaea* Pabst

Kautsky discovered this subspecies in the coastal mountains of Espírito Santo, where it grows on thin twigs and tree trunks or on rocks, often in exposed conditions. In 1976 Pabst described it as a subspecies of *S. coccinea.** Fowlie renamed it *S. mantiquierae* var. *pygmaea* in 1987 after examining *in situ* the population on which Pabst based his description. However, the main populations of *S. mantiquierae** are further westward in the Serra da Mantiquiera and flower only in summer, whereas all plants which we have grown of this taxon flower in autumn or winter. So, for the moment at least, we have opted to retain Pabst's name.

The clustered pseudobulbs of this subspecies are globose to cylindrical, and only 0.5–2.0 cm tall and 0.4 cm in diameter. Each bears a single stiff leaf 1.5–3.5 cm long and 0.5–1.2 cm wide. It is ovoid to narrowly elliptic, with some red-purple spotting beneath. The single, almost sessile flower appears from the apex of the developing pseudobulb. The 1 cm-long tepals are a muted orange-scarlet and may be recurved. The sepals are lanceolate and 0.4–0.5 cm wide, while the wider petals are diamond-shaped with a rounded or obtuse apex. The three-lobed lip, about 0.8 cm long and 0.2 cm wide, is yellow-orange with a few reddish veins. The large, almost semi-circular lateral lobes enclose the column. The narrow pointed mid-lobe is slightly deflexed and has two short ridges at the base.

Plants should be mounted and placed in an airy, cool to intermediate environment with semi-shade. Do not permit plants to dry out too much between waterings.

Actual flower size: approximately 2 cm across.

Sophronitis mantiqueirae Fowlie

Originally considered a subspecies of *S. coccinea,** *S. mantiqueirae* was given specific rank by Fowlie in 1972. Few who have grown both would disagree with Fowlie. The pseudobulbs of *S. mantiqueirae* are smaller, and, with *S. açuensis*, it is one of only two *Sophronitis* species to flower in summer. The flowers themselves differ little from those of *S. coccinea*. It grows mostly in Minas Gerais at about 1,200–1,860 m above sea level in the Serra da Mantiqueira, with isolated populations in Bahia, near Rio de Janeiro where it grows alongside *S. coccinea*, and possibly in Rio Grande do Sul. In its native habitat this species grows on moss- or lichen-covered saplings in gullies and on exposed ridges. Temperatures range in summer from about 9°–20°C and in winter from zero to 15°C. Conditions are often misty and cool, with high humidity. It shares its habitat with such species as *Dryadella lilliputana** and *Oncidium concolor,** *O. longicornu* and *O. gardneri.** So this is not a species for tropical conditions, under which it will quickly deteriorate.

We grow our plants with a winter minimum of 7°–10°C, and keep them as cool as possible in summer. The species is not particular about light levels, and seems to flower equally well in shade or bright light. It is well worth cultivating for its small size and brilliant scarlet flowers in mid-summer. Under the right conditions it quickly reaches specimen size. Plants may be potted in coarse fibrous material, but we prefer to grow ours on treefern mounts. They should be given copious water when in growth with a drier rest in winter.

Actual flower size: approximately 3 cm across.

Sophronitis species ex Espírito Santo

This unnamed sophronitis is said to come from montane tropical forests at moderate elevations in the mountain ranges of Espírito Santo in southeastern Brazil. It may prove to be a variety of *S. mantiqueirae*,* as it sometimes flowers in summer.

The terete pseudobulbs, from 2.0–4.5 cm long, are only 0.5 cm in diameter and are clustered on a branching rhizome. Covered with brown papery bracts, they are cylindrical to spindle-shaped. Each bears a single slightly fleshy leaf 4–10 cm long and about 1.0–1.7 cm wide. These sub-erect to spreading leaves are dark green, with occasional faint purple mottling beneath. They are narrow at the base, taper to a very acute apex and have a prominent keel. The single 4–6 cm flowers are produced in winter to summer on spikes about 2 cm long. The tepals are apricot-orange with dull red veins, while the three-lobed lip is yellow streaked with red. The sepals are oblong, with the dorsal strongly recurved. The 2–3 cm petals are broadly oval to almost round with slightly recurved margins. The 1.6–2.0 cm-long lip has rather large lateral lobes which meet above the column to form a narrow tube, and an oblong mid-lobe with a blunt apex.

This species grows well in intermediate to cool conditions with high humidity and moderate light to semi-shade. It may be mounted or potted in coarse freely draining material such as treefern fibre. It requires year-round moisture to prevent shrivelling of the narrow pseudobulbs, a condition to which the species seems prone.

Actual flower size: 4–6 cm across.

Sophronitis species ex Rio Grande do Sul

This species, which we imported from Brazil several years ago and which we suspect may be a variant of *S. coccinea*,* is reputed to come from the cool damp mountain regions of Rio Grande do Sul.

The pseudobulbs are egg-shaped to cylindrical, 1.5–2.3 cm tall and 0.3–0.5 cm in diameter. Each has a plain green leaf without the usual purple mid-vein of *S. coccinea*.* This lack, however, may be due to the fact that we grow the plants in semi-shade. The ovate to narrowly lanceolate leaf is 3.5–6.0 cm long and 1.0–1.5 cm wide. It is channelled above, slightly keeled below, and minutely serrated near the apex. Single flowers are borne in early spring on a 2.0–2.5 cm-long spike. Colour ranges from the normal bright orange-red of *S. coccinea* to the unusual satiny carmine of the specimen shown here. The sepals are 1.8 cm long. The 0.9 cm-wide dorsal sepal, which is oblong to elliptic, is slightly broader than the lanceolate laterals. The spreading rounded to rhomboidal petals are about 2 cm long and 1.6 cm wide. The three-lobed lip is about 1.4 cm long. It is yellow, speckled and suffused with red on the outside. The 0.8 cm-long lateral lobes are streaked and edged with red inside. They are more or less oblong, rounded at the apex, and meet above the column. The triangular, slightly deflexed apical lobe is more heavily marked and suffused with red. There are four tiny keels at the base of the mid-lobe.

This species will do well either mounted or potted. If potted, make sure that drainage is adequate. It will do well in cool to intermediate humid conditions, and moderate indirect light to semi-shade.

Actual flower size: 3.5–4 cm across.

Sophronitis wittigiana Barbosa Rodrígues

Very closely related to *S. brevipedunculata*,* this species, which was described by Barbosa Rodrígues in 1878, is often known by its synonym, *S. rosea*. It grows on mossy rough-barked trees in the state of Espírito Santo from 700–2,000 m in deep swampy gorges, sharing part of its habitat with *S. coccinea*.*

The pseudobulbs, which are arranged in two rows, may be squat and globular or more elongated, especially in cultivation. From 1.5–2.5 cm tall and up to 1.0 cm in diameter, they are covered with fibrous bracts. The stiff fleshy leaves range from broadly ovate (2.5 x 1.5 cm) to oblong (5.0 x 2.5 cm) with a sharply pointed apex. They are flat or recurved, and often suffused with purple beneath. The flower spike, produced from late autumn to very early spring, is longer than in other species, continuing to lengthen for several weeks after the flowers open. Typically 4.0–6.5 cm across, these flowers are generally sparkling pink (ranging from rosy-pink to very pale pink) with darker veins. The tepals are often recurved, especially the dorsal sepal. The oblong sepals are pointed. The large rounded to diamond-shaped lip is white or yellow with pink veins. The lateral lobes are rounded and enclose the column, and the mid-lobe is acutely pointed. A white variety has been reported.

This species does very well when mounted on cork or paperbark and grown in moderately bright light. Intermediate conditions suit it best. Give plenty of water when in growth, with a slightly drier rest in winter.

Actual flower size: 4–6.5 cm across.

Sophronitis wittigiana 'Candy Pink'

Like many other *Sophronitis* species, *S. wittigiana** exhibits a certain degree of variation in the colour of its flowers from one clone to another. Although the typical colour is pink, this may range from very pale pink to mauve-pink to dark pink or even a deep watermelon pink. Fowlie's monograph, in the *Orchid Digest*, Vol. 51, No. 1 (1987), even pictures clones which are almost pure red. Gloeden has also found an extremely rare almost pure white clone near Pedra Azul. The clone shown here, *S. wittigiana* 'Candy Pink', shows why this species is still better known by its horticultural epithet of *S. rosea*. (The latter name was published only in 1884, six years after Barbosa Rodrigues' description of the species as *S. wittigiana*, and must be regarded as a synonym.) The colour of the lip of this species is rather variable. The patch of colour in the throat may be quite small or fairly large, even extending on to the base of the apical lobe. Lip colour ranges from white to pale yellow to the darker, almost orange-yellow of the pictured clone. The veins are usually pink, but in some cases — including this one — those in the throat and on the lateral lobes are red. Any variation in the shape of the flowers is usually confined to the petals. These may be wider and fuller than either of the two clones illustrated in this book, or quite narrow with recurved margins. This species has been much less used by hybridisers than has its more brilliant relative *S. coccinea*,* but the clones of the better forms of *S. wittigiana* have great possibilities for producing more subtle coloration in their offspring.

Actual flower size: 4–6.5 cm across.

Stanhopea insignis Frost ex Hooker

Discovered by von Humboldt and Bonpland in Ecuador at the beginning of the nineteenth century, this species was first described by Hooker in 1829 using information from Frost. *S. insignis* inhabits the mountains of Rio de Janeiro, São Paulo, Paraná, Santa Catarina and Rio Grande do Sul.

The clustered ovoid to almost round pseudobulbs, which are 3.0–7.5 cm long, are grooved and bear a single leathery leaf. From 30–45 cm long and up to 10 cm wide, this pleated leaf has an acute apex and a short petiole. In autumn a pendent spike to 25 cm long carries two to three (occasionally more) very fragrant flowers. The strongly reflexed tepals are an almost translucent yellowish-white to dull orange-yellow, more or less densely spotted with violet to maroon-purple. They are about 5 cm long, with the ovate to lanceolate dorsal sepal about 2.5 cm wide and the ovate to oblong laterals much wider. The oblong petals are narrow, with wavy margins and acute apices. The very fleshy lip is about 6 cm long. The basal section, which is almost round, is purple below and whitish densely spotted with purple above. The whitish arms of the horseshoe-shaped mid-section curve inward, while the heart-shaped apical section is more or less spotted with purple.

S. insignis must be mounted or grown in baskets in order to accommodate the flower spike's habit of growing directly downward. It prefers an intermediate environment, with high humidity and moderately bright light to semi-shade. Plenty of water should be given when plants are in active growth, with a cool drier winter rest. *Actual flower size: 9–12 cm long.*

Stanhopea oculata (Lodd.) Lindley

Loddiges first introduced this species into England in 1829. It flowered in 1831, and he described it in the following year as *Ceratochilus oculatus*. Later in the same year Lindley transferred it to *Stanhopea*. It occurs from Mexico to northern South America. In Central America it is found at elevations up to 1,500 m above sea level, but in Brazil it occurs only at lower elevations in the state of Amazonas.

The ovoid to conical pseudobulbs are ridged, 3.5–7.5 cm tall and 2–3 cm wide. Each has one leathery leaf at the apex. From 27–45 cm long, this elliptic to elliptic-lanceolate leaf has an acute apex, is 8–16 cm wide, and has three very prominent veins below. From three to eight vanilla-scented flowers are borne on a pendent spike up to 25 cm long. The tepals are usually yellow to white with reddish-purple spots, but may occasionally be almost wholly white. The concave elliptic to ovate dorsal sepal is 5.5–6.5 cm long and up to 3.5 cm wide, while the reflexed lateral sepals are much wider and slightly longer. The narrow oblong to lanceolate petals are reflexed, 5.0–5.5 cm long and have wavy margins. The very fleshy lip is yellow at the base with two large reddish-purple to almost black blotches. There is a prominent hump between the basal section and the two curving 'arms' of the mid-section. The heart-shaped apical section has a tapering recurved apex.

S. oculata, like all members of this genus, should be grown on mounts or in baskets as flower spikes grow directly downward. It prefers a moderately bright spot in an intermediate to warm environment and a moderately dry winter rest. *Actual flower size: 10–13 cm long.*

Stelis species — *porschiana* alliance

This pretty stelis belongs to the subgenus *inequales* and, in that subgenus, to the *porschiana* alliance, the members of which have smooth sepals rather than the hairy ones of other alliances. We have been unable to identify it exactly, but it appears to be one of the following: *S. juergensii*, *S. paraensis*, *S. porschiana*, *S. smaragdina* or *S. tweediana*. With the exception of *S. paraensis*, which originates from the lowlands of Pará, all these species inhabit the cool mountain regions south of Espírito Santo.

The pictured species has clustered 4–15 cm stems which are covered with papery brown bracts. Each bears a single elliptic leaf from 6.5–10.5 cm long and 2.0–2.5 cm wide. It is bilobed at the apex with a minute tooth between the lobes. Flower spikes from 9.5–13.0 cm long appear from the apex of the petioles in summer and autumn. Each petiole may produced up to three spikes over time. Each spike bears twelve to twenty almost flat flowers which, at 1 cm long, are very large for the genus. They may be well spaced or overlapping and, unlike many stelis flowers, remain open in bright light. The free translucent sepals have a sparkling texture. They are very pale greenish-yellow with green tips and a few darker veins. The sepals are ovate, with the dorsal held lowermost or perpendicular to the spike. The dorsal is 0.6 cm long and 0.5 cm wide at the base, while the laterals are 0.45 cm long and 0.45 cm wide at the base. The lip and fan-shaped petals are minute.

This species may be mounted or potted, and needs a cool shady environment with year-round moisture.

Actual flower size: approximately 1 cm long.

Stelis species — *vinosa* alliance

The *vinosa* alliance of this genus contains only five species: *S. diaphana*, *S. guttifera*, *S. pendulifera*, *S. plurispicata* and *S. vinosa*, but to date we have been unable to determine the exact identity of this charming species. It comes from the cool mountain ranges of southern Brazil, where it grows as an epiphyte in the moist forests at moderate elevations.

The clustered leaves are 9–14 cm long, including the long stalks which have a few closely fitting sheaths. The leaf blade is fleshy, elliptic, and minutely three-toothed at the apex. There is a single furrow on the upper surface and a keel beneath. Spikes rise from the stalk late in spring, with several being produced from each stalk over a period of years. From 7–13 cm long, they carry about thirty well-spaced flowers about 0.3–0.4 cm across and 0.5 cm long. These are arranged in two rows. The sepals are pale green, faintly tinged with pinkish-purple, have three veins and a minutely hairy surface. The 0.3 cm dorsal sepal, which tapers to an acute point, may be held lowermost or perpendicular to the spike, depending on where the flower is situated. The lateral sepals are shorter and rounder. The minute dark purple petals, the purple-red anther cap, and the tiny white lip provide a nice contrast.

This species, like most other stelis, does well in intermediate to cool conditions in light to heavy shade. It may be mounted or potted in treefern, pine bark and sphagnum moss. Plants should be kept moist all year round.

Actual flower size: 0.3–0.4 cm across.

Trigonidium latifolium Lindley

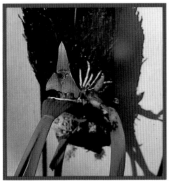

This unusual species, described by Lindley, is one of only six *Trigonidium* species found in Brazil. It occurs in the hot humid lowlands of Piauí, Pernambuco and Bahia in the north, and also in the cooler climates of São Paulo and Paraná in the south. It is usually found growing epiphytically.

The elliptic to oblong pseudobulbs are dull mid- to dark green, and strongly compressed with grooves on either side. Up to 6 cm tall and 3 cm wide, they are sometimes curved, and have a pair of sub-erect to spreading leaves. These are oblong, with an acute apex. They are folded at the base, and are up to 20 cm or more long and 2–3 cm wide. Single flowers are borne on spikes about 8 cm long from the base of the pseudobulb. The flowers are burnt-orange to brown in colour with reddish veins. The sepals are the most prominent part of the flower. They are not joined, but overlap at the base to form a tube for about half their length, with the apical halves strongly recurved to create the appearance of a triangular flower. The more or less lanceolate dorsal sepal is about 4 cm long and 1 cm wide, while the vaguely falcate lateral sepals are slightly wider. The spathulate petals, which are hidden within the sepaline tube, are 2 cm long and 0.6 cm wide with thickened very glossy maroon eye-like apices. The 1 cm-long lip has narrow erect lateral lobes and a rounded apical lobe. A linear to oblong callus runs down the centre of the lip for two-thirds of its length.

T. latifolium may be potted or mounted. It prefers a humid, warm to intermediate environment with bright indirect light.

Actual flower size: approximately 2.5 cm across.

Warmingia eugenii Reichenbach (f.)

The type for a genus with only two species, this taxon was discovered in the 1860s in Minas Gerais by Eugenius Warming, who sent a preserved specimen to Reichenbach. The latter described it in 1881. *W. loefgrenii* is conspecific. *W. eugenii* grows epiphytically at moderate elevations in the forests of Minas Gerais, São Paulo, Santa Catarina, Espírito Santo and Pernambuco.

The clustered conical to cylindrical pseudobulbs are 1–2 cm tall and about 0.5 cm wide. Each has a few brown sheaths at the base and a single fleshy leaf about 10 cm long and 2.5 cm wide. It is oblong to elliptic, folded at the base to form a short petiole, and has a prominent mid-vein. Up to thirty nodding flowers are borne in late spring or early summer on a pendent 12 cm-long spike. The lanceolate tepals are translucent white with or without a yellowish-green mid-vein. They are about 1.4 cm long and 0.4 cm wide, with long tapering apices. The sepals are slightly concave at the base, while the petals have irregularly toothed margins. The 1.0–1.3 cm-long lip also has serrated edges. The small lateral lobes are more or less rounded and spreading, while the mid-lobe is lanceolate to oblong with a tapering apex.

W. eugenii does best in an intermediate to warm environment with fairly high humidity and moderate shade. It should be kept moist all year round and never be allowed to dry out completely for more than a short period of time. It may be grown in shallow pans of treefern fibre or similar material, or mounted on treefern slabs with a little moss about the roots.

Actual flower size: approximately 1.5 cm long.

Xylobium variegatum (Ruíz & Pavón) Garay & Dunsterville

Ruíz and Pavón described this species in 1798 as *Maxillaria variegata*. In 1807 it was transferred to *Dendrobium* by Persoon. Although recognised as a synonym for *X. squalens*, it was not formally transferred to *Xylobium* until 1961, when Garay and Dunsterville made the correction, resurrecting the specific epithet because of its priority over Lindley's *Dendrobium squalens* of 1823. *X. variegatum* is a widespread species, occurring in Costa Rica, Venezuela, Ecuador, Colombia, Peru and Bolivia as well as in Brazil, where it is found in the cooler mountain regions of Pará, Rio de Janeiro, São Paulo, Paraná, Santa Catarina and Mato Grosso.

The clustered ovoid pseudobulbs are 5–8 cm tall and 2.5–4.5 cm wide. Each has two or, occasionally, three oblong to elliptic leaves 36–50 cm long and 6.5–9.0 cm wide with five very prominent veins. Many densely packed flowers are borne on a spike up to about 20 cm long, which rises from the base of the pseudobulb. The recurved tepals are cream to pink, sometimes suffused with maroon. The lanceolate dorsal sepal and the falcate laterals are about 2.6 cm long and 0.7–0.9 cm wide. The shorter narrower petals are held forward. The 1.5 cm-long lip is suffused with maroon, with the oblong apical lobe darker maroon. The lateral lobes are erect, while the apical lobe is recurved. A club-shaped callus extends from the base to the midpoint of the lip. The apical half of the lip has several wavy keels.

X. variegatum is fairly temperature tolerant, and seems to prefer shady positions. In cooler climates, reduce winter watering.

Actual flower size: approximately 2.5 cm across.

Zygopetalum crinitum Loddiges

Warre discovered this species, and sent plants of it to Loddiges, in whose nursery it first flowered in 1829. Loddiges described it as *Z. crinitum*, while Lindley later treated it as a variety of *Z. mackayi.**
Its many synonyms include *Z. stenochilum* and *Z. pubescens*. *Z. crinitum* inhabits the cool moist mountain regions of Rio de Janeiro, São Paulo, Minas Gerais, Paraná and Santa Catarina, where it grows as a terrestrial, sometimes with its pseudobulbs partly buried.

The 4–10 cm-long pseudobulbs are clustered and 2–4 cm in diameter. They are ovoid to oblong with two or three leaf-bearing bracts at the base and three to five lanceolate leaves at the apex. These are 25–45 cm long and up to 5 cm wide. From three to ten fleshy long-lasting flowers are borne from late autumn to early spring on a spike from 30–50 cm long. The fragrant flowers have green or yellow-green tepals spotted and streaked with chestnut-brown. They are oblong to lanceolate with acute apices, and usually curve inward. The sepals are 3.3–4.0 cm long and 1.0–1.4 cm wide, while the petals are slightly narrower. The 3–4 cm-long lip is white with purple or red veins, which have dense hairs of the same colour. The rounded lip has wavy margins and a very thick U-shaped callus, which is white, sometimes streaked with red, and has several grooves. The base of the club-like column is covered with tiny hairs.

Z. crinitum is an easy subject in cultivation, and prefers an intermediate to cool environment with moderately bright light. It should be potted in a coarse well-drained medium and given plenty of water when in growth.

Actual flower size: 6.5–8 cm across.

Zygopetalum intermedium Loddiges ex Lindley

Along with *Z. crinitum*,* this species was once considered a variety of *Z. mackayi*.* It was described in 1844 by Lindley using material supplied by Loddiges, who introduced it into cultivation. Other synonyms include *Z. bolivianum* and *Z. roezlii*. Also native to Peru and Bolivia, *Z. intermedium* grows mostly as a terrestrial in the cooler areas of the Brazilian states of Rio de Janeiro, São Paulo, Paraná and Minas Gerais.

The clustered olive-green pseudobulbs may be almost globose to ovoid. From 4–8 cm tall and up to 5 cm in diameter, they have one or two leaf-bearing bracts at the base and three to five apical leaves. The latter are narrowly elliptic to oblong with a tapering acute apex. They are 17–60 cm long, 2–6 cm wide, and have five to nine prominent veins below. From late autumn to early spring an erect spike 40–60 cm long carries three to five well-spaced fragrant flowers on its upper portion. The flowers are very long lasting. The tepals, which are green blotched with crimson, are 3.0–3.5 cm long and about 1 cm wide, with acute apices and sometimes recurved lateral margins. The 3.5 cm-long lip is white with violet-red veins in sometimes broken lines, and is noticeably downy near the base. The very small lateral lobes are ear-like, while the mid-lobe is skirt-like with wavy margins. At the base is a very fleshy raised callus, which is two-lobed and has several furrows.

Z. intermedium does well when potted in a fairly coarse medium, such as is used for cymbidium hybrids, and grown in a humid, intermediate to cool environment. It prefers moderate shade, and a reduction of water during winter.

Actual flower size: 5.5–7 cm across.

Zygopetalum mackayi Hooker

Often confused with *Z. intermedium*,* this species was introduced into cultivation by Mackay, after whom Hooker named it in 1827, using it as the type for the genus. *Z. mackayi* grows in cool shady mountain areas at 1,300–1,700 m above sea level in the states of Minas Gerais, Espírito Santo, Rio de Janeiro, São Paulo, Santa Catarina and Rio Grande do Sul.

The 3–7 cm-tall pseudobulbs are 3–5.5 cm in diameter and may be almost globose to pear-shaped. At the base are two or more leaf-bearing bracts, while the apex has two or three strap-like leaves 30–50 cm long and up to 5 cm wide. They have long tapering apices and several prominent veins. From four to ten fragrant flowers are borne on a spike 60 cm–1 m long which appears from the base of the new growth from late autumn to late winter. The fleshy green tepals are spotted and blotched with maroon-purple, and often have recurved lateral margins. They curve slightly inward but the acute apices are usually recurved. The lanceolate sepals are 3.3–4.0 cm long and 1.1–1.4 cm wide, while the lanceolate to slightly elliptic petals are shorter. (In *Z. intermedium* all tepals are of equal length.) The 4 cm-long lip is white with purple-blue veins, which have fine purple hairs on them. At the base are two small ear-like lobes and a very large fleshy callus, which is toothed at the apex and has a deep central furrow with several shallower grooves.

Z. mackayi grows well potted in any coarse well-drained medium and placed in a shady intermediate to cool environment. It needs plenty of water in the growing season and a drier winter rest.

Actual flower size: 6–7.5 cm across.

Zygopetalum maxillare Loddiges

Loddiges received plants of this species from Warre in 1829, and described it in 1831. *Z. hasslerianum* and *Z. mandibulare* are conspecific. *Z. maxillare* grows, mostly epiphytically on treeferns, in the cool damp mountains of Espírito Santo, Rio de Janeiro, São Paulo, Paraná, Santa Catarina, Rio Grande do Sul, Minas Gerais and Mato Grosso.

The ovoid to oblong pseudobulbs are well-spaced on a stout rhizome, 5.0–7.5 cm tall and somewhat compressed. The apical leaves, which are 20–37 cm long and about 2.5 cm wide, are lanceolate and prominently veined. From winter to spring a spike from 20–45 cm or more long bears five to eight fragrant waxy flowers the stalks of which have brownish bracts. Flowers last for about six weeks. The tepals are green, more or less heavily blotched with red-brown, and have sharp tapering apices. The lanceolate dorsal sepal and petals are about 3 cm long. The dorsal sepal is about 1 cm wide while the petals are narrower. The almost triangular lateral sepals are slightly longer and wider than the dorsal sepal. The 3 cm-long lip usually has a violet-blue apical lobe with paler edges (rather than the almost white lip of the pictured clone). The narrow erect lateral lobes are joined to the semi-circular 1 cm-tall callus, which is typically amethyst to dark purple and has several vertical furrows.

Z. maxillare resents disturbance. It should be mounted on a slab of treefern or similar material and placed in a moderately shady, intermediate to cool environment. It does not need a dry winter rest, and should be given year-round moisture.

Actual flower size: approximately 6.5 cm long.

Zygostates lunata Lindley

Described by Lindley in the nineteenth century, this species is a member of a small genus of subtropical epiphytes which is closely related to *Ornithocephalus*. Synonyms include *Dactylostylis fimbriata* and *Ornithocephalus navicularis*. It grows on mossy trees at moderate elevations in Minas Gerais, Espírito Santo, Rio de Janeiro, São Paulo, Paraná and Santa Catarina, where heavy dews are experienced almost every night.

Plants lack pseudobulbs and comprise fans of five to seven narrow mid- to dark green leaves from 4–9 cm long. They are slightly fleshy with an acute apex and a prominent keel beneath. Arching to pendent spikes about 10 cm long rise from the leaf axils in late spring to early summer and carry thirty or more closely set flowers about 0.8 cm across. The oval sepals, which are often swept back, are greenish-white. The broad fan-shaped petals are greenish-gold to golden yellow. At their widest point they are 0.4 cm across, and about the same length. The edges are deeply and irregularly serrated, and they are covered with tiny glands. The white cup-shaped lip is serrated, and has two thick calli at the base. The column has a long yellow beak-like anther and two 'arms' at the base which end in dark green knobs.

This species does well mounted on treefern or placed in small pots of well-drained fibrous material. It should be kept moist at all times, and should be grown in semi-shade or full shade in intermediate to cool conditions. It is an easy grower once established, and deserves a place in every collection.

Actual flower size: approximately 0.8 cm across.

GLOSSARY

Adventitious   Produced from an abnormal or unusual place.

Albino   Lacking in pigmentation, white.

Alliance   A loose grouping, within a genus, of species with similar characteristics.

Anther Cap   Cap which covers the sac at the top of the column which contains the pollinia.

Caatinga   Dry region covered with thorny deciduous scrub. In the Amazonian region, areas of depauperate forest growing in sandy soil which lacks nutrients.

Caboclo   A person of mixed Indian and Portuguese descent. Derived from an Indian word meaning 'out of the white'.

Callus   A hard protuberance or prominence.

Cerrado   Areas of tropical vegetation strongly influenced by seasonal factors; areas of grassland, savannah, and open woodland; trees usually stunted, evergreen, with corky bark.

Chapada   A distinctive flat-topped plateau or tableland common in the central west of Brazil.

Clone   An individual of a species, produced from a single seed, and its vegetatively reproduced progeny.

Column   Specialised formation in orchid flowers resulting from the union of stamen and pistil.

Connate   Joined together.

Conspecific   Synonymous with, identical to.

Deflexed   Turned or bent outward.

Disc   The face or flat portion of a floral segment; in orchids usually the mid-lobe of the lip.

Endemic   Confined to a distinct area, not found elsewhere.

Epiphyte   A plant which grows on another plant, but which receives no nourishment from its host.

Equitant   Leaves which are set one inside the other in two ranks.

Falcate   Sickle-shaped.

Filiform   Threadlike.

Genus   The grouping of one or more species having similar characteristics and common ancestry.

Gland   A wart-like protuberance.

Hermaphrodite   Having both male and female sexual characteristics.

Homonym   A name unacceptable under the rules of taxonomy, having been previously applied to another species in the same category.

Internode   The portion of a stem or pseudobulb between nodes or joints.

Keel   A projecting ridge.

Labellum   The lip of an orchid flower, a specialised petal.

Lithophyte   A plant growing on stone or rock.

Mentum   Chin-like protuberance formed by the bases of the lateral sepals and the column foot.

Monopodial   A plant which grows only upward from the terminal bud at the apex of the stem.

Monotypic   A genus containing only one species.

Non-resupinate   A flower not turned upside down, i.e., with labellum above column.

Paperbark   A tree of the genus *Melaleuca*; the bark of such a tree, which comprises many thin papery layers.

Petal   Part of the corolla of a flower,

usually coloured, comprising the inner and upper parts of the flower.

Petaloid   Like a petal.

Petiole   Leaf stalk.

Pleurothallid   An orchid of a genus belonging to the subtribe Pleurothallidinae.

Pollinia   The regular granular masses into which orchid pollen is compressed.

Pseudobulb   Thickened bulb-like stem possessed by many orchids; of fibrous constitution and not a true bulb.

Reflexed   Abruptly bent or turned backward or downward.

Resupinate   Inversion of a flower by a twisting of the ovary (in orchids) so that the lip is lower than the column.

Rhizome   In orchids, a stem which forms a rootstock, either above or below ground.

Rupicolous   Growing on or among rocks or stones.

Sac   A hollow bag-like depression.

Saccate   Sac-like.

Savannah   A dry plain or grassland, only lightly or intermittently wooded.

Sepal   The lower and outer parts of a flower.

Sessile   Lacking a stalk or stem.

Species   A group of plants or animals showing intergrading among its members and having in common one or more significant characteristics which separate it from all other groups. (This is a very conservative definition. Most botanists hesitate to give a definition, as the concept of a species is a very artificial one. All botanical classification is in a sense an attempt to impose a static and arbitrary framework upon a dynamic biological situation, and nowhere are the deficiencies of such an attempt made more obvious than in our attempts to arrive at a satisfactory definition of the term 'species'. However, as amateurs of orchidology, we can in practice accept that an orchid species is a representative of a group of plants possessing significant and constant similarities within the group, and distinct differences from other groups; and breeds true from sibling crosses.)

Spur   A hollow tubular extension of a floral organ, often containing nectar-producing glands.

Substrate   The material on or in which a plant grows.

Sympodial   A form of growth in which one or more new growths are produced each season at the base of the old growth.

Synanthous   Flowers appearing with new vegetative growth.

Synonym   (In taxonomy) A scientific name rejected in favour of an accepted correct name for a species.

Taxonomy   The science of classification.

Tepal   Sepal or petal.

Terete   Cylindrical in form.

Terrestrial   Growing in the earth.

Transpiration   Exhalation of water vapour.

Vandaceous   Relating to vandas; used often as a loose synonym for the term monopodial.

Velamen   A layer of tissue containing air cells which covers orchid roots.

Xaxim   A soft treefern fibre much used as a substrate in Brazil.

Xeric   Extremely dry.

INDEX

Entries in *italics* indicate synonyms. An asterisk (*) indicates that the species is mentioned in passing only.